Judging Dev

A reassessment of the life and legacy of
Eamon de Valera

IF ONLY———

'If only', *Thirty years of the Dublin Opinion* (n.d.), 277. Courtesy of the National Library of Ireland.

JUDGING DEV

A REASSESSMENT OF THE LIFE AND LEGACY OF EAMON DE VALERA

Diarmaid Ferriter

Judging Dev: A reassessment of the life and legacy of Eamon de Valera

First published 2007

by Royal Irish Academy
19 Dawson Street
Dublin 2

www.ria.ie

The author and publisher are grateful to the following for permission to reproduce the documents, photographs and illustrations in this book: UCD Archives, School of History and Archives; the UCD–OFM Partnership; the National Archives of Ireland; the National Library of Ireland; Dublin Diocesan Archives; Churchill Archives Centre; the *Irish Times* and the *Daily Times Chronicle*.

All photographs courtesy of UCD Archives, School of History and Archives and the UCD–OFM Partnership, except where otherwise stated.

Every effort has been made to trace the copyright holders of these photographs and to ensure the accuracy of their captions.

ISBN 978-1-904890-28-7

British Library Cataloguing in Publication Data. A CIP catalogue record for this book is available from the British Library.

Printed in Spain

10 9 8 7 6 5 4 3 2 1

For Muireann, Tríona and Cian

UCDA, P150/21: Blackrock College students, 1902. Modern copy of a black and white group photograph of Blackrock College students including de Valera, front row, second from right. Annotated on reverse '1902 (Feb. to July)'.

Cont

Constitution

① The name of the State
shall be ~~Eire~~

② Éire is a Sov. Indep
Democ. State

③ The Territory of Eire
shall be such as fr
time to time may com
within the jurisr dic
of Eire

Acknowledgements

At the core of this book is the archival material necessary for anyone wishing to analyse the career of Eamon de Valera. The custodians and staff of the University College Dublin (UCD) Archives, School of History and Archives, where the de Valera papers are held, deserve my warmest gratitude, particularly Seamus Helferty, who has been unfailingly helpful in facilitating access and locating relevant material. The staff of the National Archives of Ireland, especially Eamonn Mulally and Catriona Crowe, was also invaluable to the completion of this project. Catriona's friendship and support has been of immense importance for many years now, and I want to record my thanks to her for reading the manuscript, her insightful observations and suggestions and her humour, humanity and originality. Deirdre McMahon also read and commented on the manuscript and, as always, has been generous with her time and thoughts, which I greatly appreciate.

I also owe a debt of gratitude to Eoin Kinsella and Jenny Berg who helped in locating suitable archival and visual material, and Eunan O'Halpin who was generous in sharing his insights and archival research, Fidelma Slattery for designing the book and Helen Litton for the index. My thanks also to Noelle Dowling of the Dublin Diocesan Archives.

RTÉ has done much over the years to facilitate greater access to and discussion of modern Irish history and I wish to acknowledge the support and contribution of Peter Mooney, producer, and Lorelei Harris, editor of Features, Arts and Drama on Radio One.

This book was commissioned by the Royal Irish Academy; I am grateful to its President, Jim Slevin, and in particular Pauric Dempsey, Lucy Hogan and Ruth Hegarty who did much to make this project a valuable and enjoyable one from start to finish. I also wish to acknowledge the support of the Irish Research Council for the Humanities and Social Sciences and the continued support of the History Department of St Patrick's College, Dublin City University, especially James Kelly.

Sheila, Enya and Ríona deserve the greatest thanks of all; I am blessed to be amongst such wonderful and enthralling females. Thanks also to Tom and Anne Maher. My father, Nollaig, and mother, Vera, both of whom have shown fortitude and courage in recent times, deserve special mention for years of love and support. My siblings, Cian, Tríona and Muireann, have always been supportive and caring; this book is dedicated to them, with love and respect.

Diarmaid Ferriter

The Judging Dev project was devised by the Royal Irish Academy (ideas@ria.ie) and developed in conjunction with RTÉ. The Academy is grateful to UCD Archives, School of History and Archives, and the National Archives of Ireland for the support, commitment and professionalism of their staff. The Academy is pleased to collaborate with the History In-Service Team to encourage the use of these materials in the classroom.

◄ UCDA, P150/2370: Early draft of the Constitution handwritten by de Valera on squared paper, *c.* 1935/6.

I

'Stop making love outside
Áras an Uachtaráin'

UCDA, P150/3205: President de Valera on the telephone, taken to mark his seventy-seventh birthday, 14 October 1959. © Irish Press.

On 29 August 1975 as the summer drew to a close, the most polarising and significant politician of twentieth-century Ireland died a quiet death. Eamon de Valera (Dev) was 93 years of age when he passed away at Linden Nursing Home in Blackrock, Co. Dublin. His wife Sinéad had died seven months earlier, on the eve of their sixty-fifth wedding anniversary.

Five years before he died, his officially approved biography, by Lord Longford (Frank Pakenham) and Thomas P. O'Neill, had insisted that he was a creator of Ireland's destiny, and that 'it is impossible to exaggerate the extent to which de Valera submitted all his actions to a criterion which was at once intellectual and moral'.[1] In contrast, in the days following his death, journalist Con Houlihan, as if echoing conservative MP Enoch Powell's dictum that all political careers end in failure, suggested: 'One can only look on Eamon de Valera's life as a failure. By his own stated ambitions he was a failure—it is as cruelly simple as that'.[2]

Fine Gael senator Alexis FitzGerald, also writing in the immediate aftermath of de Valera's death, was much more generous, his tribute taking on an added significance given that he 'was born in the tradition which always voted against Dev'. Any portrait of de Valera, he suggested 'involves regard for the Irish political achievement since self-government. It has been real and substantial. It has been the achievement of politicians … [and] the legitimation of Irish democratic institutions'. While praising his dignity and courtesy, the methods by which he practised his political craft and his prudence and fortitude, FitzGerald acknowledged that there were defects also but that proof of such failings 'will not eliminate his greatness for there will still remain a substantial net asset worth'.[3] In the days following his death, Pope Paul VI referred to de Valera not only as a national leader, but as 'a true statesman of Europe', while the *New York Times*, in a lengthy obituary that began on page one, stressed his important role and example in the struggle of small nations against colonialism, and compared his attitude to Ireland with that of the late French president Charles de Gaulle to France.[4]

Less than ten years later, in 1982, at a conference in Cork marking the centenary of his birth, a group of leading historians of modern Ireland offered a multi-faceted overview of his career. The conference was introduced by John A. Murphy, who maintained that 'Eamon de Valera is the most significant figure in the political history of modern Ireland. This is a statement of incontrovertible historical fact'; he added the qualification that this status 'does not necessarily involve a laudatory judgement'.[5]

Anything but a laudatory assessment was developed by writers during the following decade, most notably in 1993, when a biography by Tim Pat Coogan concluded that de Valera's career was a triumph of rhetoric over reality; that he did 'little that was useful and much that was harmful'.[6]

By the beginning of the twenty-first century, a revision of such a damning judgement was beginning to emerge; this revision was part of the unease with the extent to which the phrase 'de Valera's Ireland' became shorthand for all the shortcomings of twentieth-century Ireland. Notwithstanding, Dermot Keogh, one of the editors of the 2003 collection of essays *De Valera's Irelands*, expressed the view that 'de Valera is more in need of being rescued from the uncritical prose of his admirers than from the vituperative attacks of his most ardent critics'.[7]

The resentment or reverence directed towards the legacy of de Valera existed for different reasons. The national preoccupation with the events of the War of Independence and Civil War explains why he remained so divisive a figure for those who grew to adulthood in the early decades of the twentieth century. But for many people under the age of 60, the de Valera that they witnessed was an old man; nearly blind, and seen as a symbol, almost a relic, of depressed and difficult times. In 1948 at the age of 66, when most are considering retirement, electoral defeat broke Fianna Fáil's sixteen-year grip on power. But de Valera had no intention of departing the political stage.

He returned to serve another two terms as Taoiseach in the 1950s before Seán Lemass succeeded him, and then went on to serve two terms as president, from 1959 to 1973. He was an extraordinary survivor; indeed, Pauric Travers, in his short biography published in 1994, suggested that 'the central fact of his political life was survival … judged by the criterion of longevity, even Winston Churchill, with whom he crossed swords on more than one occasion, appears as something of a pygmy'.[8] In 1972 US president Richard Nixon informed de Valera that admiration for him was 'shared by all the world's democracies, for you are our senior democratic leader'.[9]

But that longevity, which saw him leave office for the last time in June 1973 at the age of 91, was another focus of barbed comment from his detractors. The political scientist, Peter Mair, recalled a visit to Dublin as a young boy in 1963 when the news came through that Pope John XXIII had died. 'Isn't it a shame', remarked somebody to his father, 'that old saint in Rome dying and that old bugger in the Park still going on as strong as ever'.[10] Mair also observed that his longevity was matched by 'a capacity to endure that remains without parallel in the democratic world'. In de Valera's case, however, this endurance is not placed at the same level as 'other Conservative state-builders' such as Charles de Gaulle in France or Konrad Adenauer in West Germany.[11]

From the 1960s, when de Valera occupied the largely ceremonial office of Irish president, a new and different Ireland was being written and spoken about; a 'modern Ireland', and, of course, a much better Ireland, which could only, and did only come into being when de Valera had departed from the Department of the Taoiseach. Recalling his earliest foray into Irish politics, John Bruton, Fine Gael leader and Taoiseach from 1994–7, remembered:

> I joined Fine Gael late in 1965 and my first graphic political memory is of speaking, without a microphone, to Mass-goers in Culmullen, County Meath, on behalf of the late Tom O'Higgins. The presidential election of 1966, when O'Higgins came within 10,000 votes of defeating Eamon de Valera, marked a turning away from the dream of an Irish-speaking and self-sufficient Ireland towards a slightly more materialistic but more European destiny.[12]

The implication is clear; de Valera was standing in the way of modernisation, he was of no significance to a new generation, and the victory of 1966 was the faint sting of a dying, blind and irrelevant old wasp. The poet Paul Durcan imagined him as an old, cranky kill-joy in his 1978 poem 'Making love outside Áras an Uachtaráin':

> When I was a boy, myself and my girl
> Used bicycle up to the Phoenix Park;
> Outside the gates we used lie in the grass
> Making love outside Áras an Uachtaráin
>
> Often I wondered what de Valera would have thought
> Inside in his Ivory Tower;

If he knew that we were in his green, green grass,

Making love outside Áras an Uachtaráin

I see him now in the heat-haze of the day

Blindly stalking us down;

And, levelling an ancient rifle, he says 'Stop

Making love outside Áras an Uachtaráin'[13]

In a similar vein, Neil Jordan used de Valera's funeral as the background to a short story which dealt with liberation from a suffocating past.[14]

Fintan O'Toole suggested, 'In a sense, de Valera's resignation had happened long before he resigned. He had become resigned to the failure of his policies and believed that there was nothing for his people to do but endure'.[15] In the innovative RTÉ television show, *Nighthawks*, set in a fictive nightclub in Dublin in the early 1990s, de Valera used to emerge from a fridge in the background, interrupting the interviews that were taking place, frozen to resist the tides of change. There was no other figure who would have been regarded as a symbol of all that was in the past apart from de Valera, but it was also a measure of just how influential he had been that even in the early 1990s, 'Irish audiences—including those attuned to *Nighthawks* post-modern formats—were expected to be in on the joke'.[16]

The consensus is that he stayed too long, and in doing so, hindered the embrace of the policies that were finally to achieve some prosperity for the country. What is often overlooked in this assessment is that the Irish electorate returned him to office continually. Retrospectively, his critics were able to reduce him to a one-dimensional embodiment of the negative aspects of Irish independence—a civil war fought over oaths and symbols, economic stagnation, emigration, failure of the Irish language to thrive, and continued partition of the country. All of these shortcomings, it seemed, could be parcelled under the label 'De Valera's Ireland'. It was almost as if de Valera was in power on his own, whereas he was in fact surrounded by a host of strong and able politicians—Seán Lemass, Seán MacEntee, Frank Aiken and James Ryan to name but a few—who were happy to see him last the course, as was the majority of loyal Fianna Fáil voters.

On the one hundred and twenty-fifth anniversary of his birth, the seventy-fifth anniversary of Fianna Fáil's first government, and the seventieth anniversary of one of his most durable monuments—the Constitution of 1937—this book is an attempt to encourage a more sophisticated assessment of de Valera and his legacy; it reproduces some of the original personal and governmental documentation which shed light on many of the milestones of his career. A reassessment of de Valera is justified not only by the full cataloguing of his extensive personal archive, but also by the need to incorporate in an analytical framework the many scholarly studies on aspects of the twentieth century, particularly over the last ten years, that are of direct relevance to his career.

One of the advantages enjoyed by historians more recently in the context of understanding a key ambition of de Valera—the quest for sovereignty—has been the publication of volumes IV and V of the Royal Irish Academy's *Documents on Irish foreign policy* series, covering the years 1932 to 1939.[17] These volumes are indispensable in facilitating a deeper and more nuanced appreciation of what was involved in the framing of an Irish independent foreign policy. An insight into de Valera's strategy and the thinking of his colleagues, as recorded in his own papers and the documents of the National Archives, particularly the official papers of the Department of Foreign Affairs and the Department of the Taoiseach, can also add depth to any analysis.

Towards the end of his life, de Valera bequeathed his political papers to the Irish Franciscans in Killiney, Co. Dublin, where they remained until 1997, when they were transferred to the Archives Department (now UCD Archives, School of History and Archives) of University College Dublin (UCD). They remain there under the terms of a partnership agreement between the university and the Franciscans.

There are contesting perspectives on de Valera that emerge from archival research and from the secondary published material. He can be presented as a man who was of international significance; a role model in the struggle of small nations to challenge and defeat imperialism in the twentieth century, and someone who contributed handsomely to sustaining Irish democracy in the 1930s, a dangerous decade for democracy internationally. When in power, he did not shirk the need to confront violent republicans who sought to bypass their need for a mandate. He was strategically skilful, and often masterful, when it came to political tactics and Anglo–Irish negotiations in the 1930s, a leader who developed a sophisticated and moral foreign policy underpinning the sovereignty he masterminded for Ireland in the 1930s–40s, and he framed a Constitution that has endured.

This contribution to state-building has been somewhat eclipsed because of the modern tendency to disregard its significance. But listening to de Valera's recorded voice, as preserved in the RTÉ Libraries and Archives, for example, is a reminder of how it dominated his time in power. It is a voice that was presenting the case for the sovereignty of small countries in an international context, whether appealing for recognition of the Irish Republic in New York in 1920; advocating the abolition of the land annuities and Oath of Allegiance in the early 1930s; addressing the League of Nations; marking the inauguration of a new Constitution in 1937; or commenting on the effects of international war on a neutral state. His collected statements and speeches, published in 1980 and edited by Maurice Moynihan, are also testament to the degree to which 'he came to embody continuity and stability when the rest of the world was in turmoil'.[18]

De Valera was undoubtedly charismatic but can also be presented as a man who was difficult. It is argued that he did not consult his colleagues in government enough, behaved irresponsibly after the War of Independence, failed to devote enough attention to economics, and left questions unanswered about his inappropriate involvement in the *Irish Press* company while Taoiseach.[19] It has often been contended that he presided over a failed economic entity, ravaged by emigration and social and cultural stagnation, which would help to explain the hostility and occasional demonisation he has been subjected to.

During the course of his career he was also subjected to much satirical comment and deemed worthy of the title 'The Great Splitter', as 'the man who split Sinn Féin, split the IRA, split Cumann na mBan, split Clan na Gael, double split Sinn Féin, double split the IRA, split the whole country and spends the rest of his time splitting words'.[20]

The combination of his various traits left many scratching their heads. In 1989, Joe Lee, in his seminal work *Ireland 1912–1985: politics and society* acknowledged that 'it may safely be predicted that the paradoxes of Eamon de Valera will intrigue historians for generations to come. Exploration of the recesses of that cavernous mind reveals ever more complex, ever more fascinating, formations'.[21]

What were the paradoxes, as identified by Lee? De Valera was an abandoned child who enshrined in his Constitution an image of womanhood that 'confined woman to the condition of a mother living happily ever after'; he had a genuine sympathy for the poor, but 'a refusal to invest this with ideological significance'; he was a teacher by training who virtually ignored education; and a man who advised others going into politics to read economics, of which he had 'a truly profound ignorance'. He spoke nobly in 1917 of the need for Irish politics to avoid the chicanery, cliques and intrigues of modern party-machined politics, and yet he 'came in due course to preside over the most professional machine Irish politics had yet seen, its multiple "mafias" flourishing under the benignly blind gaze of the Incorruptible'; he was a man whose rhetoric centred on filling the cosy homesteads of Ireland, but 'he had no idea what to do' about the emigration that blighted his Ireland.[22]

Notwithstanding these paradoxes, Lee was by no means wholly negative in his assessment of de Valera, acknowledging the stability he brought to Irish politics, his ability to lead Fianna Fáil with 'superb tactical judgement', his imaginative use of symbolism and his ability to be a 'a marvellous manipulator of private and public minds, of individual and collective mentalities'. Arguably more significantly, he insists that:

> de Valera did not abuse his trust as leader throughout his long public life. He revelled in the cult of 'The Chief', but he used it primarily for party and national purposes … De Valera was, in a sense, greater than the sum of his parts. Behind the ceaseless political calculation and the labyrinthine deviousness, there reposed a character of rare nobility. His qualities would have made him a leader beyond compare in the pre-industrial world. It was in one sense his misfortune that his career should coincide with an age of accelerated economic change whose causes and consequences largely baffled him. But there are times in history when the stature of public men depends more on what they are no less than on what they do. That was arguably the case in Ireland for at least the first generation of independence. No modern state in Irish circumstances could flourish under a succession of de Valeras. But a small modern state that [in de Valera's own words] 'could never be got to accept defeat and had never surrendered her soul' words that still held meaning when he spoke them in 1945, indeed held meaning largely because it was he who spoke them, should speak his name with pride.[23]

Central to Lee's assessment is the notion of dignity, and Seán O'Faoláin, 50 years previously, had also identified this as central to de Valera's appeal. Despite the fact that O'Faoláin became disillusioned with him, he wrote in 1939: 'nobody will deny that one of his greatest qualities—and it contributes greatly to his influence—is dignity'.[24] This remained relevant throughout his career; in 1972 when the heavyweight boxer, Muhammad Ali, arrived in Dublin for his fight against Al Lewis at Croke Park, brandishing an oversized shillelagh, he requested a meeting with de Valera. An official in the president's office refused to entertain the request on the grounds that '*ní shílim gur chóir fear bladhmannach mar Ali a bheith ag teacht chun an Uachtaráin*' ('I don't think it is appropriate for a boastful, bombastic man such as Ali to be visiting the President').[25]

More recently, Tom Garvin, the most prolific political scientist of his generation in Ireland, in his book *Preventing the future: why was Ireland so poor for so long?* is scathing in his criticisms of the mindset which he believes was responsible for Ireland's chronic underdevelopment during the first few decades of independence. At the centre of his thesis lies de Valera and his stubborn longevity: 'A bucolic quietus was to be the solution to Ireland's incoherent yearnings towards individual freedom, self-realisation, equality, individualism and authenticity as expressed dramatically in the writings and deeds of the revolutionaries and poets'. Furthermore, change only came about when 'de Valera as Fianna Fáil's lay Archbishop, mysterious and remote in demeanour, was replaced by men of a distinctly non-charismatic stripe, managerial in style, rather than romantic or pseudo-heroic'.[26]

Undoubtedly, de Valera was acutely conscious of his legacy, concerned with policing his reputation, and influencing historians and biographers. In 1981 F.S.L. Lyons referred to his 'obsession with posterity's verdict'.[27] There were undoubted frustrations for those historians working in the absence of state legislation concerning archives (the first piece of legislation being the 1986 National Archives Act) and access to de Valera's own papers. In 1964 he invited a group of historians to Áras an Uachtaráin to discuss his career, for which questions were to be submitted in advance. One of the historians, F.S.L. Lyons, recalled being surprised that at the age of 82, de Valera 'submitted unweariedly to six or seven hours of interrogation', and 'not only possessed a phenomenal memory, but also revealed an obsessive concern to set the record straight as he saw it'. But Lyons remained unimpressed as de Valera did not seem to realise that his 'transparent anxiety might be regarded by the historians as evidence of a very different kind than that which he sought to press upon them'.[28]

In 1982 John Bowman wrote of the 'instinct not to commit the most sensitive material to paper, the rumoured destruction of some files, the occasional removal of papers by some ministers, the failure to employ professional archivists within government departments, and the generally tardy policy concerning access—all of these factors result in serious problems for the historian of Irish politics since independence'. He also suggested that de Valera preferred to 'minimise written records ... and in power tended to take initiatives which, in any "open" system of government, would have been the result of collective cabinet decisions. Reinforcing a natural instinct for privacy and secrecy was a personal sense of self-justification which dated from the Treaty and Civil War period'.[29]

This was an assertion made at a time when there was little in the way of personal or state documentation for historians to work with. The situation is now a lot better in light of the substantial amount of archival material that has been released since Bowman conducted his innovative research on de Valera and the Ulster question. But Bowman was correct in asserting that de Valera was preoccupied about the verdict of history, was sensitive to criticism and self-righteous about his own political record.[30]

De Valera himself alluded to the significance of the archival record from an early stage in his career. In January 1924 while in prison after his arrest by the Free State Army, he wrote to his personal secretary, Kathleen O'Connell: 'You know, how valuable my documents are and the care that must be taken not to endanger any of them'.[31] But the previous year, he had written to a Franciscan a month after the Civil War had ended that 'very many of the papers— important links in the chain—have had to be destroyed'.[32] Patrick Murray suggested that 'his consciousness of the importance of documents as the essential basis for historical research remained with him throughout his life'.[33]

In December 2001, in a paper published by the Royal Irish Academy, Murray elaborated on de Valera's constant preoccupation with the verdict of history, his need:

> to keep his reputation in constant repair and an anxiety to influence the interpretation of his political activity and discourse. His effort to police the evolving public presentation of his career was not a foible of old age but the settled practice of a lifetime. He consciously developed the mythpoeic significance of his career in order to emphasise his unique contribution to history along with his probity, consistency and sound judgement. There was also the obsessive, recurring focus upon a particular set of episodes in which he was the central participant.

In this, he actively engaged in 'his parallel role as supervisor of those accommodating historians whose function it was to interpret this history in terms favourable to him'.[34]

This was particularly true concerning the period around the Treaty, and perhaps even before that. De Valera seemed to play a game of cat and mouse with the Bureau of Military History, a state-backed initiative of the 1940s to collect statements from those who had been involved in Irish nationalism from 1913–21. Despite de Valera's key role in ensuring its establishment, the secretary to the Bureau, Michael McDunphy, did not succeed in getting de Valera to make his own statement. On 6 July 1949 he had a conversation with

McDunphy revealing his keen interest in the statements concerning the 1916 Rising and mentioning other witnesses who, like him, had been close to the fighting. He suggested that he knew little of the events of Holy Week and the 'facts and confusion of counsels which led up to the countermanding order', but that 'there were things within his knowledge which were not known to any other living person and he felt it was his duty to put these things on record'.[35] But de Valera ultimately chose not to, despite McDunphy pursuing him for the next eight years. Pressure of work was cited as the reason. In July 1957 McDunphy was told that prior to the general election, in March of that year, de Valera had begun recording a witness statement 'but that since he had assumed office he had not found it possible to [do] anything further'.[36]

De Valera was not alone in this reluctance; it is noteworthy that other leading politicians of his generation, such as Richard Mulcahy, Chief-of-Staff of the IRA from 1919–22 and later leader of Fine Gael, also chose to keep the Bureau at arms length.[37] This was probably because they knew that they were going to leave behind substantial private collections under the control of their own estates, rather than entrusting this material to a third party, such as the Bureau. This is a reminder that those who kept assiduous records of their political careers were in control of what was to be left behind, and who was to be allowed access to it, something that needs to be remembered regarding de Valera's archive. It may also have been the case that de Valera intended to make a statement to the Bureau but wanted it to be so comprehensive that it proved to be impossible.

Patrick Murray gives numerous examples of de Valera's determination to fashion any interpretation of the early 1920s in a way that suited him, and makes a compelling case for the idea that de Valera was particularly obsessed with that period of his career. He argued on a number of occasions for a historical commission of inquiry to independently examine the events leading up to the Civil War.[38] This desire is partly explained by the difficulty he had in coming to terms with the degree to which he personally was blamed for the violence in Ireland in 1922. In March of that year the Bishop of Dromore, Edward Mulhern, bluntly informed de Valera in a letter: 'You, and you alone are responsible for the recrudescence of the troubles in the North–East and of all the disturbances elsewhere'.[39]

De Valera was also keen in his formative political years to stress the continuity of Irish republican endeavour. Any perusal of his speeches highlights the degree to which he invoked historical figures for his own purposes, including Theobald Wolfe Tone, Thomas Davis, Charles Stewart Parnell and Patrick Pearse. At the time of the foundation of Fianna Fáil in 1926, a printed handbill detailing the aims of the party began with quotes from Wolfe Tone and James Fintan Lalor, the Young Irelander and advocate of land nationalisation.[40] But while commemorating the doctrines of militant republicans, he was always careful after the 1920s to stress the need for a mandate and an agreed objective.

Practical politics meant that de Valera, like many other successful politicians, had to effectively exploit history 'while being determined not to become its captive',[41] and had to be careful, as one of the beneficiaries of the cult of 1916, and the sole surviving battalion commander of Easter Week, to qualify references to the necessity and legitimacy of bloodshed in the pursuit of independence. As Patrick Murray acknowledges, the period of his greatest achievements—the 1930s and the 1940s—was the period he seemed to show the least interest in.[42]

Murray's observations also need to be placed in the context of the contested politics of the 1920s–40s, and the 'history wars' about the period 1913–23, which began in the early 1920s when the Free State government commissioned Piaras Béaslaí to become biographer of Michael Collins. The government gave him access to files (which was not to happen again until 40 years later) as part of its attempt to authorise an official version of its own contested recent history, by 'drawing a line of apostolic succession from 1916 and by analogy, justifying its actions in the civil war'.[43] There is little evidence that Béaslaí engaged with the anti-Treaty side, and the book was hostile to de Valera.

It was published in 1926 and marked, in the words of Deirdre McMahon, 'the opening shots of a hard-fought historical war. The civil war may have ended militarily … but some of the combatants simply moved the field of battle to the history books'.[44] These battles culminated in 1935–7 with the publication of Frank Pakenham's *Peace by ordeal*, Ernie O'Malley's *On another man's wound*, Desmond Ryan's *Unique dictator*, Frank O'Connor's *The big fellow*, Dorothy Macardle's *The Irish Republic* and a second edition of the Béaslaí biography of Collins at the end of 1937.[45] In this light, de Valera's historical policing did not occur in an 'obsessive' vacuum, as suggested by Murray, and is understandable when considered as part of a long process of action and reaction.

De Valera was worried about the extent to which the reputation of others would be built up at the expense of his overall contribution, and in this, he was right to be worried. Some historians duly obliged; Tim Pat Coogan's biography of Michael Collins, first published in 1990, sought to portray Collins as a man of ideas and a noble visionary, in contrast to de Valera 'whose talent lay in getting and holding power'.[46]

In 2005 Peter Hart published his biography of Michael Collins, and although he gave adequate attention to Collins's shortcomings, he nonetheless asserted that Collins was 'the most successful politician of modern Irish History'.[47] This is a highly questionable and ahistorical conclusion, given that Collins did not live to contribute to the building of the new state, and it diminishes the scale of work that de Valera and his colleagues completed in later years. Hart's conclusion is also a reminder of the continuing tendency to judge de Valera in the context of the early 1920s rather than looking at his career as a whole.

UCDA, P150/85: With relations in Knockmore, 1972. De Valera's cousin, Lizzie Meagher (née Coll, daughter of his uncle Patrick); de Valera; Mrs de Valera; and Lizzie Meagher's husband, Henry, standing in the doorway of the cottage at Knockmore, Bruree, in which he was reared.

UCDA, P150/3856: President de Valera being interviewed (for television) in the garden of Áras an Uachtaráin by Fyfe Robertson of the BBC, 1960s.

UCDA, P150/18: Enlargement of a school photo, 1898. Its caption reads 'Edward De Valera. Retained Exhibition, £30. Book Prize, £2, Hon. Greek, Latin, French, Arithmetic, Algebra, Euclid. Pass Trigonometry'.

THE WHITE HOUSE

WASHINGTON

June 30, 1972

Dear Mr. President:

The introduction of two men whom I deeply admire is a source of great personal pleasure for me. I ask you to receive Governor Ronald Reagan as my personal representative and friend -- and as a friend of Ireland.

In many ways, Governor Reagan exemplifies the best of the traditions that our nations share. He is both an American and a son of Ireland. He has served the United States with the kind of energy and honesty that both our peoples admire. I know that he has particularly looked forward to visiting Ireland and making your acquaintance.

Governor Reagan knows of my deep admiration and respect for you, Mr. President. This admiration is shared by all the world's democracies, for you are our senior democratic leader. In the case of the United States, I think our respect for you is especially profound because of our shared traditions and experiences.

I am especially grateful to you for your courtesy in receiving Governor Reagan, and I am pleased to extend to you, through him, my very best wishes.

Sincerely,

Richard Nixon

Iarratas ar Chuairt ar an Uachtarán ó Muhammad Ali (Cassius Cl

---

1.   Le linn do Muhammad Ali a bheith anseo le haghaidh coimhlint
dornálaíochta le déanaí, dúirt an Teachta ó Conchubhair, (Ciarraí
Theas) leis an Rúnaí Pearsanta ar an teileafón gur mhian le
tionscnóirí na hócáide a mbeidh Al ('Blue') Lewis ag dornálaíocht
leis go bhfaighfeadh Muhammad Ali deis cuairt a thabhairt ar an
Uachtarán. Mhol mé don Rúnaí Pearsanta a rá leo nárbh fhéidir
a shocrú.

        Cé go bhfuil dea-chuspóir leis an taispeántas i bPáirc an
Chrócaigh, .i. cabhair airgid a sholáthar do chás leanaí a bhfuil
ceataí meabhrach orthu, ní shílim gur chóir fear bladhmannach
mar Ali a bheith ag teacht chun an Uachtaráin go háirithe tar
éis a ndúirt sé faoina chuairt agus go háirithe a chuairt ar
an Taoiseach (cf sleachta as na páipéir nuachta faoi dhátaí
12/7/'72 agus 13/7/'72 leis seo).

2.   Cúpla lá ina dhiaidh sin bhlaoigh an Teachta Clinton,
Co. Áth Cliath, ag iarraidh an rud céanna ach dúirt an Rúnaí
Pearsanta leis "that an tUachtarán would be unable to receive
Mr. Ali within the dates on which the latter would be in Ireland
and on which it is understood he would be available".

3.   Ní dheachthas níos faide leis an scéal, ach má bhíonn
Muhammad Ali ag iarraidh coinne arís, níor mhór a bheith cúramach
faoi ghéilleadh dó.

NAI, PRES, 2003/18/64: When the heavyweight boxer, Muhammad
Ali, arrived in Dublin for his fight against Al Lewis at Croke Park, an
official in the president's office refused to entertain his request for a
meeting with de Valera, 24 July 1972. (The line 'ní shílim gur choir
fear bladhmannach mar Ali a bheith ag teacht chun an Uachtaráin'
translates as 'I don't think it is appropriate for a boastful, bombastic
man such as Ali to be visiting the president'.)

►UCDA, P150/1698: Letter from de Valera to 'a Franciscan', 22
June 1923. In it he indicates what to do with his papers in the event
of his 'death, imprisonment, etc.'. De Valera was already keenly aware
of the importance of his documents.

móí

24. 7. '72

SECRET - Contents not to be communicated to   June 22nd, 1923.
         anybody except to those mentioned
         below.
_____

Dear Rev. Father:-

        In case of my death, imprisonment, etc., I am
very anxious that you should know my will as regards the papers
and correspondence which have been deposited in the places that
you know of. Many of these papers are private and personal -
many are State papers, but until the Republic is recognised, or
until a national record office to which they could be given is
established, I want them to remain in the custody of my own
family - my wife, after my death, to fill exactly the same
position with respect to them that I fill at present.

        It is my hope that I may be able myself to superin-
tend the cataloguing and annotation of these papers some day.
If not, no one but my secretary, Miss Kathleen O'Connell, has
the intimate information which will enable the work to be
properly done. As you know, very many of the papers - important
links in the chain - have had to be destroyed. I have endeavoured
to save these in order that there may be some documentary material
for the history of this period and for a proper appreciation of
the motives and actions of the Republican Government and Army
Executive. Mrs. Childers assistance would be invaluable for this
work, and I hope that it can be obtained in case of my death.

        I need scarcely lay stress on the necessity of keeping
all the papers together. They throw light one upon another and
help to make understood what in isolation might be misconstrued
or be altogether unintelligible.

        In case I am imprisoned, it is my wish that my
secretary, with Mrs. De Valera's permission, should go through
the papers and begin work on the cataloguing, and I expect that
both she and Mrs. De Valera will be given every facility for
this purpose by the present custodians of the papers, and that
no obstacles will be put in their way should they deem it necessary
or advisable to remove the papers to some other places of safety.

                              Yours very sincerely,
                                  Éamon de Valera

P.S. Only Mrs. De Valera and Miss O'Connell have my authority
      for seeking access to these papers.

WITNESS_____

II

'Decidedly

a "personality"'

UCDA, P150/871: 'The Chief', 1919. De Valera wearing a native American ceremonial head-dress. He was made chief of a Chippewa tribe of Indians at the Chippewa Reservation Reserve, Wisconsin, when he visited it on 18 October 1919.

Born in New York on 14 October 1882, to an Irish emigrant mother, de Valera was sent back to Co. Limerick as an infant to be reared by his grandmother in a labourer's cottage. He attended the local national school and was then educated at the Christian Brothers' school in Charleville, Co. Cork. After winning a scholarship to Blackrock College in Dublin he developed a passion for mathematics that was to remain with him throughout his life. Indeed, the likely career path for him at that stage was an academic one; he took mathematics as his degree subject at the Royal University, taught at Rockwell and Belvedere colleges, and was appointed a lecturer in Carysfort College in 1906. On more than one occasion he professed to be a reluctant politician.[1] According to Donal McCartney, he remained all his life a 'crypto academic' which accounted for 'much of his style of politics'.

If the early references given on his behalf by his academic mentors are anything to go by, he was more suited to the long haul than pressurised situations. Professor Arthur Conway of UCD noted that his 'mathematic abilities are of a high order', but that he 'is adapted to excel in research work rather than do himself justice at examinations'.[2]

His lifelong devotion to the Irish language also dated from this era. Membership of the Gaelic League from 1908 provided an introduction to the nationalist movement and to a teacher, Sinéad Flanagan, whom he married in 1910. Like many of his generation, he was by no means a doctrinaire republican, but was influenced by Eoin MacNeill's articles in the newspaper of the Gaelic League, *An Claidheamh Soluis,* that urged nationalists to follow the lead given by the formation of the Ulster Volunteer Force. De Valera attended the meeting that led to the formation of the Irish Volunteers in Dublin on 25 November 1913. In handwritten notes dating from February 1950 he recalled:

> Enrolment forms were handed out after the speeches. I considered whether I should join. I was married and my wife and children were dependent on me. I had no doubt that the

formation of the Volunteers meant that there w[oul]d be an armed insurrection. The question was—was I justified in entering into an engagement to take part in an insurrection with its likely consequences. I decided that our man power was such that if the movement was confined to unmarried men it would not be numerous enough to succeed. So I crossed the Rubicon and joined. From the moment I signed my name I regarded myself as a soldier with battle inevitably in the offing.[3]

How did he fare as a soldier? In 2005 Charles Townshend produced the most comprehensive and stimulating survey of the Easter Rising to date. His forensic dissection of the activities of the various battalions in Dublin during Easter Week is authoritative and compelling, and he effectively charts the indecisiveness and inexperience of all the senior Volunteer commanders. De Valera was appointed to command the Third Dublin City Battalion, (the Southeast Dublin Unit); something of a surprise since he was not in the Irish Republican Brotherhood (IRB) and seems not to have joined until Thomas MacDonagh later appointed him brigade adjutant.

Townshend gives credence to the criticisms of de Valera's battalion in Boland's Mills, including the observation of a contemporary that 'there wasn't much of a fight, but it wasn't the fault of the men. They weren't put into the position to fight'. De Valera was the only battalion leader who specifically refused to allow women to join the fighting, even though he only had about 130 men (though the other battalion leaders 'had clearly not planned on including them' sometimes taking women on at the last minute or else ignoring them).[4] De Valera had certainly done his homework, carefully chosen his positions, and briefed his men well as to the areas each company would occupy, an indication of his ability to absorb and retrieve precise details at will.

But like other inexperienced commanders, he was unable to adapt his plans when things did not go as envisaged, resulting in the failure to intervene in support of the Mount Street Bridge outposts, waiting for an expected major assault on Boland's Bakery instead. More controversial was the detailed account of Max Caulfield in the 1960s, which included testimony from members of the Third Battalion to the effect that he was behaving erratically during the week, and, in Tim Pat Coogan's words, was a man 'on, or over, the threshold of nervous breakdown'.[5]

This has been disputed, but there were claims from Simon Donnelly and Sam Irwin, two members of his battalion, that some present thought his actions and orders strange. For example, there was puzzlement at his hyperactivity and his decision to take his men up on the railway embankment, where they could see the city in flames, a dangerous and unnecessary move, before moving them back into Boland's Bakery. Townshend points out that 'the whole incident spread bafflement throughout the battalion', but also that while de Valera's hyperactivity may have been a personal trait, 'his inexperience was common to all the senior Volunteer commanders. Indecisiveness was often a result, as they tried to grasp the real nature of the battle they had so often fought in their imaginations'.[6]

Simon Donnelly gave differing accounts at various times. In his statement to the Bureau of Military History, he sought to clear up any confusion in favour of de Valera, implying that he (Donnelly) had been misrepresented. Donnelly's own account of the Rising, given separately from his Bureau statement, makes it clear that he was puzzled by some decisions, but he goes as far in his statement as to assert that de Valera 'enjoyed the fullest and sincerest loyalty of all ranks, officers and men, without a single exception ... we were all very attached to our commandant'.[7]

This is perhaps a bit too fulsome and seeks to ignore the confusion and uncertainty that existed in 1916, and is an indication of the potential for the statements to be influenced by contemporary 1940s politics. But other, more hostile assertions about de Valera could just as easily have been politically motivated.

De Valera was the only commandant to survive beyond May 1916, and the only one to come in for any direct criticism 'and only belatedly', despite the fact that there were few casualties under his command.[8] Practically all the critical comments were made after 1922.

Thomas MacDonagh, who commanded the Jacob's Factory Garrison, seemed to be acting similarly in showing the strain, and de Valera's response to the surrender order seems to have been calm, firm and clear, and indicative of his leadership abilities.

Patrick Ward, another member of his battalion, who left a statement with the Bureau of Military History, made the point that as those in Boland's Mills were not surrounded, they could have escaped, but de Valera insisted 'as we had gone into battle on an order, the order to surrender was equally binding'. Obeying orders, it seemed, would enhance the status of the army of the Irish Republic.[9] When subsequently in prison in Dartmoor, de Valera was anxious to impress on prison commissioner Captain Eardley-Wilmot 'the fact that there was no military reason for his surrender but that as his superior officers had sent word that he was to lay down his arms, of course he had to obey'.[10] When interviewed by historian, Deirdre McMahon, in 1983, Patrick Ward, who became a devoted supporter of Michael Collins, was emphatic that the stories of de Valera having a nervous breakdown were nonsense.[11]

In June 1959 de Valera received a letter from Lieutenant Colonel G.F. McKay in Jersey, Channel Islands:

> I was your only prisoner in Boland's Mill[s] in 1916 ... I have always thought you saved my life.
>
> Do you remember once you came to see me in my little den or had me brought in front of you and said 'The English have shot some of my men on the exit from the Mill[s] to the City' which could only be covered from the roof of the hospital opposite and you sent them a message that you had me and if they shot any more of your men you would shoot me. I was scared but knew you never would.
>
> And then do you remember the surrender when you sent me out to arrange the terms under cover of a white flag and all being arranged you marched out at the head of your people and as you passed me standing on the side walk you held out your hand to say 'thank you and goodbye'. I shook you by the hand and on the spot was arrested and marched ahead of you and your men.

De Valera did, of course, remember him, and responded warmly to the letter: 'If you come at any time, ring up the office here and I will make arrangements to see you with the least delay possible'.[12]

Charles Townshend also makes the point that de Valera escaped death 'for reasons that are still not clear',[13] and does not dwell on the subject as to why his court martial was delayed for a number of days while the senior leaders were tried and executed. In documents in his own archive, de Valera was adamant that the reason often given—his American birth—was not what had spared him, despite the fact that de Valera's wife, Sinéad, had arranged for his US birth certificate to be brought to the American Consul.[14] Sinéad's own recollection of the Rising includes an account of going to the American Consul, 'and the Consul and Vice-consul were very kind to me. I went to them several times and when I apologised for my importunity, the elder man said "You are as welcome as the flowers in May"'.[15]

She may have been welcome, but de Valera's own account suggests that such gestures were not the reason for his survival. On 3 July 1969 he wrote:

> I have not the slightest doubt that my reprieve in 1916 was due to the fact that my courtmartial and sentence came late.

My sentence came just when Asquith [the British prime minister] said that there would be no further executions save those of the ringleaders, which, apparently, he interpreted as those who had signed the Proclamation. Only Connolly and MacDiarmada were executed after my courtmartial. The fact that I was born in America, would not, I am convinced, have saved me. I know nothing in international law which could be cited in my defence or made an excuse for American intervention, except, perhaps, to see that I got a fair trial.

It is, of course, true that my wife was encouraged by friends to make, and did make, representations to the American Consul here. He was sympathetic, I understand. Similarly, my mother and American friends, including Joe McGarrity no doubt, made representations to Washington. I do not know if they got any reply, but I feel certain that the Administration took no official action.[16]

Other documents in his archives reveal that Reverend Thomas J. Wheelwright, de Valera's half-brother, did attempt to get the US administration to intervene with the British government on de Valera's behalf, and there are many other letters from senators and House representatives promising to do what they could. Senator James W. Wadsworth was one of them, and he requested the US Department of State to make inquiries through the American ambassador in London, with a view to securing a modification of the sentence imposed on de Valera. But the reply Wadsworth got from the Secretary of State was unequivocal:

The fact that Mr DeValera may be an American citizen constitutes no reason for clemency in his case, or for a request by this Government for clemency on the part of the British Government. There appears to be nothing to indicate that his trial was not fair or that he was in any way discriminated against, and there would, therefore, appear to be no reason for action by this Department on behalf of Mr DeValera.[17]

Understandably, it has been maintained that his US birth may have bought time that de Valera benefited from. But the available documentation suggests that the American pressure from family and others only began to make an impression after the executions had stopped. Barrister and British Army soldier, W.E. Wylie, who was asked to prosecute at the courts martials of the prisoners, assured General John Maxwell—the man who oversaw the suppression of the rebellion and its aftermath, and who British prime minister Herbert Asquith pressured to stop the executions—that de Valera was not a ring leader and insisted that 'de Valera's American connections were not mentioned as was so often said later'.[18]

De Valera was understandably defensive about the US connection being cited as the main reason for his survival. As Owen Dudley Edwards put it, 'to be the surviving commandant was one thing; to be the commandant who survived by special pleading of individual peculiarities was a very different one'.[19]

De Valera's survival created huge political opportunities for him in terms of leadership. His imprisonment included stints in Dartmoor, Maidstone and Lewes, until his release in June 1917. David Fitzpatrick's analysis of his actions and temperament as a prisoner, based on Home Office records in London, suggest that the image of him presented by sympathetic biographers as displaying unmitigated confidence and resilience has been somewhat exaggerated; that, notwithstanding his intelligence and constant courteousness, and his occasional stubbornness and trenchant stances, he could also be sometimes 'fawning', 'emotional' and 'uncontrolled'.[20] Despite these outbursts, de Valera seemed to combine fatherliness with steeliness. The deputy medical officer at Dartmoor found him 'civil and pleasant, but he maintains the attitude of a father to his children with reference to the other Irish prisoners'. On the other hand, the governor of Dartmoor found him to be 'a real firebrand and fanatic ... he is decidedly a "personality" and others seem to look up to him as their leader'.[21]

De Valera was continually protesting, resentful of indignity and demanding that they be treated as prisoners of war, one of the reasons he was frequently transferred as a prisoner. In any case, he was recognised as the leader of the prisoners in Lewes Jail, though, like others, he was uncertain as to what should happen next. He was not quite convinced about the best course to take regarding contesting elections in 1917. This was partly because the prisoners were not always fully clear 'of the exact position at home' and were finding it difficult to read the situation. On 23 April 1917 he wrote to Simon Donnelly from prison. Written exactly a year after the Rising, the letter included the observation: 'I have not as much on my mind today as this time last year'. De Valera suggested to Donnelly that the most important issue was to send Irish delegates to the Peace Conference that would co-incide with the end of the First World War, an indication of his preoccupation with making the question of Irish independence an international one, and that their only demand at such a conference could be complete independence.

He then elaborated on the prevailing feeling about elections: 'As regards the contesting elections question, it is so extremely dangerous from several points of view that most of us here consider it very unwise. … Nobody should think however that contesting elections is the policy which the men here would advocate if they had a say in the matter'. The letter went on to stress the importance of the Irish Volunteers remaining armed and vigilant, as he believed they were going to be a part of any future solution.[22]

Nonetheless, under considerable pressure from colleagues, he agreed to contest the East Clare by-election in July 1917, and began campaigning following his release from prison, two days after he had been selected as a candidate. During that election campaign he seemed to suggest that ballots in Sinn Féin's favour could replace armed resistance—'every vote you give now is as good as the crack of a rifle in proclaiming your desire for freedom'—but reassurance about a political direction was occasionally accompanied by threatening language: 'If you cannot get arms, get that old useful weapon at close quarters—the seven foot pike'. But one thing he was clear about was the need not to alienate 'the all important support of the clergy'.[23] Two days before he was released from jail, the convention of 200 people that selected him to contest the East Clare constituency had included 60 priests,[24] and David Fitzpatrick makes much of the idea that he won over Bishop Michael Fogarty of Killaloe and that he 'paraded the pious and well connected [Eoin] Mac Neill as a mascot of Catholic respectability'.[25] De Valera received almost double the number of votes (5,010) that his opponent, Patrick Lynch of the Irish Parliamentary Party (commonly known as the Irish Party), received (2,035), a margin of victory that was wider than expected.[26]

Crucially, in the aftermath of this victory, there was a growing perception of him as a statesman with a strategy—and one which involved diluting the influence of extremists—to achieve international recognition of Ireland as a sovereign independent republic and then allow people to vote in a referendum to choose 'their own form of government'. Arthur Griffith made it clear, in stepping aside to allow de Valera to become president of Sinn Féin and the Volunteers at the end of October 1917, that de Valera's 1916 service was only part of the reason to put faith in him; the other was that he had 'the mind and capacity that Ireland will need at the Peace Conference—the mind and capacity of the Statesman'.[27]

Considerable political skill was needed in this context. Michael Laffan, in his definitive history of the rise of the Sinn Féin movement after 1916, makes the point that the greatest achievement of the campaign in 1917 was 'the emergence of a sense of cohesion and common purpose among a disparate group of people who, until then, had often suspected or disapproved of each other'.[28]

The original scepticism about the merits of fighting elections unless they could be 'almost certain of success' as de Valera had put it at Easter 1917, needed to be managed carefully.[29] Bringing such people together, or grinding them down until they agreed upon a single approach, was to remain crucial to de Valera's strategy throughout his career. His victory in East Clare was a decisive turning-point and, in some quarters, the adulation it caused seemed unbridled. Michael Laffan quotes a contemporary poem to commemorate the event:

> De Valera! My idea of what noble man should be,
>
> Calm, reserved, warm, impulsive, and strong-hearted as the sea,
>
> Laughter-loving, glad and pensive, sad and happy all combined,
>
> Scorning all the hollow shamming of the modern human mind,
>
> True to principle and honour, yet as playful as a child,
>
> As a father, soldier, scholar, always gentle, always kind

Laffan, while acknowledging the transformation of the soldier into a politician who was shrewd, skilful and revered, also qualifies the sentiments provoked by the heady days of 1917, and the above poem, by suggesting that de Valera was autocratic, and that 'his many strengths were undermined by deviousness, self-importance and narrowness of vision, but in the short term only his virtues were apparent'.[30]

De Valera also demonstrated considerable skill during the conscription crisis of 1918, after the British government had announced its intention to extend conscription to Ireland. De Valera persuaded the Catholic hierarchy to postpone any decisions about the issue until the politicians had discussed their strategy, and he went to the Archbishop of Dublin, William Walsh, rather than the standing committee of the hierarchy.[31] Tactically, he had outflanked the potential opposition and was clearly not going to be outmanoeuvred or overawed 'by the more seasoned representatives of the Irish Party'.[32] He therefore made the anti-conscription pledge his own and used the backing of Archbishop Walsh to persuade the reluctant Irish Party to sign up; he then used that support to persuade the assembled bishops at Maynooth to accept the pledge. Pauric Travers observes that 'when they raised the possibility that the Volunteers might resist by force, de Valera replied strongly that the Volunteers would resist by force, if necessary, no matter what the Bishops said'.[33] The crisis resulted in a significant boost to the membership of Sinn Féin and the Irish Volunteers, and placed Sinn Féin in a leading position in the run up to the 1918 election.

Another dramatic development was the 'German Plot' arrests in May 1918, when 73 prominent members of Sinn Féin, including de Valera, were arrested after the British Cabinet had instructed the new viceroy, Lord French, to investigate Sinn Féin's links with Germany (a pretext had been provided when a so-called 'German agent', a member of Roger Casement's Irish Brigade, had been arrested after landing on the Clare coast). The arrests were not resisted because it was believed that much political capital could be made out of the imprisonment of high-profile Sinn Féin leaders. De Valera was to remain in Lincoln Jail until his escape in February 1919.

It gave him time to contemplate the future, and his mind wandered in many directions. It was a measure of his preoccupation with the defence of Ireland that personal papers written in the jail in 1918 were transcribed by MI5 (and released by the Public Record Office in London in 2001). He had drawn up plans for a bicycle-riding 'cavalry' which would help defend Ireland against invasion as an alternative to an expensive and troublesome to train mounted cavalry: 'Cyclists would replace cavalry and could be used in considerable numbers. Cycling is very common in Ireland, the road mileage is big and the mobility of such troops could be of great use in cases of raids or even invasion'. In making the 'best possible use of the whole male population up to the age of 40 years' he suggested there might be a first line of cadets aged between 13 and 32 years old, a second line of those aged between 32 and 40 years old and a third line for those 40 years old and over. He estimated that in any given year the number of men reaching military age could be calculated at 1% of the population, or 43,000. An MI5 officer based at the Irish Command in Parkgate wrote to the War Office in London at the end of May 1918 concerning the plan: 'It is interesting and useful as an estimate of Irish manpower made by a man who knows Ireland and is a mathematical professor and likely to be accurate in his figures'.[34]

The general election of December 1918, in which Sinn Féin won 73 seats, signalled the terminal demise of the Irish Party, and was another triumph for those seeking to use the Sinn Féin movement to make a serious political impact and a compelling case for some form of Irish independence, although it occurred just six months after the 'German Plot' arrests. This sequence of events had ensured that the individuals who had evaded arrest, notably Harry Boland and Michael Collins, were left in commanding positions, and de Valera's role was temporarily more symbolic than real until he was elected president of the Dáil on his return to Ireland.

Following his brief visit back to Ireland, de Valera embarked on an eighteen-month trip to the United States in the company of Harry Boland, with Arthur

Griffith staying in Dublin as acting president. His journey there was less than edifying, an inevitability given his status as an escaped prisoner. According to the Bureau of Military History statement of Michael O'Laoghaire, a member of the IRA in Liverpool who helped to organise the clandestine sea trips of Irish republicans:

> As far as I can remember, de Valera went out as a ship's greaser. He was dressed or made up for the part and, to give him confidence, he was paraded in the trams, etc., through Liverpool. To use the words of the late Neil Kerr (who was himself at one time a seafaring man), 'he did not look the part'. However, in spite of personal disadvantages, de Valera got to the USA and back without being arrested, and that was what was wanted.[35]

The American tour was a long, exhausting, occasionally exhilarating but often frustrating journey, and it is perhaps no surprise that historians have given contrasting assessments of whether or not it was successful. On paper at least, it appeared a big success as a fundraiser, with Irish–Americans eager to contribute. The first day's collection in Brooklyn raised $150,000; a total of $2.4 million was pledged by New York City, and by May 1920, $3 million had been secured. (In 1920 $4 equalled £1stg.)[36] The trip was also a milestone in the life of Harry Boland, who, according to David Fitzpatrick, became 'de Valera's valet, shepherd and manager instead of acting as an envoy in his own right',[37] as the maze of Irish–American politics and network of organisations was negotiated. Together, they made for strange bedfellows, but de Valera thought they were 'an ideal team' as Boland got to people's hearts, and de Valera to their heads. There is testimony to the effect that some Irish–American activists found de Valera arrogant, difficult and stubborn. Harry Boland's diary entries record de Valera's exceptional attention to detail, and his lecturing of Boland on filing systems.[38] Boland also recorded that de Valera was busy buying books, working day and night ('his mind never rests'), always travelling with far too many books, and was frequently lonely due to being apart from his family.[39]

The methodical preparation and constant lobbying resulted in the trip being a considerable propaganda triumph, but it also created conflict and rows and failed to achieve the recognition of the Irish Republic or induce the American party conventions to pronounce in favour of recognition.[40] Part of the difficulty was attempting to keep a unified front and a co-ordinated effort, things which were always important to de Valera, but also, as he revealed in a letter to Arthur Griffith, monitoring the fund-raising: 'Expenses are awful here.

Cost of collecting the bonds subscriptions will I fear be very high. There is no close unit of organisation here as at home. The fund being collected by the Friends of I[rish] Freedom is a bit disconcerting'.[41] President Wilson and others were determined that the issue of the Irish Republic would remain an Anglo–Irish rather than an international concern, and de Valera's surprise appearance in New York had embarrassed both governments.

Nonetheless, as a result of the trip, there may have been up to 700,000 members of the American Association for the Recognition of the Irish Republic; de Valera campaigned coast to coast and became a celebrity, but was also apt to lose himself in points of detail (maybe he had, as Boland suggested, too many books). In his defence, it was necessary to take the Irish issue outside the somewhat narrower scope of the old-style Irish–American base as represented by the veteran supporters of Irish nationalism, John Devoy and Daniel Cohalan of Clan na Gael, and extending the appeal geographically was a significant achievement.[42] The internal rows of the Irish–American groups were also causing consternation at home, and Arthur Griffith wrote to Cohalan and Devoy in June 1920, making a personal appeal for the infighting to cease, bemoaning 'attacks being made at present by prominent citizens of America of Irish blood on the authority and credit of the President of the Irish Republic'.[43]

Some of the disagreements had to do with the extent to which the Irish–American groups were consumed by American rather than Irish politics; their support of American presidential candidates in the election of 1920; and the implications such allegiances could have for the relationship between the USA and Britain. These factors had to be considered in the context of any hoped for pressure being applied by the American government on Britain in the context of the Irish question.[44]

Many of the divisions were already gestating before de Valera arrived and there were obvious tensions between Cohalan, Devoy and Joseph McGarrity who led a rival faction of Clan na Gael in Philadelphia.[45] There was further controversy in February 1920 when de Valera suggested that Ireland's relationship with Britain regarding foreign policy could be akin to that of the USA and Cuba. This infuriated Daniel Cohalan and exposed the degree to which rival Irish–American organisations had very different views of how to integrate the Irish issue into American political life.

There were other inconveniences and flash-points also, and not just as a result of politics. De Valera was not always guaranteed an uncritical reception, and his visit to Birmingham, Alabama, in April 1920 was controversial because of the prevailing anti-Catholicism and the ingrained hostility of the 'WASPs' (White Anglo–Saxon Protestants) and more specifically the Ku Klux

Klan which was experiencing a revival at this time. He told his white audience that Ireland 'was the only white nation on earth still in the bonds of political slavery'.[46] The American trip was also significant in terms of the evolution of the cult of personality; according to Michael Hopkinson, de Valera personified the Irish question in the United States as the cause reached its height in terms of political influence,[47] and it was a measure of his impact that 'Sinn Féinism' was sometimes referred to as 'de Valeraism'. One sympathetic observer in the US, James K. McGuire, treasurer of Clan na Gael, referred at the end of August 1919 to de Valera's perceived clumsiness as masking a 'gentle, brave, kindly, noble-souled, determined idealist, like Desmoulins, St Just and the guillotined Girondists who died to make a new world and succeeded, but a most difficult man to fit in in the most selfish, self-centred materialistic great country in the world'.[48]

De Valera was also absent during a crucial stage in the War of Independence, and it is worth noting the observations of those left in Dublin regarding his absence. Writing to Austin Stack in July 1920 Michael Collins, while acknowledging the positive reception afforded to de Valera in the United States, also maintained 'yet our hope is here and must be here. The job will be to prevent eyes turning to Paris [the Versailles peace conference] or New York as a substitute for London'.[49] This was a qualification some historians have mirrored. Michael Hopkinson suggests de Valera's mission to the United States 'implied an overestimation of the role the US could play in the Irish question ... from his eighteen months' stay de Valera learned that the Irish question had to be settled in London and Dublin, rather than by mass meetings in the US'.[50]

But this may be too myopic a view. The connection with the United States remained significant, and was one of the main factors in contributing to what Owen Dudley Edwards termed de Valera's 'remarkable international sense'. His American origins and connections provided him with a source of friendship, sympathy and funds and increased his sense of the effectiveness of public opinion and the marshalling of international sentiment.[51] The American trip and dimension also added to his fame.

The summer after he had returned to Ireland he acceded to a request from a Dutch manufacturer to create a 'De Valera Series' of first-class cigars with his image on the box. A letter addressed to de Valera in July 1921 by an export cigar manufacturer, Jan van der Heijde of Eindhoven, requesting permission to create the 'De Valera' brand, was addressed to 'His Excellency Mr de Valera, Prisdent [*sic*] of the First Irish Republic'. Van der Heijde said his firm intended to issue 'a new series of our first-class cigars for which we would fain choose your name and issue these brands as the "De Valera Series". However before doing so we should like to know whether there is no objection on your part to such proceeding and we shall therefore esteem it a great favour if you would kindly drop us a few words to this effect'. Van der Heijde also asked for a portrait of de Valera to be sent to the firm for reproduction on the cigar boxes.

In the following months de Valera ordered his favourite photograph, one dating from his release from prison in 1917, to be sent to the cigar manufacturer, whose other 'special brands for every market' ironically included such imperial names as 'Royal Seal' and 'King Edward'.[52] The request confirmed de Valera's status as an international celebrity at a time when the Department of Publicity and Propaganda was sending the weekly Irish bulletin to 900 newspapers worldwide.

De Valera's return to Dublin in December 1920 perhaps inevitably resulted in pressure being applied for a change of strategy in the conduct of the War of Independence. However, Peter Hart's research would suggest that the American trip did not impair his working relationship with Collins, partly because de Valera gave him much attention and handled him and his work-load with skill and sympathy, though he did try and steer him away from confrontation: 'The overall impression given by their correspondence is one of genuine partnership, with de Valera projecting a supportive and tolerant presence'.[53] This depiction of the pair is at odds with the idea of de Valera as fearful and resentful of Collins's ambition and efficiency, concerns shared by Cathal Brugha, Minister for Defence, and Austin Stack, Minister for Home Affairs.[54]

Notwithstanding, there were many tensions. De Valera seemed keen for the IRA to reduce its reliance on guerrilla tactics. In the Dáil in January 1921, following his return from the United States, he suggested that the IRA should 'ease off as far as possible, consistent with showing the country that they were in the same position as before',[55] a suggestion that seems to have been ignored by the IRA. Later that year, the IRA GHQ staff, some of whom were distrustful of the Cabinet, rejected an attempt by de Valera and Brugha to restructure the IRA and bring it under the closer control of the Department of Defence.[56]

UCDA, P150/1079: On top of the Waldorf-Astoria in Manhattan during de Valera's contentious fund-raising visit, 1919. From left, standing: Harry Boland (honorary secretary of Sinn Féin); Liam Mellows (worked with John Devoy and was recognised as the leader of the '1916 Exiles'); de Valera; Diarmuid Lynch (secretary of Friends of Irish Freedom); and Dr Patrick McCartan (Irish envoy to Washington); Sitting: John Devoy of Clann na Gael (prominent Fenian).

UCDA, P150/503: De Valera's surrender, 29 April 1916. The Third Battalion under Comdt de Valera being escorted to Ballsbridge Barracks after de Valera's surrender to Captain E.J. Hitzen. De Valera is the figure on the far left of a group of three marching behind the flag bearer.

UCDA, P150/3817: De Valera at a ceremony commemorating the 1916 Rising at Arbour Hill Barracks, mid 1930s. De Valera in the procession to the graves from the Garrison Church is followed by Dr James Ryan (Minister for Agriculture) and Mr P.J. Ruttledge (Minister for Justice). Print captioned on reverse 'Irish Independent Photo'.

he private meetings and the art. in the Claidheamh Soluis by Eoin McNeill which led to the Pub. meeting on Nov. 25 1913 at the Rotunda are known.

I read the Art. in the C.S and went to the meeting. Enrolment forms were handed out and after the Speeches I considered whether I should join. I was married and my wife and us children were dependent on me. I had no doubt that the formation of the Volunteers meant that there wd. be an armed insurrection The question was — was I justified in entering into an engagement to take part in an insurrection with its likely consequences. I decided that our man power was such that of the movement was confined to unmarried men it would not be numerous enough to succeed. So I crossed the Rubi and joined. From the moment I signed my name I regarded myself as a soldier with battle inevitably in the offing.

Immediately in front of me at the Rotunda meeting was two persons I never expected to see there. One was my old parish priest (of Rockhill & Bruree) Fr. Eug Sheehy brother of David Sheehy MP and uncle of Mrs Sheehy Skeffington, and side by side with Father Sheehy was Larry Roche. Larry was an athlete of some note in our area, he lived on the Road near Kilmallock

He became a major in the Bos. army in the first World War. He was a nephew of Bob. Cole of Wardstown Castle

THE FAIRWAY,
GOREY VILLAGE,
GROUVILLE,
JERSEY, C. I.
GOREY 175.

Dear Mr. de Valera.

I have often wanted to send you a short note & here now is a good opportunity. To congratulate you on your election to President.

You may have looked at the signature, but even then perhaps you wont remember who I am until I remind you.

I was your only prisoner in Boland's Mill in 1916

Now you may remember the scared boy of 18, & I have always thought you

UCDA, P150/506: G.F. McKay to de Valera, 27 June 1959. Lieutenant Col. G.F. McKay, then living in Jersey, Channel Islands, was de Valera's only prisoner in Boland's Mills during the 1916 Rising. In his reply to this letter, de Valera invited McKay to visit him in Dublin.

saved my life.

Do you remember once you came to see me in my little den or had me brought in front of you & said; "The English have shot some of my men on the exit from the Hill to the Rly. which could only be covered from the roof of the Hospital opposite, & you sent them a message that you had me & if they shot any more of your men you would shoot me, I was to care but knew you never would.

And then do you remember the Surrender when you sent me out to arrange the terms under cover of a white flag & all being arranged.

You marched out at the head of your people & as you passed me standing on the side walk you held out your hand to say "thank you & Good bye. I shook you by the hand & on the spot was arrested & marched ahead of you & your men with two soldiers with fixed bayonets on either side of me. We were all taken to Balls Bridge. Horse show grounds I think it was & I was locked up in a Horse box, next to you.

Any way I am sure by now you will remember me?

I have followed with great interest your work for "Éire" & I

am glad you are now President
& perhaps can take things a bit
easier. How are the eyes?

It would be wonderful to meet
you again & have a chat, but
I fear there is no hope of that. So
we must leave it until St Peter
opens the gates to me D.V. &
says

"Come on in & meet some old friends"

With my very best wishes &
all the very best of luck

Yours Sincerely

G. F. Mackay

UACHTARÁN NA HÉIREANN
(PRESIDENT OF IRELAND)

BAILE ÁTHA CLIATH
(DUBLIN)

Reprieve of Eamon de Valera

I have not the slightest doubt that my reprieve in 1916 was due to the fact that my courtmartial and sentence came late.

My sentence came just when Asquith said that there would be no further executions save those of the ringleaders, which, apparently, he interpreted as those who had signed the Proclamation. Only Connolly and MacDiarmada were executed after my courtmartial. The fact that I was born in America would not, I am convinced, have saved me. I know of nothing in international law which could be cited in my defence or made an excuse for American intervention, except, perhaps, to see that I got a fair trial.

It is, of course, true that my wife was encouraged by friends to make, and did make, representations to the American Consul here. He was sympathetic, I understand. Similarly, my mother and American friends, including Joe McGarrity no doubt, made representations to Washington. I do not know if they got any reply, but I feel certain that the Administration took no official action.

By the way, Thomas Ashe was courtmartialled the same day that I was. He, too, would have been executed, I have no doubt, had he been tried earlier because of the part he took at the Battle of Ashbourne, Co. Dublin, where he was in charge, and where a number of Royal Irish Constabulary were killed. He was not an American citizen, and it could not be suggested, therefore, that it was on that account he was reprieved.

Eamon de Valera

3-7-69

49

United States Senate,

WASHINGTON, D. C.

July 18, 1916.

UCDA, P150/528: Letter to Fr Thomas J. Wheelwright, de Valera's half-brother, from United States senator James Wadsworth, 18 July 1916. In it Wadsworth discusses representations made to the American government requesting intervention to save de Valera from execution after the Rising.

My Dear Father Wheelwright:

I am in receipt, this morning, of a letter from the Secretary of State with further reference to the case of your brother, Mr. Edward DeValera as follows:

"The Department has instructed the American Ambassador at London to investigate this case and the Ambassador has reported that Mr. DeValera, who was Commandant in the rebel army, was convicted by court martial and sentenced to death, but that subsequently the sentence was commuted to penal servitude for life.

The fact that Mr. DeValera may be an American citizen constitutes no reason for clemency in his case, or for a request by this Government for clemency on the part of the British Government. There appears to be nothing to indicate that his trial was not fair or that he was in any way discriminated against, and there would, therefore, appear to be no reason for action by this Department on behalf of Mr. DeValera."

I regret very much to have to send you such unfavorable information but there appears to be nothing on record now on which to base a further appeal. If you can give me some additional grounds I shall be glad to address the Secretary of State further.

Sincerely yours,

J. W. Wadsworth Jr.

Rev. Thomas J. Wheelwright,
Mount St. Alphonous,
Esopus, N. Y.

M

Since writing the above, I have received your letter of the 13th with the enclosed copy of your brother's birth certificate and shall be glad to show it to those who may inquire about it.

delegates are given no powers to compromise
the independence position.

As regards the contesting elections question
it is so extremely dangerous from several
points of view that most of us here consider
it very unwise. When MacGennis was
asked for his formal consent we all
practically "considered the question and with one or
two exceptions we decided that a refusal
which gave no handle to the other side
was the safest. Still we hear that his
election his candidature is being continued.
Some felt so strongly about it that they
considered it their our duty to repudiate it
but the majority are in favour of letting
it be otherwise for the present as harm might
be done to the cause which is the only
thing we all have at heart. Nobody
should think however that contesting elections
is the policy which the men here

UCDA, P150/529: De Valera to Simon Donnelly, 23 April 1917 (pages 2 and 3 of which are reproduced here). This was written while de Valera was a prisoner in Lewes Jail. He discusses the prisoners' attitude to contesting elections and the powers that should be given to Irish delegates at a 'Peace Conference' following the First World War. Donnelly had been a member of de Valera's battalion during the Easter Rising.

would advocate if they had a say in the matter. Of course our ignorance of the exact position at home has always to be taken into account — so again whilst refusing to commit the reserve here to any policy which we cannot see our way to agree with we every hope that God may direct the actions of you all outside for the best — and we think most of us, that to refrain from actively interfering is the truest way to co-operate with you all outside

One other word do not forget the organising and in so far as it is possible the Equipping of soldiers for the Irish nation.

(6) On no account let there be any suggestions of sending us food parcels here — They might permit it. You might show these to Cathal Brugh. Hope he is well.

NAI, DE 2/36:
de Valera's
instructions on
precautions
against enemy
raids on Dáil
offices during
the War of
Independence,
May 1921.

Rough Draft

Dáil Éireann

Oifig an Príom-Aire.   President's Department.

To all Departments: — *Standing Order.*

In view of the possibility of raids on our *active*
offices, the following principles should be ~~adhered~~ to:

1. No documents which would lead directly to the
    capture of other offices or individuals to be
    filed. Lists of important persons in our
    organisation, and addresses, obviously come
    under this head.   *in correspondence*

    Officials should be addressed by their
    title in their departments rather than by
    personal name ~~or initials~~

    Documents coming from Army departments to
    Civil departments in particular must not be
    filed in the latter's offices. When communications
    from any Army department reaches a Civil office it
    should receive priority as regards attention, and
    be <u>destroyed immediately</u> when dealt with.

2. *All containing material which could be of use to the enemy*
    Files should be reduced to a minimum, only such
    documents as are absolutely necessary for reference *to*
    ~~should~~ be kept. Even in the case of these, a
    summary in rough code would do as well as the
    original documents, and would of course be much
    safer.

3. Documents which it would be difficult to replace
    should be duplicated and the originals put away
    in special places of safety. In the case of   *against the*
    documents vital for proof and evidence, it may   *enemy.*
    be necessary to have photographic duplicates made.

4. In the event of an office being raided and material
    captured which would affect any other office, the
    head of the raided office is responsible for commun-
    icating <u>at once</u> full details of the capture so as to
    enable the offices affected to take counter measures.

-2-

In addition to the above precautions the head of
each department is responsible for devising such schemes
as would prevent the enemy from obtaining important
information from the accidental capture of his offices.

Carelessness in this matter must be regarded as a
very definite neglect of duty.

Éde V.

placed.   In the cases of McCartan, de Valera and Boland,
Dick O'Neill and Barney Downes always filled the role and,
in my opinion, better men could not be found.   When the
vacancy or job in the particular ship was made, the new
member (that is, the man we intended to get away) of the
crew had to be coached, if time permitted, dressed and
presented.

As far as I can remember, de Valera went out as a
ship's greaser.   He was dressed or made up for the part
and, to give him confidence, he was paraded in the trams,
etc., through Liverpool.   To use the words of the late
Neil Kerr (who was himself at one time a seafaring man),
"he did not look the part".   However, in spite of personal
disadvantages, de Valera got to the U.S.A. and back without
being arrested, and that was what was wanted.   The same
tactics and camouflage were used in getting Dr. McCartan
and Harry Boland away.

It must be remembered that those acts were carried
out in the enemy's country, where the greatest secrecy was
important, but the I.R.A. and I.R.B. men in charge knew
their work.   Sealed lips was the order of the day.
Michael Collins knew this as well and made use of it to
its utmost, especially in Ireland where he not only
undermined but completely crippled the British Secret
Service movement there.   With men and minds like these,
all tasks were small.

Neil Kerr and Steve Lanigan were directly
responsible for the getting away of the men already referred
to.   Although I knew that these men were going abroad, I
personally had no contact with them.

In addition to wanted men, we had also bogus men -

Eamonn De Valera, President of the Irish Republic, issued the
following statement to the American press and people, at the
Waldorf, New York, Monday:

From today, I am in America as the official head of the Republic
established by the will of the Irish people, in accordance with the
principles of self-determination. Last December Ireland by a more
than three to one majority of deputies- chosen by ballot on adult
suffrage - (the exact figures being 79 to 26) demanded her rights
under this principle.

The deputies chosen on the direct issue of the establishment of
the Republic, outnumber their opponents by more than two to one (the
exact figures being 73 to 32) nor are those who consider the
Republic undesirable as numerous even as the 32 would indicate.

Irish Unanimity.

The degree of unanimity obtained in Ireland on this issue is
higher than that claimed by the American Colonies when they declared
their independence and decided that they would no longer allow
themselves to be exploited by England in the interest of her Imperialism
You had your " Tories " and your " Loyalists " to whom Washington very
properly sent the ultimatum that if they preferred the interest and
protection of Britain to the freedom and happiness of their own
country they might forthwith withdraw themselves and their families
within the enemy lines.

The degree of unanimity obtained in Ireland is higher, too, than
that by which your own glorious Union and Constitution were established
Had complete unanimity been insisted upon as a precedent to your
independence as some people pretend to believe it should be insisted
upon in the recognition of ours then you would not be today as you are
a United Nation, the greatest on the earth with a unified territory
that is a continent and a population and a prosperity that is the envy
of the rest of the world, but merely thirteen miserable dis-united
colonies with your people kept permanently divided by the intrigue of
English state craft into opposing and contending groups- Etchse the

► UCDA, P150/672: De Valera's statement issued to the American press from the Waldorf Hotel in New York, in which he announces his arrival as the 'official head of the Republic established by the will of the Irish people', 23 June 1919.

◄ NAI, BMH, Witness Statement 797, Michael O'Laoghaire, 40: O'Laoghaire was a member of the IRA in Liverpool and helped to organise the clandestine sea trips of Irish republicans. Here, he describes the efforts to smuggle de Valera to the United States in 1919. The Bureau of Military History was established in 1947 to collect statements from people involved in the War of Independence. The statements were eventually opened to researchers in 2003.

CABLE ADDRESS "WALDORF, NEW YORK".

The Waldorf-Astoria
New York

9 - VII - 19

Do Cært. O Gríobha.

a chara,

The papers will give you an account of our doings. My three present objectives are

(1) Pressing un<u>official</u> recognition of the Republic and preparation for campaign re' the Treaty. Hence the present meetings Boston, N. York, Chicago, S.F. — to try later for official — I do not underestimate the difficulty.

(2) The interesting of wealthy men of the race in the industrial development of Ireland — keeping the Commission idea in mind. (Try to get me Faw...

(3) The floating of the bonds. This requires a big organisation and the fund being collected by the Friends of I. Freedom is a bit disconcerting

The whole trouble is to organise the sympathy, for our cause which is widespread and harness it to a definite purpose.

The press is not hostile — but the English are massing their forces against us. I have to watch W. very carefully he could do us great damage were he to come out openly hostile. I am waiting till we have got the people properly first — Then even were he to attack it would not be deadly.

You ought to ask papers like New Ireland etc to be particularly careful at present. They will be re-quoted here by all the Br. agents: Show up what England has got by the war. Send me all the statistics (worked up) etc that you can.

The cases of the murders by the police — e.g. those in opening of the "Two Years Atrocities" should be written up with full detail & sent me. I am anxious about the Tipperary proclamations. I hope nothing too serious.

always in haste

E. deV.

will be glad of hints etc — that goes without saying.

UCDA, P150/728: Arthur Griffith to Daniel Cohalan and John Devoy of the Irish–American support organisation Clan na Gael, in which he pleads for an end to the infighting among Irish–American groups and an end to the attacks being made 'on the authority and credit of the President of the Irish Republic', 23 June 1920. Devoy was a veteran Fenian who fell out with de Valera in 1920 over his strategy in the United States, and later supported the Anglo–Irish Treaty. Cohalan was an Irish–American politician and Judge of the Supreme Court of New York State who also broke with de Valera. He was active in the organisation, Friends of Irish Freedom.

Private

Dáil éireann.

June 23 1920

Seoltar Litreaca cun Runaide Dáil Éireann, f/c Tige an Ard-Maoir, Át-Cliat.

Correspondence may be addressed to the Secretary, Dáil Éireann, c/o Mansion House, Dublin.

Messrs Cohalan
an Devoy

Gentlemen,

The British Propaganda is circulating through the press in this Country and abroad stories of attacks being made at present by prominent citizens of America of Irish blood on the authority and credit of the President of the Irish Republic.

The object of the enemy is to strengthen its hands for the reconquest of Ireland by the overthrow of the Republic of Ireland now in law and fact established.

President De Valera is in the United States vested with the full authority of the Cabinet and Congress of Ireland to secure ~~the~~ explicit recognition by the Government of the United States for the Irish Republic. In such circumstances any word or action which might tend to discredit his office or his mission constitutes an affront and an injury to the Irish Republic. Bitter indignation exists in Ireland at the moment over the reports of these attacks on the Irish President. Public expression of that indignation, I am seeking to avoid. I therefore write personally to appeal to you, gentlemen to give your loyal support to our President in his great work. Men and women are struggling, sacrificing and suffering day by day in Ireland with the profound heroism of the Early Christian Martyrs. I am sure I will not in vain, ask men such as you to make a lesser sacrifice and whatever causes of friction may exist not to permit them further to interfere with loyal support of our President in his work of securing explicit recognition of the Government of Ireland from the Government of the United States

(for the ministry)

Arthur Griffith Vice President.

Export Cigar Manufactory
Jan van der Heijde.

Special brands for
every market

CHOICE BRANDS:
Royal Seal.
Don Alonso.
Sport.
Marine.
Marquis
Georg V.
Janet.
William Buttler.
El Aguila Real.
King Edward.
Etc., etc.

Telegraphic addres :
JAN VANDERHEIJDE
Phone: No. 377.
Code: A. B. C. 5th edition.

*To U.S.J.a
to deal
with*

Eindhoven, July 26th, 1921.
(Holland).

To His Excellency Mr. de Valera
      Prisdent of the First Irish Republic
      Dublin

Excellency,

         We beg you to kindly excuse that we take up some
of your valuable time with such trivial matters as follows.

         We are intending to issue a new series of our
first class cigars for which we would fain choose your name and issue
these brands as the "De Valera Series". However before doing so we
should like to know whether there is no objection on your part to
such proceeding and we shall therefore esteem it a great favour if
youwill kindly drop us a few words to this effect.

         Furthemore we should like to reproduce on the
tickets for the boxes as good a portrait of your Excellency as can
be and should be infinitely honoured if your would instruct your
secretary or your photographrto send us a specimen of your latest
portrait.-

         We beg to tender our apologies for the trouble we
have put you to and our best thanks in advance for your kindness.

         In the meanwhile we beg to remain, Excellency,

                  Your most humble Servants,

NAI, DE 2/526: Jan Van der Heijde to de Valera, 26 July 1921. The summer after he had returned to Ireland from the United States, de Valera acceded to this request from a Dutch manufacturer to create a 'De Valera Series' of first-class cigars with his image on the box.

III

'I would have gone and said,

"Go to the devil,

I will not sign".'

UCDA, P150/3847: De Valera on a podium addressing a mass meeting. 1920s.

By the summer of 1921 the secret contacts and behind-the-scenes diplomacy that would prepare the ground for negotiations between Irish republicans and the British government were gathering momentum. As de Valera wrote to Collins: 'This particular "peace business" has been on for some time. They have tried so many lines of approach that they are banking somewhat on it'.[1] They were helped by the conciliatory speech made by King George V at the opening of Stormont Parliament on June 22, following the May elections in Northern Ireland. These elections arose out of the Government of Ireland Act of 1920 establishing in Northern Ireland a local 52-seat legislature modelled on that of Westminster.

At noon on Monday, 11 July 1921, a negotiated truce between the IRA and the British Army came into operation. De Valera travelled to London the next day to begin exploratory talks with British prime minister David Lloyd George, seeking to get an offer he could bring back to the Dáil. That offer was a limited form of dominion status, with no question of Irish unity without the consent of the Northern parliament, proposals that were rejected. During those meetings with Lloyd George, de Valera wrote to Collins:

> The position is simply this—that L.G. is developing a proposal which he wishes me to bring in my pocket as a proposal to the Irish Nation for its consideration.
>
> The meetings have been between us two alone as principals. ...
>
> You will be glad to know that I am not dissatisfied with the general situation.[2]

But Lloyd George's offer was rejected, and for the rest of the summer, a series of repetitive letters between Lloyd George and de Valera sought to establish a basis for negotiations, with de Valera insisting that his representatives had to be treated as representatives of a sovereign government. When the preconditions were dropped, agreement on negotiations was reached on 30 September, with the talks scheduled to begin on 11 October.

Given that de Valera was keen to define his status as an equal 'principal' to Lloyd George, it is puzzling that he, nonetheless, did not travel to London in October, but instead decided that Arthur Griffith and Michael Collins would lead the delegation. As commented by Patrick Murray, de Valera for many years afterwards spent much time trying to explain and justify his decision not to go to London for the Treaty negotiations.[3]

He offered various explanations as to why he did not attend. He needed to avoid compromising the Republic and to be in a position uncontaminated by negotiations. This distance would allow him to reopen dialogue if the conference broke down, to rally the people in the event of resistance, or to act as a kind of 'final court of appeal to avert whatever Britain might attempt to pull over'. Above all, he remained 'anxious to convey the impression that his decision not to go to London was not his alone but was somehow a collective one'.[4]

Nonetheless, the accusation that he had made a scapegoat of Collins persisted, facilitated by a much more sympathetic approach to Collins than de Valera from historians. But as Collins's most recent biographer, Peter Hart, has pointed out, of all the Dáil ministers, it was de Valera that Collins was closest to until the Treaty split. He did not want to travel to the negotiations without de Valera, but the notion of Collins as the simple soldier, unused to or unable to grasp the art of negotiations is not credible; he sat on the executive of his party, was Minister for Finance and a skilled administrator, and was not going to baulk at the prospect of being centre stage in the search for a solution.[5]

Curiously, in all his post-hoc justifications, de Valera hardly mentions one reason for staying at home which emerges from contemporary documents: the high tensions between Cathal Brugha as Minister for Defence and Richard Mulcahy as Chief-of-Staff of the IRA. Brugha had sent Mulcahy a letter on 13 September 1921 firing him, one of two occasions on which he did this, and it was quite clear the truce 'was devastating' to the relations between the two men.[6]

In 1963 de Valera corresponded with Frank Pakenham (Lord Longford) about the Treaty negotiations. An unstinting admirer of de Valera, Pakenham had published his account of the Treaty negotiations, *Peace by ordeal*, in 1935 and later co-wrote a biography of de Valera with Thomas O'Neill. De Valera's letter to Pakenham was drafted and redrafted with the assistance of Frank Aiken and Maurice Moynihan, and is part of Moynihan's collection of papers held in the UCD Archives, School of History and Archives. It elaborates on the reasons why de Valera chose to remain at home and his surprise at the attitude of Collins: 'Collins was reluctant to go but I persuaded him. I was somewhat surprised at his reluctance for he had been rather annoyed with me for not bringing him on the team when I went to meet Lloyd George earlier on in July'.[7]

He justified his selection of the negotiating team (or plenipotentiaries to give them their official title) on the basis that the group he chose, especially Collins and Griffith, representing the IRB and 'moderates' respectively, 'would form a well balanced team'. He also suggested that 'there seemed, in fact, at the time to be no good reason why I should be on the Delegation'.[8] This was disingenuous. There were very obvious reasons, including his experience, stature, and the fact that members of his own party wanted him there. He also made a reference to his 'external association' proposals (by which Ireland would be an independent country within the Commonwealth, associating with it for defence purposes, and recognising the Crown as 'external' head), observing that he knew such proposals would probably be 'unacceptable to those whose political upbringing had been based on "separatism"'.

Here, de Valera is clearly distinguishing between himself and 'separatists', but at the same time he also believed it was important that if there was a breakdown in the negotiations it 'should not come directly through me, but rather as one whom they regarded as more "moderate"'. He saw this as necessary given the fact that Lloyd George had depicted him as someone who was a diehard and impossible to do business with, and due to the hostile reaction from 'church leaders and others' who were disappointed that he had rejected Lloyd George's July proposal of dominion status.

This can be read two ways: that de Valera was a moderate who did not want to be seen as too moderate, or that this was an exercise in shifting the blame from himself. He also expected that, in the face of a settlement being reached, there would be 'a hard political campaign' and that 'my influence in that campaign would be far more effective if I myself were not a member of the negotiating team, and so completely free from any suggestion that I had been affected by the "London atmosphere"'.[9] This was an indication that de Valera was well aware of the divisions the negotiations would give rise to, and that the atmosphere in Downing Street was going to put the negotiators under considerable pressure.

It was easy for de Valera to think about all these things in the abstract, including the idea that 'it was imperative that the British should realise that they had to face here a determined people, ready to accept a renewal of the war'.[10] He also made the assertion that 'the fact remains that my staying at home was generally accepted by the Dáil and by the country as a whole'. Those last words 'the country as a whole' were crossed out in favour of the word 'people'.[11] In truth, there was opposition in the Cabinet, and he only got his decision through by using his casting vote. De Valera's conclusion to the letter to Pakenham was somewhat self-righteous: 'I hope the above will show that the reasons for the decision that I should not go to London were overwhelming, and that it was the signing of the Articles of Agreement without reference to the Cabinet in Dublin that alone threw everything out of joint'.[12]

Perhaps the real weakness in de Valera's argument was revealed in a follow-up letter to Pakenham sent in February 1963, to the effect that 'there was to my mind, always the danger that those involved in the discussions would give to the words and phrases used in any document arising out of them, such special and limited meaning as might have occurred or been attached to those words and phrases in the discussions themselves'.[13]

Given de Valera's insight in this regard, and his fastidious care with regard to words and phrases, it is quite clear that this was the kind of experience that was needed in London, rather than 'Griffith's political experience and his republican aims'.[14] In any case, to what extent did Griffith have 'republican aims'? His political aim initially had been to convert the Irish Parliamentary Party to his views on dual monarchy, and though he claimed to be a 'separatist', he still clung to the idea of dual monarchy, and his moderation alienated many of the more radical separatists.[15]

De Valera admitted to Joseph McGarrity a few weeks after the Treaty was signed 'that Griffith would accept the Crown under pressure I had no doubt … I felt certain too that [Collins] was contemplating accepting the crown'.[16]

De Valera staying at home and yet wanting to fully participate was eventually to frustrate members of the Irish delegation, as they pointed out in no uncertain terms to de Valera on 26 October 1921, in a letter in which they berated him for tying their hands in discussions and raising doubts about their powers:

> It is obvious that we could not continue any longer in the Conference and should return to Dublin immediately if the powers were withdrawn.
>
> We strongly resent, in the position in which we are placed, the interference with our powers. The responsibility, if this interference breaks the very slight possibility there is of settlement, will not and must not rest on the plenipotentiaries.
>
> As to your coming to London, we think, if you can come without being known, it is important you should do so immediately. But if you cannot come privately do not come

publicly unless we send you a message that in our opinion it is essential.[17]

It should also be pointed out that Griffith and Collins kept de Valera and the Cabinet in Dublin in the dark about their secret dealings with Lloyd George and Tom Jones, a member of the British War Cabinet Secretariat, who referred in his diaries to the 'private discussions and bargaining' that went on.[18] Robert Barton, an Irish plenipotentiary, recalled in his witness statement to the Bureau of Military History:

> Possibly Lloyd George felt that he could make more progress with Griffith and Collins than he had made with a full delegation … It was not until later that Gavan Duffy, Childers and I realised that Griffith and Collins were prepared to settle for less than we thought it possible to obtain. We had trusted them fully. We had complete confidence in them up to that time. Griffith fought magnificent actions during the full conference. We had no reason to suppose at the time that he would agree in private to anything which he had not been agreeing to with five of us present … It was decided that one of us must go to Dublin to acquaint the Cabinet and de Valera that we were not at all sure that the reports given us of what transpired at private conferences were comprehensive.[19]

But the confusion about the powers of the plenipotentiaries was partly a result of the conflicting signals being given by de Valera. His critics quite legitimately pointed to the inconsistency of his position; having prepared for compromise with Lloyd George 'he had then rushed back to the rock of republicanism' and seemed to be sending conflicting messages to the Irish negotiators. Another problem was that the Dáil had granted them plenipotentiary powers but privately, they were issued with other, contradictory instructions by the Cabinet to the effect that before signing any agreement, they would have to refer it back to the Cabinet. Not only did this mean bypassing the Dáil (something de Valera seems to have had no qualms about during the War of Independence), but given that three members of the Cabinet were in London, the 'Cabinet in Dublin' meant those who had not been prepared to go to the negotiations in the first place because of their opposition to compromise.[20]

As Michael Laffan pointed out, in the private Dáil sessions of August 1921, de Valera interpreted 'plenipotentiary' as meaning someone who was 'sent over to make peace' and who came back 'and their actions were ratified or not'. Yet, in practice, he saw their position in a different light and he was 'determined to be involved—even at a distance—in any final settlement'.[21] As late as 3 December, with a draft Treaty being discussed in Dublin, there was confusion about what the Cabinet's bottom line was, in the absence of an undisputed strategy, and this fault line was never mended.

The two months of negotiations ended at 2:30a.m. on 6 December 1921 when agreement was reached on an Anglo–Irish Treaty. The agreement caught people by surprise because for long periods it appeared that both sides were merely angling for the more favourable standpoint when the apparently inevitable breakdown arrived. On Wednesday, 7 December, Kathleen O'Connell recorded in her diary ('P', denoting President, refers to de Valera):

> Treaty published in all the papers this morning. P. in an awful state. Oh what a disappointment to our bright hopes—what a fiasco. Cabinet meeting at 11.30. President was thinking of recalling delegation, and asking for [the] resignation of Cabinet Ministers—Griffith, Collins and Barton. G's statement about 'freedom' & c. such a farce. Partition of our country and British subjects is the 'freedom' we are to have.[22]

The account of a Cabinet meeting on 8 December, held in de Valera's own papers, consists of a copy of notes taken by Erskine Childers, who had acted as secretary to the negotiators. Arthur Griffith made the point that 'we had offered to stand out. Asked Dev to come over'. Dev remarked that 'I would have gone and said, "Go to the devil. I will not sign"'.[23] It was easy for de Valera to maintain that, given that he chose not to travel. But it was later on in the meeting that inconsistencies became apparent in de Valera's position. De Valera maintained that Arthur Griffith had said at an earlier meeting that the document could not be signed 'but must go to [the] Dáil. Otherwise I would probably have gone to L.[ondon]'.[24] Here, de Valera seemed to suggest it was for the Dáil and not the Cabinet to ratify.

De Valera bears a responsibility for allowing such confusion to develop. There can be no doubt that the title of president of the 'abstract' republic was taken extremely seriously by de Valera, but his gamble—that he could stay at home, untainted by the negotiations and then sell his 'external association' compromise—involved a serious underestimation of the pressure his colleagues were under—pressure he had directly contributed to by refusing to go to London. The British and Northern Irish prime ministers always represented themselves at such important Anglo–Irish negotiations, and Lloyd George too had Cabinet considerations. Joe Lee is probably correct in asserting that de Valera's choice in 1921 was less conspiracy than miscalculation.[25]

De Valera, Cathal Brugha and Austin Stack rejected the Treaty, de Valera stating he could not support the agreement which was in 'violent conflict' with the wishes of the majority. By January, after almost 100 TDs had spoken at thirteen days of the Treaty debates held in University College at Earlsfort Terrace, the Treaty was supported by 64 votes to 57. De Valera led his supporters out of government and Sinn Féin's carefully constructed unity lay broken.

Regarding de Valera's position early in 1922, Owen Dudley Edwards has correctly asserted that, given the depth of republican militarism, 'the civil war would have happened if he had supported the Treaty'.[26] This is indeed likely, given the difficulties that de Valera already had in dealing with the militants and his honest admissions about his own lack of extremism. It is a reminder of the danger of isolating de Valera as the embodiment of intransigence in the immediate aftermath of the Treaty.

In the subsequent fall-out from the signing of the Treaty, Michael Collins consistently outclassed and out-performed de Valera. Of course, the divisions in the republican movement after the Treaty were painful and difficult, but one of the main characteristics of Collins was his sheer decisiveness once a decision had been made.[27] The same could not be said of de Valera during this period; it is likely the reason that he kept returning to the subject of the Treaty and the Civil War was to impose a retrospective decisiveness on his actions that was simply not in accordance with his mind or with the sequence of events as they unfolded. De Valera's determination to win any public opinion or propaganda battles was evident very quickly. Two weeks after the Treaty was signed, according to Kathleen O'Connell's diary, he was 'determined to have a paper "Republic of Ireland" with [Erskine] Childers as editor'.[28]

But he had little influence over his republican colleagues who occupied the Four Courts in April, and he did agree an election pact in May to attempt to create a national coalition of pro- and anti-Treaty Sinn Féin, relative to their existing strength in the Dáil, which did not work in practice during the election of June 1922 (pro-Treaty Sinn Féin won 58 seats, anti-Treaty Sinn Féin won 36 and labour, farmers and independents the remaining 34).

As Patrick Murray points out, de Valera occasionally gave the impression that 'violent insurrection by a minority ... may be deemed legitimate provided a majority comes to approve of it at some later stage'.[29] In this, he was not unusual as a member of the Irish republican family in 1922, but contradictions and inconsistencies abounded during these years. Maybe there is also a tendency to view some of his speeches in early 1922 through the prism of the outbreak of Civil War rather than putting them in the context of a Civil War that had not yet started, was not seen as inevitable, and took him by surprise,[30] although in holding to the belief that he could still unite the two sides he was being unrealistic and stubborn.

By the end of the twentieth century it became fashionable to retrospectively impose a contemporary definition and interpretation of democracy and to project it back to 1922. It was also often forgotten that the Treaty settlement came about as a result of the threat of 'immediate and terrible war' if the Irish plenipotentiaries did not sign, and this was something that the British Treaty delegates were very sensitive about in later years. In 1928 Lionel Curtis, who had acted as secretary to the British delegation, warned Churchill not to mention the threat in a forthcoming memoir.[31]

Any account of these times that seeks to blame any one person or party for the Civil War involves simplifying a confused time, and it is fair to describe de Valera during the Civil War as being led rather than being the leader. This is one of the reasons why written accounts of this period that are sympathetic to de Valera—most obviously Dorothy Macardle's *The Irish Republic*, first published in 1937—focus on the failures in the Irish Free State rather than the divisions, despair and turmoil within Irish republicanism, which is completely ignored.[32]

De Valera's contemporary references to the homogeneity within republicanism were delusional or disingenuous, or both. His true feelings on these subjects were apparent in his correspondence with Mary MacSwiney, included in his personal papers. During the Civil War, he sought to explain why he could not share her uncompromising republicanism:

> Reason rather than Faith has been my master. …
>
> I have felt for some time that this doctrine of mine unfitted [*sic*] me to be leader of the Republican Party. … Nature never fashioned me to be a partisan leader in any case and I am sorry that I did not insist on Cathal's [Brugha] assuming the leadership when the party was being formed. For the sake of the cause I allowed myself to be put into a position which it is impossible for one of my outlook and personal bias to fill with effect for the party. … Every instinct of mine would indicate that I was meant to be a dyed-in-the wool Tory, or even a Bishop, rather than the leader of a Revolution.[33]

It was an extraordinary letter—raw and honest—that revealed much about his vulnerability, frustration and hopelessness during the Civil War, and the lowest point in his public life, where he was unable or unwilling to control the momentum of events. The biography of de Valera by Seán O'Faoláin, published in 1933 (a book O'Faoláin later described as 'arrant tripe'),[34] was sympathetic to de Valera on the subject of the Civil War, suggesting it was 'most cruelly unjust to blame him … over the militarists he had no control [over] and they avoided or rejected his influence, so that when he issued his cease fire order in May 1923 he only did so because the chastened militarists were only too glad to accept his control that they had once rejected'.[35]

This was a view that went out of fashion. Tom Garvin's survey of this period makes much of the fact that republicanism and majority rule did not sit very comfortably together at this point, and he adds that de Valera had 'a paranoid misunderstanding of the actual sovereign status of the Free State'; that he had a 'sneaking regard' for the republican diehards in the south and west of Ireland, and was apt to present himself as a humble soldier (he rejoined the IRA Dublin Brigade's Third Battalion following his resignation as president of the Irish Volunteers) following the men of 'faith' rather than reason, which he saw as a much more noble stance, because 'reason' could not give him the truth.[36]

Garvin's criticisms of the activities of de Valera during the Civil War are valid, but the tendency to project a twenty-first century view of democracy to the 1920s in Ireland is still problematical. In truth, the distribution of anti-democrats was quite even between pro- and anti-Treaty sides.[37] As well as certainty in the minds of some, there was confusion in the minds of many, including de Valera. He was not one of the 'abstract fanatics' of the republican movement referred to dismissively, or impatiently, by Seán O'Faoláin's wife, Eileen,[38] and while it may be true that 'he slid into incoherence' at times in mid 1922,[39] it was also the case that such incoherence was born of ambivalence about the side he was now stuck with, and they in turn were sceptical about his republican credentials and appetite for the fight. As Michael Laffan observed, 'De Valera might appear intransigent to supporters of the Treaty, but to sea-green incorruptible republicans his views were suspiciously moderate'.[40]

Such 'incorruptible republicans' would, it is likely, have fought regardless of whether de Valera rejected the Treaty or not, but it has remained a common belief that while de Valera did not start the Civil War, neither did he do enough to stop it. The killing of Michael Collins in an ambush in August 1922, when he was head of the new National Army, gave further ammunition to the critics of de Valera's Civil War conduct.

But had he really lost the plot completely? Was he a shivering, broken-down wreck as depicted in Neil Jordan's 1996 film, *Michael Collins*, which did much to create, or perhaps sustain, that image of him, and was a thorough hatchet job? On one occasion, the barman asked the 'de Valera' who used to emerge from a fridge on RTÉ's *Nighthawks* if he wanted a drink, to which he replied that he would have 'A Mick Collins'. 'A Mick Collins?', the bewildered barman inquired. 'One shot—and hit the road', said Dev. As Luke Gibbons noted wryly: 'It is difficult to know whether the joke is at his or Michael Collins's expense'.[41]

But whatever about indigenous black humour, the Jordan film, in introducing de Valera to a younger generation for the first time, ensured the Hollywood treatment was at de Valera's expense. Alan Rickman, the skilful actor who portrayed de Valera, broached this issue when interviewed by Hugh Linehan of the *Irish Times*:

> It's not so much a question of characterisation, though, as of certain scenes being left out. If I were sitting here with the de Valera family, I'd say: 'Believe me, I spent a lot of time and energy fighting his corner, in terms of not judging him. But I can't answer for what the director or the studio do'. In the script, there was a very important moment—which was cut—which made it clear that he was not involved in the death of Collins. But other forces wanted the film to end on a romantic notion rather than a political one. ... What's the point of whingeing about it? It's the sort of story that would need about 12 hours to tell properly, but that isn't going to happen.[42]

The verdict of Harry Browne is accurate: 'Too much of the movie relies on flawed plot and characters resting on a complex—nay, contrived—structure of relationships that can't bear the weight', particularly in the context of the triangle of Harry Boland, de Valera and Collins.[43] As Joe Lee pointed out when reviewing the film, there was nothing that Collins stood for in the film—including his ambivalence about the status of the Republic and partition—which was not adopted by de Valera ten years later.[44]

During the Civil War, de Valera, it seems, felt the need to continue to repeat the republican mantras of incorruptibility, in exchanges that now seem bizarrely delusional, as evidenced by his letter to Joseph McGarrity in Philadelphia on Dáil Éireann notepaper in February 1923:

> The Free State[rs] are starting the old villainous misrepresen-tation. I have always tried to think that our opponents are acting from high motives, but there is no doubt there is a bit of the scoundrel in O'Higgins.

Some more of our good men are falling by the way, but there can be no turning back for us now. One big effort from our friends everywhere and I think we would finally smash the Free State. Our people have a hard time of suffering before them, and we have of course to face the possibility of the British forces coming back and taking up the fight where the others lay it down—But God is good! …

The critical moment here has just arrived. Both sides are strained to the utmost, but I think we can bear it better than our opponents can … Already they are divided into a war party and a peace party, almost of equal strength, I am told. We are a far more homogenous body than they are. If this war were finished Ireland would not have the heart to fight any other war for generations, so we must see it through.[45]

Allowing for the morale boosting that was a part of this letter, contrast these expressed views with the de Valera sanctioned 'official' republican version in Dorothy Macardle's *The Irish Republic*. Only one line is devoted to de Valera's apparent paralysis during the Civil War: 'He did not believe it probable that the IRA could prevail or that any good could come to Ireland by continuing this war and he expressed this view to some of the military leaders, earnestly asking them to consider whether victory was not clearly out of reach'.[46]

In his letter to his republican comrades requesting them to dump arms in May 1923, de Valera reserved his most damning criticism for the church, with scathing references to the 'moral leaders especially, whose influence in a crisis like this would be beyond price, have allowed themselves to be so entangled in the conflict that they are now useless. … they have displayed a spirit of hate and vindictiveness more narrow and bigoted even than that of the professional politicians'.[47]

The same month, he was conscious of the extent to which the Civil War had narrowed his options and left him bereft of control, and the need to try and regain the semblance of unity that had existed in 1917. He sent a letter to the Organising Committee of Sinn Féin concerning their resolution that a political organisation—The Irish Republican Political Organisation—be formed. De Valera objected to this on the grounds that 'purely republican needs' were already catered for by the IRA:

We wish to organise not merely Republican opinion, strictly so-called, but what might be called 'Nationalist', or 'Independence' opinion in general. If we do not do it, the other side will and the loss will be immense. ...

To attempt to found a further Republican organisation would be wasteful duplication that would serve no purpose whatever. ...

The position is in many respects similar to that we had to face in the middle of 1917. If we act as wisely and as energetically as we acted then, we shall win the people over once more.[48]

UCDA, P150/1875: Joking with a guard in Arbour Hill, between January and July 1924. Austin Stack (former Sinn Féin Minister for Home Affairs), de Valera and 'Keegan' (from Limerick) with a Free State officer/guard aiming his revolver at them in jest.

UCDA, P150/3618: Back row: Richard Mulcahy (IRA Chief of Staff); Michael Rynne (aide-de-camp to Richard Mulcahy). Front row: Cathal Brugha (Minister for Defence); Rynne's grandfather, Stephen O'Mara (former Parnellite MP); de Valera; and Rynne's mother (and O'Mara's daughter), Mary, 6 December 1921. This was taken at Strand House, Limerick, home of Stephen O'Mara on the morning that the Treaty was signed. De Valera had received the freedom of the city of Limerick the previous day.

UCDA, P150/1874: In prison in Arbour Hill, 1924. Austin Stack,
de Valera and 'Keegan' sitting in the prison yard.

UCDA, P150/3666: De Valera outside Áras an
Uachtaráin examining a copy of the American edition
of Dorothy Macardle's *The Irish Republic*, 5 October
1965. Found in an envelope labelled 'President taken
with copy of American edition of *The Irish Republic*.
5th October, 1965 day of publication'.

NAI, DE 2/244: De Valera to Michael Collins, 15 July 1921. De Valera expresses optimism about his preliminary discussions with British prime minister David Lloyd George.

TELEPHONE:- VIC... IA 9940 (12 LINES.)
TELEGRAMS:-GR... ENOR HOTEL, LONDON."

17 JUL 1921

GROSVENOR HOTEL

LONDON

S.W.1.

Secret.

July 15

To Min of Finance,

I am sure you are anxious to hear whether any important developments have taken place. The position is simply this — that L.G. is developing a proposal which he wishes me to bring in my pocket as a proposal to the Irish Nation for its consideration.

The meetings have been between us two alone as principals. The general idea on which we the ministry started out remains unchanged.

You will be glad to know that I am not dissatisfied with the general situation.

The proposal will be theirs — we will be free to consider it without prejudice.

Hope to see you about the middle of the week

Dev.

P.S. We must put back D. meeting Am writing D.H.

(English translation)

NAI, DE 2/302: De Valera to Lloyd George, 30 September 1921. In accepting the decision to send delegates to London to discuss a political solution, de Valera brought to an end the long drawn out correspondence between himself and the British prime minister during the summer of 1921.

Mansion House,
Dublin,
30th September, 1921.

Rt. Hon. D. Lloyd George,
Gairloch.

Sir,

We have received your letter of invitation to a Conference in London on October 11th "with a view to ascertaining how the association of Ireland with the community of Nations known as the British Empire may best be reconciled with Irish national aspirations."

Our respective positions have been stated and are understood, and we agree that conference, not correspondence, is the most practical and hopeful way to an understanding. We accept the invitation, and our Delegates will meet you in London on the date mentioned "to explore every possibility of settlement by personal discussion."

Faithfully yours,

EAMON DE VALERA.

It was thus made clear that during the negotiations there would be constant contact between the Delegation and the Cabinet at home. Indeed I do not believe that until the last moment before signing any member of the Delegation regarded himself otherwise than as bound by these instructions.

But, perhaps, I should begin at the beginning. When the question of choosing a Delegation first arose my thought was to send Brugha and Stack with Griffith and Collins. Brugha and Stack were unwilling. Further, I myself realised on reflection that these four would not work well as a team unless I accompanied them. That would mean, apart from other considerations, taking five members, practically the whole Government, out of the country for a considerable period at a most critical time. In this connection I may remark that it was our purpose unless agreement were reached to prolong the negotiations so that in the case of a "break" it should occur at a time favourable to operations by our army.

This left me with Griffith and Collins. They by themselves alone, it seemed, would form a well balanced team. Griffith would have the confidence of the"moderates" and Collins that of the I.R.B. and the Army, and the latterss being on the Delegation would, I thought, keep this section of public opinion steady, a matter of no small importance, during the negotiations. Griffith was our Minister for for Foreign Affairs. Collins was our Minister for Finance as well as our Director of Army Intelligence.

With these two as the leaders no one could suggest that the Delegation was not a strong and representative one. and it would be so regarded if sent by any other state.

They were both able men who had given great service to our country and were well fitted, I thought, to stand up for Irish rights against any British arguments. Griffith was a man of considerable political experience, and in his book, The Resurrection of Hungary, and in the papers he had edited had shown that he was well aware of British diplomatic wiles. The two men had worked together, so far as I was aware, in harmony when I was out of the country.

Lest my feference to the regard which the "moderates" had for Griffith might create any wrong impression I should point out, perhaps, that since the Convention of the new Sinn Féin in 1917 Griffith had accepted the Republican aim, and in all my intercourse with him from that time I had not known him to recede from that position. He had on more than one occasion in my absence signed official documents as Acting President of the Republic.

Collins was reluctant to go but I persuaded him. I was somewhat surprised at his reluctance for he had been rather annoyed with me for not bringing him on the team when I went to meet Lloyd George earlier on, in July. I now considered it essential that he should go with Griffith.

Having fixed on Griffith and Collins as the leaders, we added Barton, our Minister for Economic Affairs; and to strengthen the legal side Gavan Duffy, who had been one of our representatives abroad and had, I knew, a keen legal mind and was well acquainted with diplomatic procedure. Duggan, a solicitor, was a further aid on the legal side. He had been out in Easter Week and was, I believed, a member of the I.R.B. All, had, of course, finally Cabinet approval.

UCDA, P122/119: De Valera to Frank Pakenham (Lord Longford), 24 February 1963 (pages 2–7 of which are reproduced here, page 7 is incorrectly labelled '6'). De Valera defends in detail his reasons for not being a part of the delegation that negotiated the Anglo–Irish Treaty in 1921. Pakenham, who revered de Valera, published his account of the Treaty negotiations, *Peace by Ordeal*, in 1935 and was joint author, with Thomas P. O'Neill, of the officially approved biography of de Valera, published in 1970.

Childers, I knew, would be an admirable secretary, painstaking, methodical and brilliant; one who with Barton would be likely to understand the British mind and methods and be a further safeguard were there to be any British manoeuvring. We appointed him.

With such a team in constant contact with the Cabinet in Dublin I believed that my presence on the Delegation was unnecessary. There seemed, in fact, at the time to be no good reason why I should be on the Delegation, but I expected to be in the closest contact with it.

There was, on the other hand, a host of good reasons why I should remain at home. One had, above all, to look ahead and provide for the outcome of the negotiations. They would end either in a "make" or a "break" - in a settlement based on the accepted Cabinet policy of external association, or in a failure of the negotiations with a probable renewal of war. In either case I could best serve the national interest by remaining at home.

If the outcome were to be the settlement we had envisaged, that based on external association, it was almost certain that it would be no easy task to get that settlement accepted wholeheartedly by the Dáil and by the Army. The arrangement was a novel one. The kind of association involved was new to our public opinion.

Although such a settlement would leave independence and the Republic intact and give a united Ireland, nevertheless an association in which Britain was involved, even though the association was to be with the States of the Commonwealth rather than with Britain alone, was bound to be unpalatable to those whose political upbringing had been based on "separati The whole idea was foreign to the "separatist" way of thinking.

I had, therefore, no doubt at the time and have no
doubt now, that had the settlement we had agreed on in the
Cabinet been concluded, a hard political campaign would lie
ahead of us.   My influence in that campaign would be far
more effective if I myself were not a member of the
negotiating team, and so completely free from any suggestion
that I had been affected by the "London atmosphere".

Moreoever, whilst the negotiations were in progress
it was imperative that the British should realize that they
had to face here a determined people, ready to accept a
renewal of the war rather than give way on the essentials.
For this reason, my presence at home was desirable so that
I might play my part in keeping public opinion firm and in
doing everything possible to have the Army well organised
and strong.   Besides, I apprehended that rumours of "surrender"
were sure to be rife the moment it was reported that a
settlement was in sight.   It was important that I should
be at hand to deal with any public uneasiness to which these
might give rise.

On the other hand, if the outcome of the negotiations
were to be a "break" it was vital that public opinion here
should be properly prepared for it and the Army in as fit
a state of readiness as possible to meet the resumption
of hostilities.   The views of the "moderates", Church
leaders and others, those who would have been willing to
accept some form of "home rule", had in this case of a "break"
obviously to be kept in mind.   To meet their case it was
better that the "break" should not come directly through me,
but rather through one whom they regarded as more "moderate".
My action in turning down out of hand the Lloyd George proposals
of July 20th 1921, when I was with him in London, had met with
strong disapproval from this section of our people.

From the time of my meeting with him, Lloyd George had done everything in his power to create the impression that I was an impossible person, one with whom no one could do business, and this some of the "moderates" here were accepting and propagating as a fact. Were there to be a "bfeak" with a section of our people discontented and restless, the national position would be dangerously weakened ~~on the resumption of hostilities~~ *when the war was resumed.* I was providing for this contingency much better by remaining at home than by leading the Delegation.

$\otimes$

It was, I am sure, considerations like the above that secured acceptance of my view that I should not go to London. I had no doubt myself that my view as the right one. The fact/~~is~~ *remains* that my staying at home was generally accepted by the Dáil and by the ~~country as a whole~~ *people*, and the question did not become a serious issue until the Articles of Agreement were signed and *the* political division in Dáil Éireann had occurred.

It is possible that opinion was somewhat affected by the almost universal view at the time that President Wilson had made a fatal mistake in going himself to Paris to participate in the Peace and League of Nations discussions, and there was an inclination to ~~apply an analogy to~~ *regard* the case here *as analogous.*

I must add that notwithstanding all the initial reasons for my not going to London, I had *at the Cabinet meeting of Dec 3rd,* when the position had become critical made up my mind to go until Griffith stated that he would not sign the British proposals ~~and~~ *but* would leave it to us and Dáil Eireann to reject them. *The cabinet then decided that I should not go.*

Among further considerations which I might mention was that we had to emphasise from the outset that we were entering into these negotiations in the same manner as any established state would enter into negotiations with another state. For

this reason all the fomralities of letters of credence, etc.,
were ~~scrupulously~~ observed in the appointment of the
delegation.   ~~Itxis~~   There is nother point: the fact that
I was here and that referring home was necessary added
strength to the position of the negotiators.   In cases
of difficulty, they could always look for time to refer back.

It was Lloyd George's constant ~~aim~~ *endeavour* to get Irish
representatives regarded merely as members of a British
domestic political party, instead of as representatives of
a nation that had declared its independence.   We had to
combat this endeavour and to insist, as I had done in
the long correspondence with the British Prime Minister
preceding the negotiations, that it was only as the
representatives of a State which had declared its independence
that we had any authority to negotiate.   This insistence
led, ~~as you may remember,~~ to the breakdown at Gairloch,
and, as you know, the negotiations were ~~actually~~ *finally* entered
upon without either side accepting the position of the other
side or abandoning its own.   It was more in consonance with
our position as an independent State, and emphasised it, that
the Delegation should be led by the Minister for Foreign
Affairs rather than by one who was not merely head of the
Government but also President and head of the State.

I hope the above will show that the reasons
for the decision that I should not go to London were
overwhelming, and that it was the signing of the Articles
of Agreement without reference to the Cabinet in Dublin
that alone threw everything out of joint.

P.S. I am sure it is not necessary
for me to deal with the absurd claim
that because the delegates were called
"Envoys Plenipotentiary" they were free
to act as they pleased. Their "full powers"
were of course subject to their credentials
and to their instructions.

87

Dáil Éireann.

9.

IRISH DELEGATION OF PLENIPOTENTIARIES.

SECRETARIAT.

October 26th, 1921.

A. E. A Chara,

Your letters reached me this evening.   It is impossible for me, with the engagements we have this evening and the time at my disposal to deal with all the matters.

I have got a meeting of the delegates and secretaries. The delegates regard the first paragraph of your letter No. 7 as tying their hands in discussion and as inconsistent with the powers given them on their appointment and Nos 1 and 2 of "Instructions to Plenipotentiaries from Cabinet" dated 7th October.

Obviously any form of association necessitates discussion of recognition in some form or other of the head of the association.   Instruction 2 conferred this power of discussion but required before a decision was made reference to the members of the Cabinet in Dublin.

The powers were given by the Cabinet as a whole and can only be withdrawn or varied by the Cabinet as a whole.   Having regard to the stage discussions have reached now, it is obvious that we could not continue any longer in the Conference and should return to Dublin immediately *if the powers were withdrawn.* *A.G.*

We strongly resent, in the position in which we are placed, the interference with our powers.   The responsibility, if this interference breaks the very slight possibility there is, of settlement, will not and must not rest on the plenipotentiaries.

As to your coming to London, we think, if you can come without being known, it is most important you should do so immediately. *But if you cannot come privately do not come publicly unless we send you a message that in our opinion it is essential – A.G.*

* Art O Gríobhtha*

Riobárd Bartún

Seorsa Gabháin uí Dubhthaigh

E. S. Ó Dúgáin

Mícheál O Coileáin

Oáil éiReann.

7th October, 1921.

INSTRUCTIONS TO PLENIPOTENTIARIES FROM

CABINET.

(1) The Plenipotentiaries have full powers as defined in their credentials.

(2) It is understood however that before decisions are finally reached on the main questions that a despatch notifying the intention of making these decisions will be sent to the Members of the Cabinet in Dublin and that a reply will be awaited by the Plenipotentiaries before the final decision is made.

(3) It is also understood that the complete text of the draft treaty about to be signed will be similarly submitted to Dublin and reply awaited.

(4) In case of break the text of final proposals from our side will be similarly submitted.

(5) It is understood that the Cabinet in Dublin will be kept regularly informed of the progress of the negotiations.

Éamon de Valéra

----------oOo----------

4 SUNDAY [338-27]
2 in Advent

✗ visit Galway from Loughrea

5 MONDAY [339-26]

President was presented with Freedom of Limerick. Stayed at Strand House

6 TUESDAY [340-25]

✗ No Dante celebration tonight. 7.30
President returned home from Clare at about 2.30. Had lunch at 5.3. Went to Greystones & returned about 7. About 8.30 Duggan called. He had returned from London with the Treaty. President did not meet him until 7.15 at the Mt. That was first time he saw final draft. He got a shock.

7 WEDNESDAY [341-24]

Treaty published in all the papers this morning. I in an awful state. Oh what a disappointment — to our bright hopes — what a fiasco. Cabinet meeting at 11.30. President was thinking of recalling Delegation

UCDA, P155/138: Kathleen O'Connell's desk diary, 7 December 1921. On the day following the signing of the Treaty she expresses her disappointment.

UCDA, P150/657: De Valera to Mary MacSwiney during the Civil War, 11 September 1922. In it he expresses doubts about his suitability for a life in politics, and his inability to make common cause with extreme republicanism. Trenchant in her opposition to the Anglo–Irish Treaty, MacSwiney had been elected to the Dáil in May 1921 and served as president of Cumann na mBan. She was imprisoned twice during the Civil War and released after a 21-day hunger strike. She refused to support the new Fianna Fáil party after its foundation in 1926.

<u>Private</u>   September 11, 1922.

Miss McSwiney,

A Chara:

        I recd. your letter - letters I should have said. I
have done my utmost to be angry with you since I got the first
of them, but it is impossible -- you are incorrigible!

        As long as you keep on the plane of Faith and Unreason
and maintain that position consciously, so as to make yourself
inaccessible and drive all who would reason with you to despair,
-- I can understand it perfectly as a ruse of expediency - no one
can ever possibly weaken <u>you</u>. They must blow you up, and the
F.S. are saying just this as excuse for their militarism.

        Unfortunately for me, Reason rather than Faith has been
my master. I do not believe we have any right to expect the
Almighty to work miracles for our special benefit. If they come
by the way and help us, we can be grateful but it is presumption
on our part if we set reason aside and rely on them.

        I have felt for some time that this doctrine of mine
unfitted me to be leader of the Republican Party. I cannot think
as you and Count Plunkett and in another way as Liam Mellows
thinks. Nature never fashioned me to be a partisan leader in
any case, and I am sorry that I did not insist on Cathal's assuming
the leadership when the party was being formed. For the sake of
the cause I allowed myself to be put into a position which it is
impossible for one of my outlook and personal bias to fill with
effect for the party. I must be the heir to generations of
conservatism. Every instinct of mine would indicate that I was
meant to be a dyed-in-the wool Tory or even a Bishop, rather than
the leader of a Revolution.

        I have honestly and faithfully endeavoured to discharge
the duties of every position I occupied so as to realise the ideals
of those who elected me to these positions. I have made myself a
slave at times in order to do so. As soon as I can do it without
injuring the cause, I intend to claim my own personal freedom again.

        I find I have written you a letter such as I have never before
written to anybody -- but I let it go. You will assume on reading
it that I am in the depths of despair, and you will be wrong. To
see things as they are is not to dispair. There are difficulties
for both sides in this struggle, and if I see our own, I see also
those of our opponents. Nor do I forget the margin for miracles --
dont be too confident they may be thrown in on the scale on the
other side as well as on ours. The side that most deserves them
will get them. And to deserve them each of us must act as our

reason and our conscience or our higher instincts prompt u

    And now having made such a lengthy confession, it would be natural to look for absolution, but I ask only fo absolution for my sins of typewriting. I trust the margin for miracles will not turn out as unsatisfactory as this. Note that it is caused by not putting the sheet in straigh and point the moral.

    Kindest regards to Annie - she may see this.

                    E. de V.

► Seán Cronin (ed.), *The McGarrity papers* (Tralee, 1972), 124: De Valera to Joseph McGarrity, 10 September 1922. De Valera writes optimistically of the republican cause during the Civil War. A prominent member of Clan na Gael, McGarrity formed Friends of Irish Freedom with John Devoy and Daniel Cohalan, to provide assistance to Dáil Éireann during the War of Independence and also ran the American Association for Recognition of the Irish Republic. He managed de Valera's tour of the US in 1919–20. He was an implacable opponent of the Anglo–Irish Treaty, and remained a supporter of the IRA.

COPY   I5

D A I L   E I R E A N N

IRE UM DNOTHA COIDRIOCHA   BAILE ATHA CLIATH

Joseph McGarrity, Esq.,   February 5th, 1923
3714, Chestnut St.,
PHILADELPHIA

My dear Joe:

              Just a line.   I find it necessary to
publish that confidential letter I wrote you December a year
ago, but not the postscript of course.

              The Free State are starting the old
villainous misrepresentation.   I have always tried to think
that our opponents are acting from high motives, but there is
no doubt there is a bit of the scoundrel, in O'Higgins.

              Some more of our good men are falling by
the way, but there can be no turning back for us now.   One
big effort from our friends everywhere and I think we would
finally smash the Free State.   Our people have a hard time of
suffering before them, and we have of course to face the possibility of the British forces coming back and taking up
the fight where the others lay it down - But God is good!

              I am very anxious about our chief repre-
sentative over there.   I want you to keep an eye on him, and
prevent him from being rushed into any foolish adventures, or
from being made the instrument of the designs of any cliques.
I have repeatedly told him that he must rely on you for
honest disinterested advice, and to keep in touch with you
constantly.

              The critical moment here has just arrived.
Both sides are strained to the utmost, but I think we can bear
it better than our opponents can, tho' at this very moment we
received the biggest blow we have got since we started.   If
they find that it doesn't knock us out they will despair, I
think.   Already they are divided into a war party and a
peace party, almost of equal strength, I am told.   We are a
far more homogenous body than they are.   If this war were
finished Ireland would not have the heart to fight any other
war for generations, so we must see it through.

              This is only a scrappy note, but you will
understand.   Kindest regards to Mrs. McGarrity and the
family.   I hope you are all keeping well.

                              Yours very sincerely,

          (sgd.)   EAMON DE VALERA.

<u>Confidential</u>

A Chara:-

   The Government and Army Command have unanimously
decided that the Republican cause can no longer be defended
successfully by military effort. It has become necessary
to transfer the contest to another plane. Accordingly, in
a few days an order to "dump" arms and to cease military
activities against the Free State will be issued to our
forces.

   This will mean peace if our men are not pursued
and harried by the Free State. If they are, it can only
mean the beginning of a far more horrible type of warfare
than that which we have so far experienced. The split in
the nation is already deep and the bitterness between the
opposing parties intense. If this new fighting starts
it will persist, I fear, until the nation is completely
crippled and all hope in the future lost.

   Good-will on our part alone cannot prevent this.
We are sorely in need of the help of all who have learned
to think broadly in terms of the nation. This is why I
write you. The particular help that you can give you will,
yourself, be best judge of.

   The transition has to be effected. But, for this
most dangerous passage, those who could be of value for the
steering are for the most part already arrayed as partisans
in hostile camps. The moral leaders especially, whose
influence in a crisis like this would be beyond price, have
allowed themselves to be so entangled in the conflict that
they are now useless. Instead of an all-embracing love which
would be a balm to all the wounds, they have displayed a
spirit of hate and vindictiveness more narrow and bigoted
even than that of the professional politicians. As for the
people in the mass, there is little hope from them. They are
disorganised, worn out, and disheartened. They have become
inert and apathetic - very many even cynical. There has been
so much misrepresentation and lying that they have trust in
no one and see no direction towards which they can turn with
confidence. It is also sad when the future could be so bright
Some special way of helping may occur to you. Please give it
thought.

all so

I suppose you have heard how our *our* recent visitor fared here.
His attitude was so sympathetic that all people thronged to
visit him with the result that you know of. I had one interview
with him, in which we discussed matters generally. He came,
unfortunately, at a bad time for us. The peacemaker has always
an almost irresistible temptation to try to effect his object
by bringing pressure on the weaker side to give in. I am afraid
our visitor was succumbing to it when he should have stood
rigidly for impartial justice. However, his task was almost
superhuman and it is easy to criticise.

What his ecclesiastical mission was, I do not know, but
he seems to have received scant courtesy from the Bishops.
Some of our people seemed inclined to petition for a permanent
delegation. I had some difficulty in pointing out to them that
that might be very far from a blessing. It is much easier for
a powerful Empire to secure friends than it is for a
struggling "small nation". I know that these are your views
on this matter.

The conspicuousness of the absence of the representatives
of a certain College at recent ceremonials has not passed
without comment here and its significance is fully appreciated.

I am sure you realise how much we would all appreciate
any help or suggestions which you can offer. We are in sore
need of the assistance of all our friends everywhere.

        Le meas mor,

                Mise,

P.S. I enclose you authentic copies of recent attempts at
negotiation, with interviews, etc. which will assist you in
appreciating the present situation.

S I N N   F E I N

May 31st, 1923.

To the Organising Committee:

I have received short reports of your meetings and noted the subject of your discussions.

As regards the resolution ---

"That we recommend to Pres. De Valera that a political organisation to be called in English the Irish Republican Political Organisation be formed"

.... it is quite clear that the Committee do not appreciate the purpose we had in view in suggesting the formation of the Committee. We wish to organise not merely Republican opinion, strictly so-called, but what might be called "Nationalist", or "Independence" opinion in general. If we do not do it, the other side will and the loss will be immense.

Purely Republican needs are already catered for in

a. The I.R.A., the organisation of young men which will persist as the Volunteers persisted after 1916, aided by its auxillary women's organisation (CUMANN Na mBAN).

b. CUMANN Na POBLACHTA, a political organisation formed over a year ago. This meets the purpose of the resolution. It will remain a rallying centre for strict Republicans if th should find later that the broader national movement does not fulfil the same aims. Republicans have here a safegua which they didn't have in (1916.) 1917

To attempt to found a further Republican organisation would be wasteful duplication that would serve no purpose whate As I have indicated, what is needed at the moment is a broadly national organisation which will embrace all who put the cause national independence and general national interests above all sectional or party interests. This seems so obvious to me that I am surprised that there is any difference of opinion about it I can quite understand why you should be undecided as to

1. Should it be a brand new organisation with an appropriate name, e.g. The Irish Independence League, or The Irish Self-Determination League?

2. Should it be a reorganisation and revival of the old organisation "SINN FEIN"?

Some months ago, the Government and Army Executive considered this question with its many pros and many cons, and finally came to an unanimous decision that reorganisation xxxxx

UCDA, P150/1818: Communication sent by de Valera to the Organising Committee of Sinn Féin, 31 May 1923. De Valera argues for a more moderate republicanism in order to rebuild support for the party.

SINN FEIN was the better. At that time what we feared most
as that our opponents would set out deliberately to get hold
Sinn Fein and try to swamp the Republican element in it.
at danger has been since removed practically by the formation
~~xxxxxxxxxxxxxxxxxxx~~ Cumann na nGaedhal which leaves Sinn Fein
o us.

When the decision above referred to was arrived at, we
t about the work of reorganisation and have been at it ever since.
e work has been impeded in every way. It had to be done under-
round; the offices were raided and organisers arrested, etc, etc.
new situation has, however, now arisen, and progress will be
ry rapid if we can secure a Committee such as yours to come out
the open and direct it. You can widen out and add to your
mbers as time goes on. At present it would be well not to
clude anyone too closely associated with the military movement.
ese would serve as an excuse to the others for raiding and
mpering the Committee, and might also frighten off just those
wish to attract into the organisation.

If any members of the Committee consider that they cannot
associated with the reorganisation of Sinn Fein in this way,
would be much better that they should leave the Committee.
od work can only be done by those who believe in what they are
ing and who can accordingly put heart and soul into their effort.
any time is lost by the Committee in getting under way, the tide
ll be missed.

The position is in many respects similar to that we had to
ce in the end of 1916 and the beginning of 1917. If we act as
sely and as energetically as we acted then, we shall win the
ople over once more. If we think narrowly in terms of party,
shall condemn our movement to a policy that will be little
tter than factionism and the national cause will be set back
n, twenty, perhaps fifty years. We should set out to organise
t a party, but the nation. To me, Sinn Fein meant the nation
ganised. I never regarded it as a mere political machine.

As regards the question raised by Mrs. Ceannt, no decision
s yet been made as to the policy we shall adopt with regard to
e pending elections. We may declare them illegal and ignore them,
we may deal with them as we dealt with the elections proclaimed
the British, that is, use them for our own ends. We are thinking
er this question, but it would be very wrong to arrive at a final
cision until we have to. The situation is changing and may be
ry different in a month or two from what it is now. The obvious
urse to pursue is to make all our preparations as if we were going
contest them. These preparations can very well be made under the
gis of Sinn Fein. To attempt them under the Republican auspices
ld, to a certain extent, commit us and tie our hands.

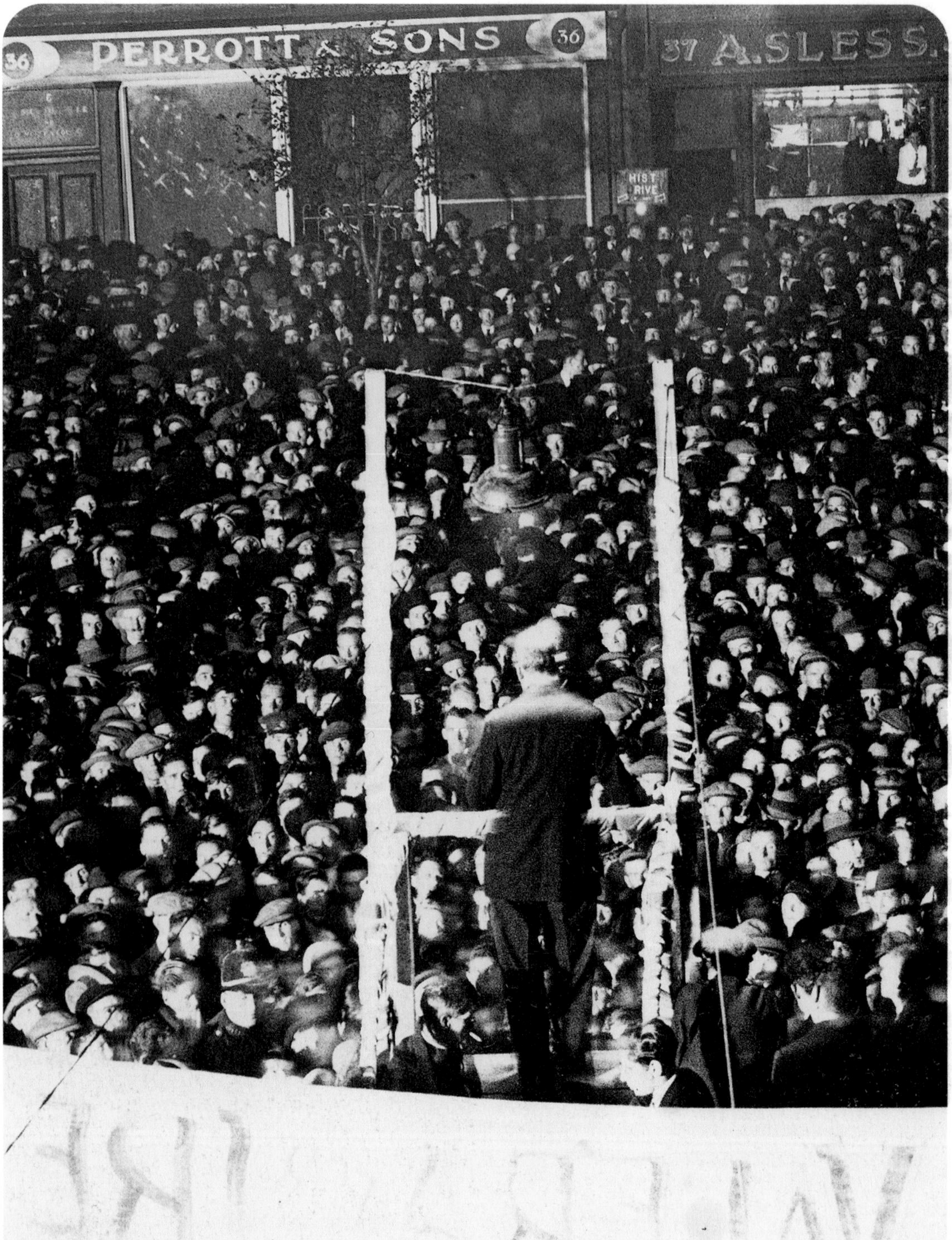
36
PERROTT & SONS
36
37 A.SLESS

IV

'Appearing on platforms at
twilight illuminated by
blazing sods of turf'

UCDA, P150/3848: Large crowds at an election rally, 1920s.

De Valera was in hiding for much of the Civil War and re-emerged to fight the general election campaign of August 1923, during which he was arrested when addressing an election meeting at Ennis, Co. Clare, amidst gunfire and confusion, 'enabling republicans to portray him plausibly as the victim of a repressive and undemocratic administration'.[1] Sinn Féin performed well in this election, winning 44 seats (which they were not going to take up), but de Valera was to remain in prison in Arbour Hill for a year, and any optimism that the results gave rise to did not last too long. De Valera was surprised by the election result; the previous month he had written to a colleague that 'the F[ree].S[tate] people have got behind the shield of popular approval and we must get inside it before we can hope to make any real progress'.[2] But he was also aware that for anti-Treaty Sinn Féin to get popular approval in the long term, they would have to get behind another shield—the Dáil. The challenge, in seeking to abandon abstentionism, was to carry with him as many of his colleagues as possible.

But before that, the imprisonment he endured during this period, in Arbour Hill, including solitary confinement (he was in a wing separated from other prisoners and prevented from exercising in their company)[3] undoubtedly afforded him an opportunity to analyse what had gone wrong, to mourn the loss of colleagues and friends killed, including Harry Boland, Michael Collins, Cathal Brugha and Liam Lynch, and to perhaps question his own arrogance. He had to reflect on what road he should take in the future and formed, it is fair to assume, a determination not to make the same mistakes again in terms of political management and strategy. His incarceration at this stage of his career was arguably of crucial importance in making him the astute politician he became on his release. His good physical health and stamina also worked to his advantage; in this, he was much more fortunate than some of his colleagues, particularly those who, unlike de Valera, went on hunger strike.[4] On his release from prison, many of his former Sinn Féin colleagues, now leading members of Cumman na nGaedheal, probably believed that he had no future in politics.

As observed by John Regan, 'By 1925, anti-treaty Sinn Féin republicanism seemed to be on its last legs, especially when seen through the prismatic intelligence reports of both the army and the Garda Síochána'.[5] There was ongoing internal debate about the policy of abstention. At the Ard Fheis in November 1925 de Valera made it clear that he was in favour of entering the Dáil, a position 'much to the surprise of army intelligence which gleefully noted that the republicans' party organisation was now in decline'.[6] A new opportunity to win the people over came in March 1926, when de Valera made it clear that he would enter the Dáil, as a matter of policy, not principle, if the Oath of Allegiance was abolished. The Sinn Féin Ard Fheis subsequently rejected this, which led to his resignation as president of the party.

He quickly established his new party, not just to mark the change of policy on abstention, but also because, as pointed out by Pauric Travers, this 'gave de Valera unfettered control, which he had not enjoyed with Sinn Féin'.[7] On 17 April 1926 De Valera outlined to a representative of the United Press the five aims of the new Fianna Fáil party:

1) Securing the political independence of a united Ireland as a Republic.

2) The restoration of the Irish language and the development of a native Irish culture.

3) The development of a social system in which, as far as possible, equal opportunity will be afforded to every Irish citizen to live a noble and useful Christian life.

4) The distribution of the land of Ireland so as to get the greatest number possible of Irish families rooted in the soil of Ireland.

5) The making of Ireland [as] an economic unit, as self-contained and self-sufficient as possible—with a proper balance between agriculture and the other essential industries.[8]

But the dilemma facing the new party, after they won 44 seats in the general election of June 1927, was whether or not to enter the Dáil. De Valera busied himself giving statements to various newspapers in June 1927 following the results of the election. He received a telegram from the editor of the *Daily Chronicle* in London congratulating him on the results and asking him for his response, to which he replied 'that no question is ever settled until it be settled right is the lesson English people should learn from these elections'.[9] In one sense, de Valera was fortunate that events dictated how he should progress, following the assassination of the Cumann na nGaedheal justice minister Kevin O'Higgins, and the introduction of legislation requiring all election candidates to commit themselves in advance to taking their seats.

On 11 August 1927 the president of Fianna Fáil and his colleagues took the oath, simultaneously dismissing it as an empty formality. As Travers put it, 'On such fine distinctions rests the foundation of modern Irish political democracy'.[10] Behind the scenes, de Valera went to considerable trouble to find a solution to the dilemma of the oath, seeking theological interpretations of it, views as to the validity of an oath taken under duress, and whether an oath taken in a qualified way had actually been sworn. He corresponded with a number of people, including Michael Browne, Professor of Moral Theology at Maynooth who went on to become Bishop of Galway. In a letter dated 6 October 1927 Browne wrote the following (this section of the letter was highlighted by vertical lines added either by de Valera or a colleague):

> In regard to duress: the obligation of an oath taken under duress or fear holds. Fear does not invalidate an oath. It does however justify the swearer in taking the oath in a qualified or restricted sense that will make it compatible with his rights, provided the reservation is not purely mental but such as a prudent man would suspect to exist. If the swearer makes public the sense in which he takes the oath and is allowed to swear then there is no question at all that he is bound only in this sense and to its extent.[11]

Fianna Fáil evolved into an exceptionally successful political party, not just in national, but also in international terms. Peter Mair makes the observation that Fianna Fáil's electoral record in almost 80 years of its existence, securing an average of 45% of the vote over 24 general elections, is 'virtually without equal across the western democratic universe'.[12] Ironically, they achieved this without delivering successfully on most of their professed aims as outlined in 1926. An ideology that was 'petty bourgeois' has been accurately identified by Richard Dunphy as being the essence of their success, making it populist, but not a vehicle for the advancement of socialism despite the accusation by the Labour Party leader, Thomas Johnston, that it had drawn twelve of its fifteen manifesto pledges from earlier Labour programmes.[13]

The creation of the party was also about validating the institutions of the Free State, and in the process, proving the validity of Michael Collins's interpretation of the Treaty. The party also, in its ability to attract previously disillusioned republicans, ensured that more people voted; in the 1923 Free

State election only 58.7% of the electorate voted; by the time of the 1938 election, 75.7% of the electorate voted, with Fianna Fáil taking 51.9% of the vote.[14] The energy put into rallying support and arranging publicity was phenomenal; Henry Patterson described it as 'a Leninist approach to organisation and propaganda'.[15]

As the parliamentary party minutes for the foundation years make clear, the main preoccupations of the party at that time were discipline and the importance of building and maintaining its grass roots support. This structure was modelled on that of old Sinn Féin which had a local cumann in each parish, constituency organisations and a national executive. By 1927, a year after the formation of the Fianna Fáil party, organisers had succeeded in getting 1,307 cumainn established; by 1929 this had receded to 703, but under the direction of Seán Lemass, the party mobilised 1,404 cumainn in the crucial 1932 and 1933 general elections.[16]

The parliamentary party was also obliged to make its presence felt in the Oireachtas, present a unified front, offer alternative policies, behave with dignity, abstain from alcohol, and not mix with the enemy. They were informed in 1928 that 'the carrying on of conversations with Free State ministers in the halls of Leinster House is unbecoming and demoralising'. But these rules were not just imposed by a dictatorial de Valera. As Eunan O'Halpin noted:

> The minutes are also revealing about the contributions and approach[es] of individual members of the parliamentary party. They suggest that proceedings were surprisingly democratic, with the party leadership generally content to listen to the members rather than hector them. If these minutes accurately reflect proceedings between 1927 and 1932, then the conventional portrayal of the first generation of the party's parliamentary rank and file as a collection of nodding dogs who simply took their lead from de Valera and did whatever he told them to, requires some revision.[17]

Brian Farrell's assessment of de Valera's leadership style was that he was not a unique dictator, despite the fact that party discipline 'appeared magical'. While it is clear that there was little toleration of public dissent, de Valera also worked not to alienate his Cabinet colleagues. This was a crucial lesson he had learned from the Treaty split and it permeated his dealings and relations with his Cabinets after 1932. His relationship with Seán Lemass for example, could not, according to Farrell 'have survived without a considerable degree of conciliation and compromise and concession on both sides'.[18]

Looking at the figures of Dáil first-preference votes by party in the twelve general elections contested by Fianna Fáil while led by de Valera, the consistently high performance is striking, particularly after they first achieved power in March 1932, and these results are an indication that de Valera's abandonment of abstentionism was the correct choice electorally. In 1922 anti-Treaty Sinn Féin recorded a first-preference share of 21.7%, but Fianna Fáil in the second general election in 1927 recorded a share of 35.2%. By 1932 in the election that brought them to office, the share rose to 44.5%. Thereafter, the figures were as follows: 1933 (49.7%), 1937 (45.2%), 1938 (51.9%), 1943 (41.9%), 1944 (48.9%), 1948 (41.9%), 1951 (46.3%), 1954 (43.4%) and 1957 (48.3%).[19] Although Jack Lynch came close in 1977, when Fianna Fáil won 50.6% of the vote, no other leader of Fianna Fáil was able to sustain the sort of electoral performance presided over by de Valera. Even the popularity of Lemass did not allow him to eclipse de Valera; under Lemass's leadership, the figures were 43.8% in 1961 and 47.7% in 1965. The very high figure of 1938 is no doubt partly applicable to de Valera's conduct of Anglo–Irish relations, but the 1944 figure is equally impressive, given that Fianna Fáil had then been in power for twelve consecutive years.

In 1933 political scientist, Warner Moss, located four sources of Fianna Fáil's strength: the support of young people (who would modify their views in parallel with the party as they got older, thereby limiting deserters); those who took the anti-Treaty side in the Civil War and were now advocating social reform; the sizeable number of the electorate who were disgruntled with Cumann na nGaedheal; and those seeking to benefit from the 'local patronage and favours' that could be dispensed when Fianna Fáil was in power.[20] As observed by Maurice Manning, the most important factor contributing to its subsequent long-term success was the extent to which it continued to command support from its traditional core of supporters.[21] Richard Sinnott, in analysing Irish electoral behaviour, argued that the party transcended the limitations of its original support base at a very early stage, highlighted by the fact that as early as 1933, it secured 43% of the vote in Dublin and Dún Laoghaire.[22]

According to Richard Dunphy in his book *The making of Fianna Fáil power in Ireland*, Fianna Fáil's electoral success was also aided by the growth in numbers of the 'protected national bourgeoisie' and the working class, as well as an increase in trade union membership; its interrelations with these different groups became pronounced. Much of their initial appeal came from the small-farmer class which was already in decline, but support from the other groups enabled it to escape over-dependence on that stratum.[23]

In relation to support for the party according to social class, it was not until 1969 that detailed data became available, when Gallup carried out the first major opinion poll in Irish politics. It revealed that in the 1969 general election, Fianna Fáil achieved virtually identical levels of support among the three main social categories: middle class (45%), working class (42%) and farmers (42%). In contrast, the figures for Fine Gael were: middle class (28%), working class (16%) and farmers (20%). The figures for the Labour Party were 13%, 14% and 15% respectively, making it clear that they were dependent on the same middle- and working-class support base as Fianna Fáil, but did not receive as much support from farmers.[24] The 1969 figures clarified the extent to which Fianna Fáil successfully became a 'catch-all' political party.

In terms of the electoral contests, minute attention to detail is revealed by the thorough schedule of meetings drawn up for de Valera.[25] In his *Begrudger's guide to Irish politics*, Breandán Ó hÉithir observed that 'there is a cultivated myth which would have us believe that de Valera won elections by putting on a big black cloak, appearing on platforms at twilight illuminated by blazing sods of turf, and casting spells on people in bad Irish'. The truth, however, as recognised by Ó hÉithir, was that de Valera had a 'life-long devotion to the essential dull details of how the bottom rung of the ladder to power is hammered into place'[26] which included canvassing, compiling lists of supporters, ferrying passengers on polling day, organising public meetings and creating banners. Whatever about casting spells, Dev was an important electoral asset and his formidable presence in black was guaranteed to ensure a big turnout at election rallies.

In terms of his impact on the public, de Valera was in the curious position of not being a naturally gifted orator, but of commanding an extraordinary hold over his audiences. In the second volume of his autobiographies, the playwright Seán O'Casey, struggled to figure out the attraction of de Valera as a politician, the fact that audiences reacted so strongly to him and that women seemed to be drawn towards him. He was not a crowd worker, but tended to keep his gaze firmly fixed ahead and seemed to create a sense of distance between himself and people.[27] This was all in spite of the fact that in O'Casey's view, de Valera 'knew, like Griffith, next to nothing about the common people. He was outside of everything except himself. There seemed to be no sound of Irish wind, water, folk chant or birdsong in the dry, dull voice … De Valera's voice was neither cold nor hot—it was simply lukewarm and very dreary'.[28] But this perceived lack of shared characteristics with the Irish population was also something that was depicted as rather fascinating and exotic; in the memorable phrase of the British dominions secretary, J.H. Thomas, de Valera was 'the Spanish Onion in the Irish stew'.[29]

Like many of his colleagues, de Valera remained dismissive of coalition governments throughout his career. During his last general-election campaign in February 1957, when addressing an election meeting in Mallow, Co. Cork, he dismissed the idea of a 'national government' or 'national coalition', insisting that coalitions led to weak governments with 'rickety foundations' and that 'when Coalitions are formed behind the people's backs after the Election is over all the policies and promises made by the individual Parties are thereby thrown overboard'.[30]

Two years later, Fianna Fáil's attempt to abolish proportional representation (PR) was narrowly defeated (48% of the electorate voted in favour) in a referendum on the same day that de Valera was elected president. In 1968, the year the second proposal to abolish PR was defeated, Seán Lemass recalled in an RTÉ interview that there was a discussion in 1937 on whether or not PR should be established as a constitutional requirement rather than leaving the electoral system to be determined by law. While he thought it was best to leave it to be determined by law, he believed that 'de Valera came to the conclusion that PR was not suitable to Irish circumstances long before he actually proposed to the Dáil legislation to actually change the system, but there was always the political question as to whether it was feasible to make the change, and when it was desirable'.[31] On both occasions, 1959 and 1968, it was made clear that in relation to the electoral system, Irish voters did not want what de Valera wanted: a straight-vote electoral system that would lead to 'strong government' (large majorities for the governing party) and rid the country of coalition governments 'making policy by compromise'.[32]

UCDA, P150/3811:
De Valera leaving
Ennis Cathedral
surrounded by a large
crowd, 1920s.
Annotated on reverse
'Leaving Ennis
Cathedral. In front in
tweed suit "Dodger"
Considine'.

▲ UCDA, P150/556: De Valera with supporters, 1917. Taken during the East Clare by-election.

► UCDA, P150/1842: A bearded de Valera and Pat Creagh, 10/12 August 1923. Creagh was 'temporary occupier of Ciamaltha house at which Pres. stayed for tea on 12/8/23 on his way to Ennis. He slept at Hartigans on bank of river at Castleconnell. Pres. cut his beard off on Aug 14th having cut his beard he left his mustach [*sic*] on until a snap was taken'.

UCDA, P150/2949: Departing a religious institution in Philadelphia, March 1948. De Valera smiling, with his hands up to his face with unidentified clergy and others during a visit in Philadelphia.

At the Show
118.P.

UCDA, P150/3814: De Valera with Lord and Lady Powerscourt seated in the stands at the Royal Dublin Society Horse Show, 1920s. Captioned 'At the Show'.

► UCDA, P150/2011: Statement on the aims of Fianna Fáil, 17 April 1926. This was issued a month after the Extraordinary Ard Fheis of Sinn Féin which resulted in a split in the party over the issue of abstention from Dáil Éireann. The new party was formally launched at the La Scala Theatre in Dublin on 16 May 1926. De Valera explained that he chose the name Fianna Fáil (Warriors of Destiny) to symbolise 'a banding together of the people for national service, with a standard of personal honour for all who join as high as that which characterised the ancient Fianna Éireann, and a spirit of devotion equal to that of the Irish Volunteers from 1916-21'.

Aims of Fianna Fáil.

The new Republican organisation, FIANNA FAIL, has for its purpose

the re-uniting of the Irish people, and the banding of them together for the

tenacious pursuit of the following ultimate aims, using at every moment such

means as are rightfully available:

1. Securing the political independence of a united Ireland
    as a Republic.

2. The restoration of the Irish language, and the development
    of a native Irish culture.

3. The development of a social system in which, as far as
    possible, equal opportunity will be afforded to every
    Irish citizen to live a noble and useful Christian life.

4. The distribution of the land of Ireland so as to get the
    greatest number possible of Irish families rooted in the
    soil of Ireland.

5. The making of Ireland an economic unit, as self-contained
    and self-sufficient as possible - with a proper balance
    between agriculture and the other essential industries.

The conviction on which the new Organisation is based is this:

That in the heart of every Irishman there is a native undying desire to see

his country politically free, and not only free but truly Irish as well, and

that the people recently divided are but awaiting an opportunity to come

together again and give effective expression to that desire. They are

conscious that if real unity can be secured, Ireland is theirs for the taking.

[Why name chosen]

The name FIANNA FAIL has been chosen to symbolise a banding together

of the people for national service, with a standard of personal honour for all

who join, as high as that which characterised the ancient Fianna Eireann, and a

spirit of devotion equal to that of the Irish Volunteers from 1913 to 1921.

[Immediate political objective]

In order to get an authoritative national policy, and unity of

direction in the carrying out of it, it is essential that the elected/representatives of

the people be brought together in a common assembly. The Free State Assembly

might be used as a nucleus for such an assembly, were it not for the oath of

allegiance to the King of England which is imposed as a political test on all

who become members of that assembly. That oath no Republican will take, for

it implies acceptance of England's right to overlordship in our country.

The Free State oath is then the primary barrier to national

unity, and must go if unity is to be attained. The removal of it is the immediate

Maynooth

Oct. 6th 1927

a cara

In reply to your queries, fidelity in Moral Theology may refer to the general virtue of faithfulness to promises or to a specific form of that virtue dealt with under the Fourth Commandment in connection with Civic and Political Duties. In this last connection Fidelity has a precise meaning and is contrasted with the obligations of Reverence and Obedience. Fidelity to lawful authority does not involve positive as much as negative obligations : its force is that it prohibits rebellion, treason conspiracy. Theologians agree it does not prohibit active resistance to unjust law neither does it exclude the use of constitutional means : it rules out violent or unconstitutional measures.

Hence an oath of fidelity to a government or authority must be taken strictly in this precise sense and in no other

In a loose sense people speak of fidelity or loyalty as a term covering all the duties of citizens but in theology in this connection it always is contrasted with and distinguished from the duties of reverence and obedience. An oath is to be strictly interpreted, according to canon 321. Hence in law and conscience an oath of fidelity is to be understood in the sense referred to above.

In regard to duress : the obligation of an oath taken under duress or fear holds. Fear does not invalidate an oath, ~~but~~ It does however justify the swearer ~~in~~ taking the oath in a qualified or restricted sense that will make it compatible with his rights, provided the reservation is not purely mental but such as a prudent man would suspect to Exist. If the swearer makes public the sense in which he takes the oath and is allowed to swear then there is no question at all that he is bound only in this sense and to its extent.

Yours faithfully,

M. J. Browne

Jan. Election 1933

UCDA, P150/2097: Fianna Fáil's list of campaign meetings at which de Valera spoke during the general election of 1933, 10–23 January 1933 (pages 1 and 3 of which are reproduced here).

1933

MEETINGS PRESIDENT DE VALERA.

			Cumann Secretary.
Tuesday 10th Jan.	✓ Navan	7-30 p.m	Peter Connaty, The Square, Navan
	✓ Kells	9-30 p.m	John English, Carrick St. Kells.
Wednesday 11th "	✓ Elphin	12 noon	E.J. Scott, Kinard Ho. Elphin.
	✓ Manorhamilton	8 p.m.	J.J. O'Rourke, Main St. Manorhamilton.
Thursday 12th "	✓ Glenties	12 noon	Berd. McMenamin, Glen Rd. Glenties.
	✓ Letterkenny	7 p.m.	Patk. Cullen, Rosemount, L'kenny
	✓ Ballyshannon	9-30	P. Campbell, Bishop St. ~~Bisham~~ Ballyshannon.
Friday 13th "	✓ Drumshambo	12 noon.	M. Conifry, Drumshambo.
	✓ Sligo	8 p.m.	Ml. Kerrin, Grattan St. Sligo.
Saturday 14th "	✓ Headford	12 noon	Jas. Dolan, Bridge St. Headfo:
	✓ Castlebar	7 p.m.	Jos. Mongan, Mount Gordon, Castlebar.
	✓ Baile an Róba ~~Westport~~	~~9 p.m.~~	M C Ellen ~~Ed. Scott. Bridge St. Westport~~
Sunday 15th "	Ballina	~~12 noon~~ 1 p.m.	
	Ballyhaunis	4 p.m.	F. Waldron, Adarig, B'haunis.
	✓ Ballinasloe	7 p.m.	M. MacAodagain, Scoil na gCeard, Ballinasloe.
	✓ Portumna	9-30 p.m.	S. Layng N.T. Dominick St. Portumna.
Monday 16th "	✓ Roscrea	12 noon	E. O'Donnell, Limerick St. Roscrea.
	✓ Waterford	8 p.m.	F. Heylin, 3 Bath Tce. W'ford.
Tuesday 17th "	✓ Fethard	Noon	S. O'Floinn, Burke St. Fethard
	✓ Cahir	7 p.m.	S. Hennessy, Gurteen, Cahir.
	✓ Mitchelstown	9-30	C. O'Riain, New Sq. Mitchelsto
Wednesday 18th	✓ Dungarvan	12 noon	P. Ormond, Mitchell St. Dungarvan.
	✓ Middleton	7 p.m.	Maurice Horgan, Cork Rd. Middleton.
	Cork	9 p.m.	
Thursday 19th	West Cork		
Friday 20th	Kerry		

MEETINGS   PRESIDENT DE VALERA.

Tuesday 10th Jan.	Navan	7-30	(b)
	Kells	9-30	
Wednesday 11th "	Elphin	12 noon.	
	Manorhamilton 8 p.m.		
Thursday 12th "	Glenties 12 noon.		
	Letterkenny 7 p.m.		
	Ballyshannon 9-30		
Friday, 13th "	Drumshambo 12 noon		
	Sligo	8 p.m.	
Saturday 14th "	Headford	12 noon	
	Castlebar	7 p.m.	
	Westport	9 p.m.	
Sunday 15th "	Ballina	12 noon.	
	Ballyhannis 4 p.m.		
	Ballinasloe 7 p.m.		
b	Portumna	9-30 p.m.	
Monday 16th "	Roscrea	12 noon	
	Waterford	8 p.m.	
Tuesday 17th "	Fethard	noon	
	Cahir	7 p.m.	
	Mitchelstown 9-30		
Wednesday 18th "	Dungarvan	12 noon	
	Middleton	7 p.m.	
	Cork	9 p.m.	
Thursday 19th "	West Cork		
Friday 20th "	Kerry.		
Saturday 21st "	Clare		
Sunday 22nd "	Birr	12 noon —	Mass
	Portlaoighise 4 p.m.		
	Athlone	7 p.m.	
	Mullingar	9-30	
Monday 23rd	Dublin — Kilkenny, Carlow		

In the course of his speech at Mallow on Feb. 20th. Mr. de Valera said:
1957

17/2/57

In my broadcast on Sunday night last I spoke of that admirable summary of the evils of Coalition, which appeared some years ago as an advertisement by Cumann na nGaeldeal. The nGaedheal time allowed for the broadcast was, however, too short to permit of my dealing with it as I desired.

The advertisement ran, you may remember, as follows:

"Coalition Government

"This is what you are voting for if you
give your first vote to Independents,
Farmers or Labour.

It means:

(1) Bargaining for place and power between
irresponsible minority groups.

(2) A weak Government with no stated policy.

(3) Frequent changes of Government.

(4) Consequent depression in trade and industry.

(5) No progress, but stability, security and
credit in constant danger."

In reference to the first point it is unnecessary for me to refer to the bargaining that takes place when these Coalitions are being formed. Many of you may remember the scurrying of the envoys that went from Party to Party when the first Coalition was being arranged - sadly reminiscent to some of us of the scurrying of envoys that took place at another important juncture in our history. But, it was not on that that I commented in my broadcast. It was rather on the fact that when Coalitions are formed behind the people's backs after the Election is over all the policies and promises made by the individual Parties are thereby thrown overboard. Each Party, being in a put minority in the Dail, can ~~foist~~ on the other Parties the ~~fall~~ blame for the non-fulfilment of its Election

UCDA, P150/3097: Speech given in Mallow, Co. Cork during the last general election that de Valera fought as leader of Fianna Fáil, in which he outlines his opposition to coalition government, 20 February 1957.

V

'Our international
position will let the
world and the people
at home know that
we are independent.'

When Fianna Fáil formed their first government on 9 March 1932 de Valera assumed the position of Minister for External Affairs as well as President of the Executive Council and from that point onwards the main issues that dominated his political life related to the pursuit of sovereignty and the attempt to carve a niche for Ireland in international affairs. His initiatives included the abolition of the Oath of Allegiance and ending the payment of land annuities, which led to the Economic War with Britain. His quest for sovereignty also resulted in the abolition of the governor generalship, the creation of the Irish Nationality and Citizenship Act of 1935 which replaced British citizenship with Irish, and the introduction of a new Constitution in 1937.

Volume IV of the Royal Irish Academy's *Documents on Irish foreign policy*, covering the years 1932 to 1936, brings together over 400 documents which go to the heart of de Valera's quest to establish an independent role for Ireland in international affairs during a tumultuous decade. What is striking is the clarity of thinking that existed within the government and the civil service about these matters, and the growing realisation within the British government that they would have to deal with a de Valera who was there to stay, having won a further general election in 1933, giving Fianna Fáil 77 seats in a Dáil of 138 members.

Other, perhaps overlooked, reasons for de Valera's success included Cumann na nGaedheal's creative diplomatic action within the terms of the Treaty and developments within the Commonwealth through the Statute of Westminster which had secured sovereign independence for the dominions, though the issue of neutrality was left unclear. Also as important was the speed with which the new Fianna Fáil government secured the confidence and trust of Irish civil servants. For many of them, the changeover in power in 1932 was challenging, as they had helped to establish the state during the Civil War and were now being asked to take direction from those who had fought with the anti-Treaty side during that war. Tensions may also have been eased by a 'no fraternisation' instruction said to have been issued after the change of government by the

Secretary of the Department of Finance, requiring the termination of personal relationships with former ministers. In 2002 Garret FitzGerald recalled a conversation he had with Vivion, son of Eamon de Valera, as Vivion recounted a conversation he had with his father in a car ten days after the change of government in 1932: 'During the discussion, Eamon de Valera told his son how impressed he had been with the response he had received from officials of the Department of Foreign Affairs to his ideas for moving beyond the terms of the 1921 Articles of Agreement, commonly known as the Treaty'.[1]

The skill and determination of de Valera and his officials in the 1930s made Irish neutrality possible, and he also displayed 'a clever tactical awareness and a shrewd sense of when to act and how far to go'.[2] But he had never been absolutist about foreign policy; indeed there had been a certain caution attached to de Valera's approach to foreign policy which was reflected not only in his desire for neutrality during great power conflicts, but also in the fact that he did not incorporate neutrality into the Irish Constitution; a recognition, that, whatever about the desire for an independent foreign policy, it could not be pursued by ignoring the interests of its stronger neighbour. According to Joe Lee, 'that meant that its course could not be set precisely in advance. That was why he did not make neutrality a constitutional imperative. This was realism carried to the point of principle'.[3]

Lee has also argued that in much of his foreign-policy thinking he was ahead of his time; his 'Document no. 2' at the time of the Treaty—so often mentioned but then glided over—was a document with a tone of compromise, which was far-sighted about the future of the British Empire. It stated specifically that Ireland would be associated with the Commonwealth for 'purposes of common concern', and these were many, including defence, peace and war, and political treaties. There is no mention of the Empire, that the notion of Commonwealth equals.

While it recognised the Crown as head of the association, it included a specific commitment to repel any force against Ireland and to repel any attempt to use Ireland 'for any purpose hostile to Great Britain and the Associated States'. In other words, here was the making of a defence pact, particularly if Irish resources could not resist the invasion of a force hostile to Great Britain. The irony, as pointed put by Lee, is that Britain rejected this, instead insisting on the military clauses of the Treaty. Had 'Document no. 2' been accepted, de Valera would not have been in a position to renegotiate his own document in the way that he was able to renegotiate the ports clauses of the Treaty.

This analysis of de Valera's defence options might be contested, but Lee was correct in seeking to depict de Valera as being much more cautious than was presented by his opponents: 'His British enemies, and even some of his Irish ones, were prone to portray him as a wild man, even a mad man, on the subject of Anglo–Irish relations, a doctrinaire so wedded to arcane abstractions that it was impossible for sane, rational creatures—themselves of course—to do business with him'.[4]

On 18 January 1932 the Irish high commissioner in London, John W. Dulanty, reported George V's views on de Valera to Joseph Walshe (Secretary of the Department of External Affairs). The king, it was clear, was an admirer of William Cosgrave, but not so keen on his opponent, though he did, it seemed, possess a degree of insight about what de Valera's strategy might be: 'Whilst an Opposition was a necessary part of any Parliament he thought it a pity that the Fianna Fáil party should be led by somebody who was, as far as he could discover, not an Irishman at all'. After the king asked what should be done if de Valera was elected, Dulanty continued, 'Like Pilate, he did not wait for a reply but went on to say that whilst "shooting would be no good", he would not be surprised if a trade boycott were attempted'.[5]

Those in charge of Irish foreign policy in the mid 1930s not only tore up the Anglo–Irish Treaty of 1921, they also prepared the ground for the return of the ports controlled by Britain under the terms of the Treaty, in 1938. Ronan Fanning suggested that de Valera's achievements in Anglo–Irish relations should not be overlooked, as without them 'we might never have achieved independence and we certainly would not have achieved it before the Second World War'.[6] It took a generation of independent-minded and ideologically driven public servants to make this possible. De Valera's relationship with Joseph Walshe was particularly important; it has been described as one that 'developed from initial apprehension to unshakeable faith',[7] which was also a measure of de Valera's considerable charm. He seemed to have an ability to win over those who were initially sceptical, an accomplishment at odds with David Fitzpatrick's description of him as 'notoriously gauche in manner and convoluted in thought and speech'.[8]

Another individual of exceptional importance was Maurice Moynihan, one of twentieth-century Ireland's most important public servants. As recorded by Deirdre McMahon, when de Valera initially asked Moynihan to be his personal secretary in the Department of the Taoiseach, Moynihan was surprised and reluctant (he had supported the terms of the Anglo–Irish Treaty). He told de Valera frankly that he did not agree with some of his policies to which de Valera replied that it did not matter. According to Moynihan, 'He didn't ask how I voted and he never did'. Moynihan, like many others, was won over by de Valera's professionalism, attention to detail, and found him stimulating, but

Moynihan was also capable of standing up to him.[9] There was also a strong element of personal devotion, and this was something de Valera managed to command in so many people throughout his career, including his secretaries Kathleen O'Connell and Marie O'Kelly.

Joseph Walshe quickly became enthused by de Valera's foreign-policy vision, and he contributed much to its implementation. As early as 12 March 1932, following conversations the previous day, he wrote to de Valera about the abolition of the Oath of Allegiance:

> Your mandate must be as clear to the British as it is to the people at home. But your mandate is twofold—on the political side— not merely to remove the oath but to take steps to achieve the independence of the whole of Ireland. ...
>
> I believe that you can achieve the Unity of this country within seven years and that we can have our complete independence without calling this country by any particular const[itutiona]l name. 'Ireland' will be our name, and our international position will let the world and the people at home know that we are independent.[10]

This letter indicates that de Valera had made a significant impact on Walshe.

The following June, when Walshe was in Cologne for medical treatment, he reiterated his belief in the importance of de Valera continuing the policy of:

> creating new and salient historical facts which is the only effective way [of] getting the ear of the world.
>
> I most earnestly hope, President, that your recent experiences have still further convinced you that you must remain Minister for External Affairs. In the trying years before us especially the same mind must directly control what are, really, only two facets—the external and the internal—of the same group of activities of our State life.[11]

This kind of correspondence reveals many things, including a preoccupation with Ireland's international status, the confidence in articulating that place, a determination to succeed as an independent nation, and the centrality of the mind and determination of de Valera to all of that.

Irish diplomats in the 1930s were observing many of the hugely important political developments in Europe also. Seán MacEntee, who served as Minister for Finance and later in a variety of other ministries, articulated the importance of laying 'the foundation of a European block, which would practically neutralise British influence on the continent and in co-operation with America in the Atlantic'.[12] MacEntee may have been over ambitious and optimistic in this regard. The real foreign policy successes were going to lie in complete independence from Britain and the declaration of neutrality, though Joseph Walshe's optimism regarding the North ('I believe you can achieve the Unity of this country within seven years')[13] was misplaced. Irish diplomats also accepted that they had to be realistic about lack of Irish influence in Washington and absence of American support for Irish independence. As Walshe put it in October 1932: 'We must therefore frankly regard ourselves as definitely isolated from any support from America … no publicity that we can do in America will secure us the sympathy of more than a very small and impotent section of the population'.[14]

Another reason for de Valera's success in Anglo–Irish relations was the warm personal relationships that he built with senior members of the British establishment, and the tone of his correspondence with such figures is at odds with some of the cutting assessments made by historians. David Fitzpatrick, for example, in relation to de Valera's foreign policy in the 1930s, argues that Fianna Fáil were 'applying confrontation to achieve what might otherwise have been painlessly negotiated … goading the former enemy into surly if half-hearted reassertions of imperial authority'; adding that Chamberlain 'rashly surrendered sovereignty over the Ports'.[15]

This was not the case; there was nothing rash about the manner in which the ports agreement came about, as demonstrated by Deirdre McMahon. Chamberlain consulted his colleagues closely, and his tactical generosity had undermined de Valera's strategy of linking the ports issue with partition; Chamberlain was conscious of the ideological tensions within his own government, and managed them and the negotiations well, ensuring that the ports agreement got a positive reception in the British media.[16]

Contrast Fitzpatrick's assessment with the friendliness of the correspondence of Malcolm MacDonald of the Dominions Office with de Valera in May 1938:

> I do congratulate you and our Prime Minister on what you have done in the cause of friendship between our two peoples, and I shall always feel proud that I was privileged to play some part in the negotiations. I cherish especially the memory of our friendly and fruitful talks together. If the personal relations which we

established are a symbol of the friendship which will gradually grow between the peoples of the two islands, then indeed is the future bright.

De Valera replied, 'It has been such a pleasure to have one as understanding as you to deal with in the difficult matters of the relations with the two countries'. He could not resist adding an asterisk beside the words 'Dominions Office' with a note at the end of the letter reading: 'By the way, this inappropriate title should now be changed'.[17] De Valera was also, however, determined to chide the administrators of British imperialism about their racism. In August 1935 he wrote to J.H. Thomas, Secretary of State for the Colonies, criticising a section in the *Annual report on the social and economic progress of the people of Somaliland*, printed by the Stationery Office. The offending passage read: 'In this condition the Somali may be compared with the traditional Irishman when well primed with the liquor of his country. The latter brandishes his shillelagh and looks for heads to crack; the Somali sharpens his spear and begins to think of blood feuds to settle and flocks to loot'. De Valera felt obliged to protest that 'such an example of extreme bad taste and mean racial propaganda' could still appear in an official report, believing that such an attitude 'belonged to another age'.[18]

That same confidence and independence was also of relevance in the context of de Valera's approach to the League of Nations, the international organisation established in 1919 to preserve peace and settle disputes by arbitration. De Valera received much publicity for his opening address to the League Assembly in Geneva in September 1932, when the Irish Free State held the presidency of the League Council. He spoke from his own text, having dispensed with that prepared for him by the League Secretariat, arguing strongly that the League had to maintain the letter of its covenant to remain relevant in international affairs.[19] He highlighted his disquiet about the larger powers dominating international organisations:

> Let us be frank with ourselves. There is on all sides complaint, criticism and suspicion. People are complaining that the League is devoting its activity to matters of secondary or very minor importance, while the vital international problems of the day, problems which touch the very existence of our peoples, are being shelved or postponed. People are saying the equality of the states does not apply in the things that matter, that the smaller states whilst being given a voice have little real influence.[20]

Part of the reason for de Valera's relative disinterest in the Commonwealth in the 1930s was his focus on the League of Nations, and the fact that the increasingly professional Irish foreign service now had an alternative focus to the Anglo–Irish issue. Michael Kennedy's study of Ireland and the League of Nations makes clear the degree to which de Valera was dependent on senior officials like Seán Lester and Francis Cremins, and their differing opinions were sometimes reflected in ambivalent statements from de Valera about the League.[21] The League of Nations involvement was not just significant as an exercise in nation-building, but also provided an opportunity to go beyond the constraints (and presumably, sometimes the tedium) of Anglo–Irish relations, or as Deirdre McMahon put it more bluntly, the League of Nations offered an escape from 'the constitutional navel-gazing of the Imperial conferences and more exciting opportunities for a new, small state'.[22]

Ultimately, the failure of the League was to mean a return to the Anglo–Irish stage. De Valera was disillusioned by the failure of collective security in the League of Nations as seen in the case of Manchuria, and Italy's invasion of Abyssinia. At home, de Valera also displayed independence in his approach to the Spanish Civil War, despite domestic opposition, by supporting non-intervention and initially refusing to recognise the Franco regime.

UCDA, P150/2536: Taking over the Treaty Ports, 11 July 1938. De Valera accompanied by Frank Aiken; Seán MacEntee; Gerald Boland (Minister for Lands and Fisheries) and his son, Kevin; Vivion de Valera; and five unidentified individuals arriving by boat at Spike Island. © Irish Press.

UCDA, P150/2509: De Valera;
Thelma Cazalet, MP; and Malcolm
MacDonald (far right, British
Labour Politician and Secretary of
State for Dominion Affairs), 24
April 1938. Taken 'the day before
the signing of the happy [Anglo–
Irish] agreement—at Malcolm's
house' (Upper Frognal Lodge,
Hampstead, London), sent to de
Valera by Thelma Cazalet in 1939.

UCDA, P150/2810: President of the Assembly, September
1938. De Valera listening to speeches at the League of Nations.

UCDA, P150/3818: De Valera with members of the Irish diplomatic service, 1930s. Identified on reverse as follows: 'Front row L. to R.: [John W.] Dulanty [Irish High Commissioner in London, 1930–49]; Joe Walsh[e] [Secretary to the Department of External Affairs, 1927–46; Ambassador to the Holy See, 1946–54]; President; Bob Brennan [Minister to the USA, 1938–47]; [Tom J.] Kiernan [Secretary of the High Commission in London, 1925–35; Minister of Plenipotentiary at the Holy See, 1946–54]. Back row L. to R.: John Hearne [High Commissioner to Canada, 1939–49; Ambassador to the USA, 1950–60]; Frank Gallagher [Director of the Government Information Bureau, 1939–48]; F.H. Boland [Secretary to the Department of External Affairs, 1946–50; Ambassador to Great Britain, 1950–5]; [Michael] McWhite [Minister to Italy, 1938–50]; Seán Murphy [Minister to France, 1938–50]; L.[Leo] Kearney [Minister to Spain, 1935–46]; & Michael Rynne [Legal Advisor, Department of External Affairs, 1930–50; Ambassador to Spain, 1954–61]'. © G.P. Beegan.

UCDA, P150/2789: Crowds cheering de Valera at London's Waterloo Station on his way to Geneva, 19 September 1932. De Valera was present at the first meeting of the Assembly as President of the Council.

ROINN AN UACHTARÁIN
DEPARTMENT OF THE PRESIDENT

BAILE ÁTHA CLIATH
DUBLIN

saorstát éireann

12th March 1932

My dear President,

Judging from our conversation yesterday I think you will be glad to have a personal note on some of the main issues affected by the method of removing the oath.

It is all a question of method. The oath can be abolished. Your mandate cannot be as clear to the British as it is to the people at home. But your mandate is twofold — on the political side — not merely to remove the oath but to take steps to achieve the independence of the whole of Ireland. I am convinced that the latter & more important part of your mandate can be rendered impossible of achievement by the slightest imprudence with regard to the method of carrying out the first.

There is serious doubt as to whether the oath is or is not in the Treaty. The Treaty debates which I have had examined for this purpose very largely stultify our present argument that the oath is not in the Treaty. One of the biggest difficulties we have had with the British on the P. Caruinal question was the fact that Mr Blythe had made a statement in the Seanad that it was part of the Treaty. Thomas quoted the statement at us in the midst of a big

NAI, DT, S2264: Joseph Walshe to de Valera, 12 March 1932. A private letter written only three days after Fianna Fáil took office in 1932, containing the embryo of the strategy of constitutional change which de Valera was determined to embark on. This letter is an illustration of the speed with which Walshe, Secretary of the Department of External Affairs from 1927 to 1946, embraced de Valera's foreign policy aims. Walshe subsequently served as Ambassador to the Holy See from 1946 to 1954.

St Elizabeth Krankenhaus,
Köln
Hohenlind,
13th June, 1933.

My dear President,

Many thanks for your very kind letter written from Paris.

I followed your journey as closely as one can from the papers and I was delighted to see that it was such a wonderful success from beginning to end. I am looking forward to hearing your personal impressions.

The results in our home and external affairs are found to be exceedingly good. It is another big break in the "paper wall", and another big push forward of our first line of defence against English interference.

There is no doubt whatever that your reception in Rome and Paris in your full official (pace The Irish Press) capacity — was an event of the very first importance in our relations with Great Britain. It has brought a favourable — perhaps a pen-ultimate settlement — distinctly nearer

137

I hope you are already considering the question of an early visit to America — an official visit to Washington in the first instance, we must not hesitate to make every possible use of our present status to reach our goal, even though that method may cause misunderstandings (which you can dissipate in one speech) amongst some of our people, especially in America.

If I were at home, I would urge you very strongly to spend at least a week at the London Conference and to find an opportunity for making a speech there. It is a great chance to continue the policy of creating new and salient historical facts which is the only effective way getting the ear of the world.

I most earnestly hope, President, that your recent experiences have still further convinced you that you must remain Minister for External Affairs. In the trying years before us to specialize the same mind must directly control what are really, only two facets — the external and the internal — of the same groups of activities of our State life.

My heart has been — and still is — undergoing very vigorous treatment which at times, is very prostrating in its effects, but the Dr who's a tip top man has my case well in hand and I feel, at last, certain that I shall be cured. Unfortunately, I shall have to stay in Germany somewhat longer than I expected when I left Ireland, but it is good to go home with the sure feeling that I can take up my work without fear of further interruption. I am going to practice the motto you suggest —

17th May, 1938.

Personal

Dear Mr de Valera,

I am sending this note just to say that
our legislation will be through both Houses of
Parliament in time for The King's Assent to be
given to it tonight.   I should like to add, in no
mere formal way, an expression of my pleasure at the
final accomplishment of what we have been patiently
endeavouring to do over so many months.   I do
congratulate you and our Prime Minister on what you
have done in the cause of friendship between our
two peoples, and I shall always feel proud that I
was privileged to play some part in the negotiations.
I cherish especially the memory of our friendly and
fruitful talks together.   If the personal relations
which we established are a symbol of the friendship

which

on de Valera, Esq., T.D.

which will gradually grow between the peoples
of the two Islands, then indeed is the future
bright.

With kindest regards

Yours very sincerely

Malcolm MacDonald

UCDA, P150/2517: Malcolm MacDonald to de Valera, 17 May
1938. MacDonald expresses his pleasure at the successful outcome
of the negotiations that led to the 1938 Anglo–Irish Agreement.
This agreement contained provisions for the removal of barriers to
British–Irish trade, the resolution of the dispute over the payment
of land annuities and provisions for the handing over of the Treaty
Ports—Cobh, Berehaven and Lough Swilly—which had been
retained under the defence annex to the Anglo–Irish Treaty of 1921.

May 30th, 1938

Personal

Dear Mr. MacDonald,

       I am very glad to have your letter expressing your pleasure at the outcome of the negotiations.

       I feel that were it not for the happy combination on your side, of yourself and the Prime Minister, the negotiations could not have been successful, or begun.

       I have no doubt the happy ending of the disputes in question has begotten a new attitude of mind on the part of our people, and if we could only now succeed in solving the problem created by partition, a happy future of mutual understanding and fruitful co-operation in matters of common concern lies ahead before our two peoples.

       It has been such a pleasure to have one so understanding as you to deal with in the difficult matters of the relations between the two countries that I regret your departure from the Dominions Office. I hope most sincerely that in the equally difficult task you have undertaken, your knowledge and zeal will serve you equally well.

       Sincerely yours,

The Rt. Hon. Malcolm MacDonald, M.P.,
Secretary of State for the Colonies,
Colonial Office,
Downing Street,
LONDON, S.W.1.

By the way, this inappropriate title should now be change

E. de V.   d

20th September, 1932

Copy

The President.

Attached is the first draft of your speech in opening
the Assembly. While it is not generally regarded as the
national speech of the acting President it obviously
cannot contain anything which is unacceptable to you. The
draft has been prepared by the Secretary Gerneral, and may
be modified, of course, as you wish. It would be desirable
to exercise special care regarding the paragraphs relating
to Disarmament, the Sino-Japanese dispute, and the Economic
Conference.

Should you not wish specially to make another speech
at the Assembly the draft could, perhaps, be modified to
include your views, indicating that at such points you
speak as "the Representative of the Irish Free State".

Draft addition prepared by S Lester re. Secretary General's resignation.

The year which has passed since the close
of the last regular meeting of the Assembly has
been one of great difficulty for most, if not all,
of the countries which we represent.   Internal
problems, economic or political or both, would
alone have been more than enough to occupy the
full attention of every Government.   But under
the conditions of the modern world, practically
every decision of importance which any Government
has to take must [depend to a great extent on] the
action of other Governments, and it is, therefore,
in strict accordance with the logic of existing
facts that the year in which each Government has
to face in its own country, difficulties of exceptional gravity, should also be a year of unparall-
eled activity in international relations. We may
regret that this should be so, and long, as many
individuals long, for a return to days which seem
to have been simpler and happier than our own. But
we must face the facts, and it is an inexorable
fact that to-day no Government can carry out its
duty to its own people unless it is prepared for
constant consultation and co-operation with the
Governments of other countries.

Such consultation and co-operation is, as
the years pass, increasingly concentrated in Geneva —
a proof, if proof were needed, of the soundness of
the fundamental lines on which the League has been
organised. But this is only a beginning. It is

one thing to bring the world's problems to the
League; it is a still different thing to solve
them.   League membership and mechanism have grown
[gratifyingly]; its difficulties, however, have
increased correspondingly.   The period of theoretical construction is over.   Now comes the moment
of test, the time when the world desperately awaits
results.   And there could not be a grimmer moment,
a more difficult period: a world economic depression dragging all nations down to the end of a three
years exhaustion, fundamental differences of opinion
and policy threatening the world-wide hopes centered
in the Disarmament Conference and perhaps even the
Economic Conference, political disputes cleaving
apart the nations in Europe, Asia, Latin-America.
Two vast currents seem to be sweeping world-life.
On the one hand the economic depression is driving
the nations to tariff walls, economic separatism,
and self-sufficient nationalism such as was hardly
dreamed of a few short years ago; on the other,
the march of progress, the fertility of invention,
and the spread of capital is weaving them irrevo-
cably into an economic whole.   These forces are
diametrically opposed, the one centripetal, the
other centrifugal; the nations are buffeted back
and forth between them.

     Let it never be forgotten, as it so often is
forgotten, that the League is not an outside,
detached, extraneous organisation functioning of
and by itself; it is, on the contrary, an association of states bound together for mutual goodwill

and co-operation and able to act only as the
governments of those states give it power to act.
The League undoubtedly represents something
spectacularly new in international relations; it
provides the platform and the facilities for a
far more enlightened approach to the problems of
the world; but it can never be far ahead of the
governments who give it life and power.   Public
opinion should appreciate this; public opinion
should much more frequently place responsibility
for its disappointments, not on the League which
provides the mechanism but on the governments which
fail fully to use it.

The outstanding event of the past year has,
of course, been the Disarmament Conference.   There
is still a long road to be travelled, and many
difficult problems to be solved before the first
Convention for the Reduction and Limitation of
Armaments is placed on the Statute Book of the
world.   The decisions taken hitherto are not so
comprehensive as many had hoped; and they constitute a pledge rather than a concrete result.
But I fully believe that the pledge will be redeemed
at an early date, and that more far-reaching
proposals will be entertained when the Conference
meets again.   If we view the situation in this
light, and always bear in mind the novelty, range
and complexity of those endeavours, we cannot
doubt that great progress has been made, and that
with the exercise of patience and good-will a

VI

'An affair of hasty improvisations,

a matter of fits and starts.'

UCDA, P150/2949: Waving to supporters, March 1948. 'Cheered by thousands who lined the streets to see him, former Eire Prime Minister Eamon De Valera waves his hat in answer as his car follows a parade through Boston. With him (wearing mustache) is General Frank Aiken, one time Eire Minister of Finance [*sic*]'. Aiken had in fact been Minister for Defence. © Daily Times Chronicle.

The forthright claim in the Constitution of 1937 of the legitimacy of the state's right to rule all of Ireland was immediately qualified by the reassurance that there would be no attempt to implement the claim. This was about disputing the right of Britain to control Northern Ireland, while also allowing a clause that suggested Stormont (Northern Ireland's home-rule parliament) could continue, or as Article 15.2 stated: 'Provision may be made by law for the creation or recognition of subordinate legislatures'. This, seemingly, did not exclude some federal type of state as an alternative to partition, while aggressively asserting the principle of unity.

De Valera and his colleagues were not always consistent in their attitude to Northern Ireland and their thoughts on how to end partition. As John Bowman revealed, even in the brief period 1917 to 1921, de Valera oscillated concerning this issue. Between 1917 and 1918, he advocated the expulsion or coercion of Northern Unionists, but by 1919–20, when in the United States, he modified his stance by suggesting that the Unionists could be assimilated; while in 1921 he suggested they could be accommodated in a federal island externally associated within the Commonwealth.[1]

In January 1921, in correspondence with Michael Collins, de Valera argued that the dilemma for Sinn Féin was whether to boycott the election in Northern Ireland in May of that year, 'Unless … we were certain of a quarter, or at least one-fifth (say ten Members) of the total representation … If we secured anything less it would be boomed abroad that these counties were practically a homogenius [sic] political entity, which justified partition'. The alternative was to contest the elections, so that 'the unity of Republican Ireland will be preserved—letting the elections go by default would seem to be the abandonment of the North as hopeless for us, and the acceptance in a sense of partition'.[2] This encapsulated the difficulty of striking a balance between not recognising the legitimacy of partition, and yet not abandoning the Northern Nationalists.

In a private session of the Dáil in August 1921 de Valera said force would not be justified in relation to Ulster because it would not be successful and would amount to making 'the same mistake with that section as England had made with Ireland'. But he was not consistent in this view in the years to come. In the Senate in 1939 he denied that he was a pacifist, and said that he would be justified in using force if he could do so effectively, to 'rescue the people of Tyrone and Fermanagh, South Down, South Armagh and Derry City from the coercion they are suffering', but he left unanswered the question he had asked himself in that speech: 'Would I go further than that?'.

By the end of the 1940s he had emphatically rejected force and seemed to acknowledge that the problem was one between the North and South of Ireland, and not Britain: 'If there were agreement between the peoples of the two parts of Ireland, British consent to do the things that they would have to do could be secured'.[3] In July 1958 he said simply that he accepted force 'would not be the right method'.[4] Force, he knew, even if it achieved a united Ireland, could only achieve a temporary, unstable solution, but the international anti-partition tour he undertook after the loss of the 1948 general election could not have come at a worse time in terms of interesting a wider world recovering from the Second World War.[5]

John Bowman's account of *De Valera and the Ulster question* depicts him as a pragmatist under considerable pressure from ideological republicans both inside and outside his government,[6] but the research of Deirdre McMahon has also uncovered the degree to which some of his fellow ministers thought he needed to be more pragmatic. Not just Seán MacEntee, but also Lemass and James Ryan, Minister for Agriculture, expressed concerns about the economic effects of the Anglo–Irish disputes and would have been prepared to settle the financial issues without reference to constitutional issues.[7] Terry de Valera's memoir makes it clear that de Valera had an affection for MacEntee, who, as Minister for Finance, was known in the Cabinet as 'The Leader of the Opposition', and both Seán Lemass, Minister for Industry and Commerce, and Frank Aiken, Minister for Defence, could be argumentative also.[8]

MacEntee was not shy in articulating his opposition, even if he continually showed a reluctance to follow through on his many threats of resignation (there are six such incidents recorded in his private papers held in UCD Archives, School of History and Archives). His protests are a reminder that de Valera was surrounded by men of strong views who were willing to assert themselves forcefully. As early as 1938, MacEntee, a Belfast-born Catholic, drafted a long letter of resignation to de Valera (which was never sent) regarding talks with the British government and the idea that any solution to the trade dispute would have to involve Britain taking 'effective steps' to end partition.

He insisted that the:

Partition problem cannot be solved except with the consent of the majority of the Northern non-Catholic population. It certainly cannot be solved by their coercion ... We are relying on England's big stick and it will fail. ...

I know that you will understand why I have had to write this letter. In our relations of more than twenty years there has not so far as I know been any reserve between us when we have been discussing matters affecting the nation. We have had differences of opinion as to the wisdom or unwisdom of a line of policy and I have always been prepared in the last resort to defer to your judgement. But I cannot concede that full deference now, because in regard to Partition we have never had a considered policy. It has always been an affair of hasty improvisations, a matter of fits and starts. We are giving it first place now in the practical business of Government. ... we are prepared to subject our farmers and our people as a whole to further and intensified hardship in order to compel Great Britain to force the Northern non-Catholics to associate with us, when with our connivance every bigot and killjoy, ecclesiastical and lay is doing his damnedest here to keep them out. Where is the reason in asking us to pursue two policies so utterly at variance with each other? It is because I believe that some of us are subordinating reason to prejudice, that prejudice which may be blameless in the heart of an individual, but should be banished form [sic] the minds of statesmen, in regard to this matter of defence, and are only raising the Partition issue now to coerce their colleagues to defer to their prejudices that I feel the essential unity and confidence of the Cabinet has been destroyed.[9]

Despite de Valera's foreign policy successes, or perhaps because of them, in particular the return of the Treaty Ports, he banged the anti-partition drum whenever possible. As noted by John Bowman, he always kept a map of the partitioned island close at hand to impress his views on visitors, but one of the most senior Irish diplomats with long experience of de Valera's attempts to interest London in the issue concluded that de Valera's error was he believed that partition 'could be solved by logical argument'.[10] He was also occasionally emotive when writing about partition. When in correspondence with Malcolm MacDonald after the Ports agreement, while they wrote fulsomely of each other's good faith, he added that 'if we could only now succeed in solving the problem created by partition, a happy future of mutual understanding and fruitful co-operation in matters of common concern lies ahead before our two peoples'.[11]

Likewise, in a handwritten and emotive letter to Neville Chamberlain in April 1939, with the outbreak of the Second World War just five months away, de Valera urged him to continue his policy of appeasement, 'notwithstanding the pressure that will be brought upon you. Once this war is begun no man can see the end'. But his main concern was partition:

> I cannot refrain from writing to you. You and I have worked to bring about conditions which would make it possible to lay the foundations of good neighbourly relations between the British and Irish peoples. The agreement, a year ago was a notable advance in that direction, but the failure to deal with Partition has largely offset what was then accomplished. A free united Ireland would have every interest in wishing Britain to be strong, but when Britain's strength appears to be used to maintain the division of our island no such consideration can have any force: a large section of our people, particularly the young are led to see hope only in Britain's weakness. Can something not be done and without delay?
>
> The Consequences of failure in the past to act in time are clear to see and should be a warning.[12]

Chamberlain, of course, had other things on his mind, but this letter was a prime example of de Valera's determination to raise the issue at what could be considered the most inappropriate times, particularly for a foreign audience. One of the most powerful recordings of de Valera's speech-making exists in the RTÉ Archives and dates from 1950, when he addressed the Council of Europe. Speaking initially about the battle against Communism, he became more and more impassioned as he turned to the subject of partition:

> We have heard here recently suggested that the best way of beating Communism is not necessarily by force—that there is something else also which is required; that we have got to show the people who are going to resist Communism that there is a way of life which is worth defending. We believe that that is true and we want to be, in Ireland, to be in a position in which we will feel that we are defending *all* the things that are worth defending;

that we are defending the liberties of our people and as long as the powerful nation which is near us by force, divides that ancient nation and subjects a large proportion of the people that are cut off to a foreign rule against their will, then as long as that exists, so long will Irishmen feel that if there is liberty to be defended, it has first to be defended on Irish shores.[13]

In talking about Communism, he very quickly turned it into an attack on partition, and had taken this message to the USA, Australia, France and Italy amongst other places while in opposition between 1948–51, leaving Lemass, in the words of Pauric Travers as 'a one man Opposition in the Dáil'.[14]

The anti-partition message continually espoused by de Valera was simple, and was frequently termed 'the restoration of the six counties' which, it was maintained, would come sooner rather than later, and was always 'the one remaining obstacle to ending the quarrel of centuries'. The view was continually asserted that 'the British government alone ... if they really have the will, can bring about a united Ireland in a very short time'.[15]

According to John A. Murphy, 'The great irony in all this is that, for de Valera, the priorities of the 26-county state always took precedence over the vision of an aspirational 32-county Ireland'.[16] In the same vein, Garret FitzGerald asserted that de Valera's real achievement was the fact that sovereignty became the means by which he secured the assent of those who had previously not accepted the legitimacy of the 26-county state.[17]

The Second World War resulted in the possibility of an end to partition in return for Ireland giving up its neutrality. On 26 June 1940 Malcolm MacDonald arrived in Dublin and handed de Valera a one page memorandum with an offer from the British government of a declaration accepting the principle of a united Ireland, offering a joint body of representatives of the two parts of Ireland to look at the constitutional implications of such an entity, and a joint defence council, on the proviso that the 26 counties joined the war effort. The weakness in this plan was reflected in the hopelessly naïve opening paragraph: 'If the plan is acceptable as a whole to the Government of Éire, the United Kingdom Government will at once seek to obtain the assent thereto of the Government of Northern Ireland, in so far as the plan affects Northern Ireland'.[18]

De Valera did not bite, probably because he was aware that Northern Ireland would react with great hostility. He also knew that there was a danger of splitting his own party, and an uncertainty about whether Britain would be victorious, or, in Henry Patterson's phrase, echoing John A. Murphy's words, 'de Valera's preference for defending the integrity of the existing 26 county state and the unity of Fianna Fáil over what might have been a historic opportunity to undermine partition'. But Patterson also argues that in terms of potential intransigence from Northern Ireland, Unionists were perhaps not in a position to be as strident as they would have wished, feeling perhaps that if they refused, they would be blamed 'for whatever disasters ensued' and putting local concerns before that of the British Empire.[19]

There was a further offer by telegram from Churchill—'Now or Never. A Nation Once Again'—on the night of the Pearl Harbour attack, but this was sent when Churchill was drunk, and was judiciously ignored. That it was an alcohol-induced message seems to be confirmed by Terry de Valera's account of a conversation between Sir John Maffey (later Lord Rugby) and his father when Maffey called to the house and told him of Churchill's intoxication.[20]

Apart from Britain, de Valera did not visit any part of the Commonwealth until after 1948, and although, as pointed out by Deirdre McMahon, the Irish relationship with the Commonwealth was almost invisible by the end of the Second World War, de Valera was not intrinsically hostile to the Commonwealth. He had allowed officials to attend meetings of Commonwealth delegations to the League of Nations (though this was kept quiet) and he informed Malcolm MacDonald in 1936 that he would not take Ireland out of the Commonwealth.[21]

It should not be assumed that British politicians and officials negotiating with de Valera throughout the 1930s were aghast at the notion of a united Ireland. There was a belief on the part of people like Chamberlain and MacDonald that unity was likely in the long term and they would have been happy to facilitate it if Northern Ireland was willing. Perhaps less representative were the views of Sir Warren Fisher, Permanent Secretary to the British Treasury, who seemed to have a guilt complex about the division of Ireland, and favoured 'the termination of the present wholly uneconomic partition'.[22]

Hiding behind the cloak of partition, de Valera reacted with pettiness to the notion of acknowledging the shared heritage of the main political parties in the decades after independence. In 1949 John A. Costello as Taoiseach of the coalition government, in a magnanimous gesture, invited de Valera to join him in a broadcast to mark the occasion of the declaration of the Irish Republic, which de Valera rejected on the following grounds:

> We in Fianna Fáil are glad that henceforth there will be agreement amongst all parties in Dáil Éireann that the state shall be described as a Republic. We cannot convince ourselves however that the act merits that its coming into operation should be marked by national celebrations. Indeed, when the constitution came into

operation in 1937, we decided that celebrations such as those now proposed ought to be reserved until the national task which we have set ourselves is accomplished. We still believe that public demonstrations and rejoicings are out of place and are likely to be misunderstood as long as that task remains uncompleted and our country partitioned.[23]

De Valera also built a warm relationship with Sir John Maffey (later Lord Rugby), the UK's representative in Ireland during the Second World War, and corresponded with him on the subject of partition. De Valera's personal papers contain the correspondence between them right into the 1950s, another indication of the positive impact that de Valera made on people, who were initially distrustful of and irritated by him. In February 1948 Rugby wrote to de Valera: 'You have always been accessible, patient, frank and sincere, and at the end of more than eight years of association I keenly realise how deep and warm a regard I have for you as a man and as a fellow-traveller through anxious times'.[24] In April 1957 de Valera wrote to him expressing the view that hopes of reconciliation between Britain and Ireland in his own lifetime were fading, urging Rugby to apply pressure to get partition on to the British government's agenda:

> The first step, in my opinion, is as I think I suggested to you already, to get your Government to admit publicly that it is a British no less than an Irish interest to see partition ended. Chamberlain agreed that this was so, but events moved so rapidly that he was denied a favourable opportunity for making this declaration. Can we get your Government to make it now?[25]

Interestingly, Rugby blamed John A. Costello's declaration of the Irish Republic in 1949 for lack of progress, by cutting all ties with the Commonwealth ('His wild words have stimulated the gelignite group'). It is quite surprising to read a senior British diplomat writing to de Valera to depict Fine Gael as unreconstructed republicans, but his solution to the problem was that de Valera 'should once again get your knees under a table in London'. De Valera, in his reply, did not think this was practicable, but he did leave Rugby with the comment that 'I must I suppose, submit to your inevitability of gradualness'.[26]

Even at the end of the 1950s, the possibility that Ireland might rejoin the Commonwealth (it had ceased to be a member with the declaration of the Republic in 1949) was being discussed, during de Valera's last term as Taoiseach, though he made it clear that it would have to be contingent on an end to partition. In March 1958 de Valera and Aiken proposed to the Commonwealth secretary Lord Home that Northern Ireland would agree to a United Republic of Ireland within the Commonwealth, recognising the Queen as its head, a proposal that was rejected.[27] As revealed by Deirdre McMahon, the British prime minister Harold Macmillan was not enthusiastic, doubting if 'a united Ireland—with de Valera as a sort of Irish Nehru—would do us much good'.

This reference to the Indian situation was one which British observers occasionally made and with good reason. De Valera had an important influence on the Indian struggle for independence; the MI5 file on de Valera revealed a continuing unease after 1922 at 'the links between Irish and Indian radicals',[28] while in 1947 an Indian delegation was sent to Dublin to consult de Valera about the country's future constitutional status, and de Valera urged them to seek some form of external association.[29] The following year, in the summer of 1948, de Valera broadcast a radio talk from New Delhi, in which he reiterated the common cause between Indian and Irish nationalists: 'For more than 30 years many of us in Ireland have followed with deepest sympathy the fortunes of the people of India in their efforts to secure freedom. We regarded the people of India as co-workers and allies in a common cause and we rejoiced exceedingly when India's right to independence was fully acknowledged'.[30]

Writing later to thank de Valera for his visit, Indian prime minister Nehru reiterated that 'for a long time past, several generations in India have followed closely and with deep sympathy events in Ireland. We have drawn inspiration from many of the happenings there and you have been admired by vast numbers of our people'.[31] As late as 1968 the Indian Embassy in Dublin was requesting a copy of De Valera's 'Document no. 2'.[32]

After the conflict in Northern Ireland erupted in 1969, when de Valera was president, partition and violence were the issues that defined the country in the eyes of some outsiders. In 1972 C. Brooks Peters, a senior, now retired journalist at the *New York Times*, living in Dublin, was assigned to write a series of articles to coincide with de Valera's ninetieth birthday. De Valera's secretary refused to give permission for the interview on the grounds that de Valera as president stuck rigidly to the practice of not giving interviews for publication. It was probably just as well, as the first question on Brooks Peters' list of proposed questions was the following: 'In view of the opinion widely held all over the world today that Ireland is an island populated by gunmen and religious bigots, how, Mr President, do you foresee the future of this island?'.[33]

UCDA, P150/2955: Prime Minister Nehru and De Valera, June 1948. Taken during de Valera's visit to India (stamped 'Press Information Bureau, Government of India').

UCDA, P150/2534: Eamon de Valera with his Cabinet, appointed June 1938. '(Only fully autographed copy)'. Standing, left to right: Gerald Boland, Oscar Traynor, Frank Aiken, Dr James Ryan, P.J. Little, Maurice Moynihan (Secretary to the Government). Front row, left to right: Thomas Derrig, Seán Lemass, Seán T. O'Kelly, de Valera, P.J. Ruttledge, Seán MacEntee.

de Valera

mac aₐgáⁿ.   Ryₐₙₐⱼₐⱼ,   deₑⁱₘᵤₑᵤtₜₑₑ.

maₓ Okₑₐₘ   Dₐₐ Líttᵢ   m. ommₐₘⱼₘⱼₑₒcₐₐ

▲ UCDA, P150/3806: De Valera working at a desk in Geneva, *c.* 1932. Taken by C. Ed. Boesch, Genève.

▶ NAI, DE 2/266: De Valera to Michael Collins, 13 January 1921. De Valera outlines the various possible strategies open to Sinn Fé[
relation to the elections in Northern Ireland to the new Stormont Parliament. The Government of Ireland Act of 1920 establish
Northern Ireland a local 52-seat legislature modelled on that of Westminster. Collins was Minister for Finance as well as Direct
Organisation and Intelligence for the IRA, and had a good working relationship with de Valera before the Treaty negotiations.

Dáil Éireann

| AIReaċt AIRʒI'O. | | Department of Finance |

Ⅽⅰṡ an ÁRO-ṁaoⅰR,
áⅽ-ⅽlⅰaⅽ

MANSION HOUSE,
DUBLIN.

13th January, 1921.

TO: M.C:

      With regard to the Ulster Six Counties Question -
I have been thinking over it again this morning - I will consider
it further, but at the moment my view of it is that our decision
should ultimately be determined by an analysis of our political
strength in these counties, unless, for instance, we were certain
of a quarter, or at least one-fifth (say ten Members) of the
total representation, I would be for boycotting the Election
altogether, that is sending no Candidates forward. If we secured
anything less it would be boomed abroad that these counties were
practically a homogenius political entity, which justified
partition, but if we were certain of a Quarter or over, I think
we should contest all the Seats. The analysis which will enable
us to determine this can be made by an examination of the last
Parliamentary and Local Elections, and I am asking O'Keeffe to
have it made at once.

      As the matter stands now the considerations in
favour of each of the alternatives appear as follows - at least
to me :-

      In favour of :

(1)   Contesting the elections with a view to abstention, or
      rather joining up with the Dail in the South :

     (a)   That the unity of Republican Ireland will be
          preserved - letting the Elections go by default
          would seem to be the abandonment of the North
          as hopeless for us, and the acceptance in a
          sense of Partition; it would help to kill the
          Republican movement in the North by throwing
          Sinn Feiners practically into the Camp of the
          Nationalists - this might produce, later, a
          dangerous re-actionary affect on the South.

(b)   That the Republican Movement in the North
will be strengthened, overshadowing and,
perhaps, eliminating the other National
group, which will have a certain favourable
re-action, of course, on the South - just
as of an opposite character to that which
I have referred to in the last paragraph.

(c)   The abstention of the entire National groups
from the Parliament will put the Labour and
Capitalist section of the Unionists
struggling with each other for control in
the Parliament; Unionists will understand,
of course, even before the Election Campaign
commences that our representatives will not
enter the Parliament, and so they will be
able to realise in advance, each section of
them, that on the elections will depend
whether Unionist Capital or Unionist Labour
will have control in the Parliament - hence,
we would have by this course the advantage
of the contest between Capital and Labour
in the Election Campaign itself as well as
later in Parliament. This gives the first
course, in my opinion, the advantage practicall
in full, which Mr. Griffith claims for (2)

(d)   This course would be the most directly in line
with our past Policy, and would best be understood both at home, and in Foreign countrie.

(e)   A Moral Effect - Mr. G. seems to claim this in
some special way for No.2. To me the balance,
as far as moral effect, is altogether in favour
of No.1, for, surely, the effect is rather in
the Boycott of the Parliament, and the
repudiation of its authority, than in the
Boycott of the Elections, which would be engage
in by us solely for principle, and to show our
numerical strength. The extent of our
repudiation of the moral right of the Northern
Parliament will be much clearer to the World
when expressed in terms of a definite number
of elected representatives, and a definitely
ascertained electorate, than in the vague
statistics on which we would be forced to rely
if we failed to take advantage of the Election
Our failure, despite anything we could say, wou
be attributed to a conviction on our part
that we had no chance whatever. Hence, as I
have said to me this seems a supplemental

(f)   Our going forward would prevent the going up of
      Nationalist Independents who could hardly be
      blocked otherwise, and who, if they go up are
      certain to attract a substantial section of the
      Republican or Nationalist Vote, owing to the
      political animosity that exists in the North, and
      this would undoubtedly weaken our moral position.

(a)   The only argument that I can see which gives a
      balance in favour of this course is that our
      abstention from the elections will make it more
      clear to the average Labour-Unionist that the
      real struggle for power in the Parliament will
      be between him and the Capitalist, and that
      accordinglyb that it is between him and the
      Capitalist that the real struggle in the Elections
      should be also. It will be our business to
      prevent the Labour element from being confused
      by our entry into the elections - we ought to be
      able to make him to see that we are contesting
      these elections for principle, and not for actual
      power in the Northern Parliament, seeing that we
      will not go near that Parliament.

            I think further that the fact that the
      elections will be held under the Proportional
      Representation system will diminish the danger of
      our entry solidifying or amalgamating the two
      Unionist groups.   I have not, so far, studied
      closely the P/R system, and cannot say offhand
      to what extent greater results can be got by the
      amalgamation of two groups, than by the groups
      separately.   If the system were even
      approximately "proportional" there should be but
      little advantage in amalgamating. In the old
      system what would throw the Unionist Groups
      together would be the fear of the results of a
      three cornered contest. I think the P/R system
      must tend to eliminate that fear, and so our
      entry into the contest would not materially tend
      to drive the Unionist groups together. If there
      be, of course, any analogy to the dangers of the
      3 cornered contest in the P/R system, and if,
      never the less, the Unionist groups xxxx could be
      induced to keep separate, whilst our Candidates
      are also in the field, the result would be in our
      favour, as it might give us some extra representatives
      This could not, of course, occur at all if the
      system be genuinely proportional.

                              B

(President de Valera)

I know that you will understand
why I have had to write this letter. In
our relations of more than twenty
years there has not so far as I know
been any reserve between us when
we have been discussing matters
affecting the nation. We have had
differences of opinion as to the wisdom
or unwisdom of a line of policy +
I have always been prepared in the
last resort to defer to your judgement.
But I cannot concede that full deference
now, because in regard to Partition we
have never had a considered policy. It has
always been an affair of hasty
improvisations, a matter of fits and
starts. We are giving it first place
now in the practical business of
government. When did we do that
before in regard to any of those activities
by which our citizens are
consolidating + intensifying Partition.
Why we would not risk
antagonising one Gaelic Leaguer
or G.A.A. cramk in order to undo
Partition — as it could be undone in

sports and amusement. And yet
we are prepared to subject our farmers
and our people as a whole to further +
intensified
~~hardship and as I believe if the policy~~
~~be pursued~~ hardship in order ~~that~~ to
~~Great Britain~~ compel Great Britain
to force the Northern non-Catholics
to associate with us, when with our
connivance every bigot and kill-
joy, ecclesiastical and lay is doing
                    here
his damnedest to keep them out.
Where is the reason in asking us to pursue
two policies so utterly at variance with each
other. It is because I believe that ~~some~~ of us
and subordinating reason to prejudice, that
prejudice which may be blameless in one heart
of an individual, but should be banished from
the minds of statesmen, in regard to this
matter of defence, + are only raising the
Partition ~~Partition~~ issue now to coerce their
colleagues to defer to their prejudice that
✓ I feel the essential unity + confidence
of the Cabinet has been destroyed

UCDA, P67/155: Draft letter from Seán MacEntee to de
Valera, 17 February 1938 (pages 10 and 11 of which are
reproduced here). MacEntee announces he is resigning in
protest at de Valera's policy on partition and Northern Ireland.
This letter was never sent. MacEntee, a native of Belfast,
served as Minister for Finance, 1932–9; Minister for Industry
and Commerce, 1939–41; and Minister for Local
Government and Public Health, 1941–8. He threatened to
resign on a number of occasions.

Shown to Mr McD
as type of statement that
would be useful. Shebasis
copy?

Saturday, March 12. 19

The Gov. of the U.K declare that it is no
part of the policy or intention of the Gov. of the U·
to oppose any arrangement which may be freely a
voluntarily entered into between the Gov. of Éire
the Gov. of N.I. * The Gov. of the U·K will
accordingly
welcome every improvement in the mutual rel
of Éire and N.I and far from raising any de
will on the contrary be ready to take any
practicable steps that may be necessary to face
                                                              Government
any arrangement desired by the two ~~parties~~ for th
development of closer relations between them or
for the establishment of a united Ireland.

* The Gov. of the U·K recognise that such an
arrangement would be a valuable contribution to
friendly relations between G·B and I. and to
world appeasement.

UCDA, P150/2501: Handwritten note by de Valera, shown to Malcolm MacDonald, suggesting the kind of statement that de Valera would favour from the British government regarding the relationship between the North and South of Ireland, 12 March 1938. MacDonald, a British Labour politician who came to greatly admire de Valera, was Secretary of State for Dominion Affairs, 1935–9.

Personal & Confidential

éire

Dear Prime Minister,

I cannot refrain from writing to you. You and I have worked to bring about conditions which would make it possible to lay the foundations of good neighbourly relations between the British and Irish peoples. The agreement, a year ago was a notable advance in that direction; but the failure to deal with Partition has largely offset what was then accomplished. A free united Ireland would have every interest in wishing Britain to be strong, but when Britain's strength appears to be used to maintain

UCDA, P150/2548: Handwritten personal and confidential letter from de Valera to British prime minister Neville Chamberlain, 12 April 1939. De Valera urges Chamberlain to tackle the partition question, following the previous year's Anglo–Irish Agreement.

the division of our island no such consideration can have any force: A large section of our people, particularly the young are led to see hope only in Britain's weakness. Can something not be done and without delay?

The consequences of failure in the pas to act in time are clear to see an should be a warning. Will the generation that succeeds us have again to deplore the unwisdom of those who did not act wh action would have meant success. I kn your difficulties and your present pre-occu with events farther afield and deeply sympa with you. But the intensification of feeli here and amongst our people in the United States makes it imperative to act quickly lest it be too late to save the situation.

I remain   dear Prime Minister

    Yours Very Sincerely

        Éamon de Valéra

May I express the hope that you will
remain firm in your efforts for Peace
notwithstanding the pressure that will be
brought
placed upon you. Once this war is begun
no man can see the End.

            EdeV.

169

*Brought over
Mr. Malcolm MacDon
+ handed to Taoiseac
on June 26th, 1940..*

The United Kingdom Government would be glad t
be informed what would be the attitude of the Governmen
of Eire towards the following plan.   If the plan is
acceptable as a whole to the Government of Eire, the
United Kingdom Government will at once seek to obtain
the assent thereto of the Government of Northern Irelan
in so far as the plan affects Northern Ireland.

The following are the proposals which, taken
together as a whole, constitute the plan referred to in
the preceding paragraph.

(i)   A declaration to be issued by the United
Kingdom Government forthwith accepting the principle
of a United Ireland.

(ii)   A joint body including representatives of
Government of Eire and the Government of Northern
Ireland to be set up at once to work out the
constitutional and other practical details of the
Union of Ireland.   The United Kingdom Government
to give such assistance towards the work of this
body as might be desired.

(iii)   A joint Defence Council representative of
Eire and Northern Ireland to be set up immediately.

(iv)   Eire to enter the war on the side of the
United Kingdom and her allies forthwith, and, for th
purposes of the Defence of Eire, the Government of
Eire to invite British naval vessels to have the use
of ports in Eire and British troops and aeroplanes t
co-operate with the Eire forces and to be stationed
in such positions in Eire as may be agreed between
the two Governments.

(v)   The Government of Eire to intern all
German and Italian aliens in the country and to take
any further steps necessary to suppress Fifth
Column activities.

(vi)   The United Kingdom Government to provide
military equipment at once to the Government of
Eire in accordance with the particulars given in
the annex.

UCDA, P150/2940: Lord Rugby to de Valera, 18 February 1948. Lord Rugby, formerly Sir John Maffey, was the UK representative in Éire during the Second World War and corresponded with de Valera in relation to partition and Anglo–Irish relations. This letter was sent to de Valera on his final day in office before being succeeded by John A. Costello's inter-party government.

File with reply

**FARMHILL,
DUNDRUM,
Co. DUBLIN.**

DUBLIN 96397.

18 February '48

Dear Mr. de Valera,

From what you have often told me I know that the prospect of some respite from the strain of office will not be unwelcome to you.

I was present in the Dáil to-day. I had a speech in me, but it had to stay there.

Perhaps some day I shall put on record some of my experiences and thoughts here during these eventful years. I promise you that, if I do, it will be with friendly intent & with no blazing indiscretions.

Meanwhile before February 18th

1948 draws to a close I want to let you how deeply I feel today's swift closing of the chapter.

You have always been accessible, patient, frank & sincere, and at the end of more than eight years of association I keenly realise how deep & warm a regard I have for you as a man and as a fellow-traveller through anxious times. &

F. Bland promised me some time ago that he would try to get a photograph of you for my masterpiece. I should much like that & I will ask him again.

If I or my office can be of any service at any time we stand ready to help.

With my thanks & best wishes

Yours very sincerely

Rigby

17th April, 1957

he Right Honorable Lrd Rugby,
uay House,
alesworth,
uffolk,
ngland.

ear Lord Rugby,

On looking through our letter files I find
ere a dictated draft of a letter which I intended sending you
n reply to your kind acknowledgment of my Christmas greetings
ast December.   Somehow the dictation was interrupted and the
etter, I expect, was not sent.   If so, please accept my
pologies for my seeming ungraciousness.

I am back once more at the desk in the Taoiseach's
ffice, over the corner of which we had so many serious talks
uring the war.   As I sit here I can, in imagination, see you
ull from your breast-pocket the long reminder slip.   Those
ere anxious times for us both, but they have left with me not
npleasant memories.   I hope it remains the same with you.   I
eeply regret Mr. Eden's ill health.   If you should be writing
im will you please convey to him my heartfelt good wishes for
is speedy recovery?

As the years pass my hope that complete recon-
iliation between Ireland and Britain would come in our time is
eginning to fade.   That this reconciliation will come ultimately
 have no doubt.   But, delays are dangerous and particularly in
he world of today.   Were Eden still at the helm in your country
 should be disposed to make a last desperate effort to see my
ope realized.   But, he is ill and at the other end of the world,
nd of your present Ministers I know little.

Lord Salisbury, or as I knew him Lord Cranborne,
as, I see, resigned from the Government.   That means another
ink gone.   Lord Mountbatten, whom I met before he left India, is

the only other person over there who might be in a position
to do anything.   I saw your present Prime Minister in Strasbour
but only met him casually.

I am writing you all this in the hope that you
might be able to get some move on towards the solution of this
exasperating problem.   The first step, in my opinion, is as I
think I suggested to you already, to get your Government to
admit publicly that it is a British no less than an Irish intere
to see partition ended.   Chamberlain agreed that this was so,
but events moved so rapidly that he was denied a favourable
opportunity for making this declaration.   Can we get your
Government to make it now?

With assurances of my highest regard both for
Lady Rugby and yourself.

Very sincerely yours,

QUAY HOUSE,
HALESWORTH,
SUFFOLK.
HALESWORTH 3210.

18 . 5 . '57

My dear Taoiseach,

If I have not sent my promised reply to your letter of 7 April you may be sure it is not because I have put it out of my thoughts.

I must admit that the question of Partition, always difficult enough, is now even more difficult than it was when you and I confronted each other at the familiar table, and very much more difficult than when you discussed it with Neville Chamberlain.

Your External Relations Act shewed the workings of your mind in seeking a plan to preserve a bridge-head for operations and a link between our two islands. It was a statesmanlike conception. Unhappily its machinery in action — though a mere formality —

could be used in political warfare for bitter attack. It was so utilised, even by James Dil who in his heart knew better.

Heaven knows, the procedure was humilia enough from our point of view! Still the basic idea was sound, — somehow to keep up a bridge, however slender.

You in your experience know that Lon is not unreasonable in these matters. When you think what you have been able to achieve over the annuities, the ports &c you must feel that the British Government is not bad to deal with or is often found on the side of the angels.

Then, at a most vital point, in our neighbourly relations and in world history, when all people, and I most fervently, were hoping that the War chapter would move into a new chapter of closer understanding in which all problems could be considered with due regard to the needs of neighbourly co-existence and the inevitability of gradualness, in comes John Costello and crashes the delicate fabric, all mainly, so far as I could see, to gu

176

pitch for you and the Fianna Fail opposition.

Not one word to me as to the desirability of re-examining the difficult procedure of the External Relations Act, no suggestion of any discussion in London.

And apart from that, in order to show that he could go one better than you, he proclaims a form of warfare upon us, — a campaign to damage us in our pride, our pocket and our prestige.

It seemed to me that our attitude towards Eire during & after the War deserved something better than this. I was staggered by it.

The leader of Fine Gael brought about a position in which all the bridges went down between Eire & the Commonwealth and he created a situation in which it was not possible for the head of the Irish Government to visit London. His wild words have stimulated the peligrate group and you now succeed to the difficulties which he created.

This long preamble is necessary as I regard my mind as a test mind for you to work upon in considering the problem to-day.

can foresee how the end will come about.
Politicians dislike "the inevitability of gradualness"
But it is the best of all processes. Politician
like the Grand Slam. But I do not think
is on the cards here for either side.

Anyhow, how can the first move be ma
You think that the ball is in our court or th
we must make the stroke. I do not think tha
is possible. I think the ball is in your
court and that you must make the stroke.

What I would suggest is that, without
making any bargaining points, you should seek
to re-enter the Commonwealth. You could take
this up with other member countries before
London if that suited you best. You —
and all Ireland — have very close links with
Canada, Australia — New Zealand.

My idea is that you should once
again get your knees under a table in
London where you could feel your way.

I fully recognise that the terms of admission
would be in conformity with a republican
status.

178

New Delhi, India,
18 June 1948.

My dear Mr. de Valera,

It was a great pleasure to meet you during your
very short visit to Delhi and India. There were so many
people here who were anxious to meet you. But it was
difficult to find time for it and many of them are rather
annoyed with me because of this. For a long time past,
several generations of India have followed closely and
with deep sympathy events in Ireland. +We have drawn
inspiration from many of the happenings there and you
have been admired by vast numbers of our people. For
them it was an event that you visited India and their
only regret is that they could not take advantage of
your visit.

I enclose some photographs that were taken at
the time of your visit to Delhi.

With all good wishes,

Yours very sincerely
Jawaharlal Nehru

Eamon de Valera, Esq.,
Dublin.

UCDA, P150/2955: Letter from Indian prime
minister Jawaharlal Nehru, 18 June 1948. De Valera
visited India in 1948 as part of his anti-partition tour.

Day in the life of the President

1.   Early breakfast; listens to radio news bulletins.

2.   Mail and correspondence - that on private matters dealt with in conjunction with Personal Secretary; correspondence of an official nature referred to the Secretary to the President.

3.   Daily Mass in Áras oratory.   This is also attended by Mrs. de Valera, members of the family when in residence, the Aide de Camp on duty, and members of household staff.

4.   Necessary time given daily to deal with official correspondence and matters in consultation with Secretary to the President.   Usually a number of documents to be signed - warrants of appointment, army commissions and bills as they are presented from the Taoiseach's Department; messages to and from other Heads of State; other official correspondence and matters arising from powers and functions conferred on President by Constitution or law; invitations and arrangements for public engagements - personal attendance or representation at public ceremonies and functions;* reception of State or other distinguished visitors; presentation of Letters of Credence etc. as occasion arises.

5.   Luncheon (private or official as the case may be).

Afternoon

6.   Receives overseas and other visitors, at their direct request and by appointment: (Visitors, from time to time, include representatives of international bodies and of Irish organisations with which President is connected as Patron or in whose work or aims he has a special interest).   Public engagements;* visits friends in hospitals.   Receives Taoiseach, at least once a month, who keeps him generally informed on matters of domestic and international policy.

Tea; listens to Radio, television; readings.

Occasional walks in grounds.

Receives personal friends.

Official dinners occasionally; formal attendance at opera or other cultural event periodically.

Usually in his study until 10 p.m.

(Public engagements - i.e. memorial ceremonies, cultural events, opening of more important or national conferences, etc. may take place in morning or afternoon).

Examples of the questions I would appreciate having President
e Valera answer in writing:

) In view of the opinion widely held all over the world today that
reland is an island populated by gunmen and religious bigots, how,
r. President, do you foresee the future of this island?

) In your personal view, Sir, is religion the main barrier to re-
nification of the island?

) Which, Mr. President, of the many world renowned statesmen of the
Oth. century you have known did you find most interesting and congenial?

) What, in 1972, is the schedule of a typical day in the life of the
resident of the Irish Republic.

) Would you care to send a special greeting to the people of North
merica? South America? Africa? Asia? Australia and New Zealand?

uggested pictures to accompany the three articles on President de
alera:

) The President at work at his desk.

) The President with his Cabinet.

) The President with his family.

) The President awarding the Aga Khan trophy at the R.D.S. Horse
how, August, 1972.

) The President with President de Gaulle.

) The President with President Kennedy.

▲ NAI, PRES, 2003/18/66: C. Brooks Peters to de Valera, 12 June 1972. The American
ambassador to Ireland, John D.J. Moore, forwarded these questions to de Valera on behalf
of journalist, C. Brooks Peters.

◄ NAI, PRES, 2003/18/66: 'Day in the life of the President', sent to C. Brooks Peters, a
retired *New York Times'* journalist living in Dublin who wanted to write a profile of de
Valera to mark his ninetieth birthday, June 1972. His request for an interview was refused.

VII

'The policy of patience

has failed and is over'

UCDA, P150/3834: De Valera delivering a speech, *c.* 1940s. Sitting at the table to his right are Martin O'Sullivan (Labour Party TD for Dublin North West, 1943–8) and to his left, Seán MacEntee (Minister for Local Government and Public Health, 1941–8).

M uch significance has been attached to the peaceful transfer of power in 1932, but not enough, argues Peter Mair, to de Valera's 'decisive role in ensuring that democracy survived in the new Irish State—against the odds'. Mair argues that the snap general election of 1933, seeking to consolidate his own and the country's interest, and his decision not to opt for a non-democratic solution, were of the utmost significance, and de Valera's great historic achievement, particularly when seen 'within a context of a long international history of democratic consolidation and breakdown'.[1] During a decade that witnessed the collapse of democracy in such countries as Italy, Portugal, Greece, Germany and Spain, Mair further argues that historians and political scientists have taken Irish democracy for granted.

This is a point that had earlier been made by J.G.A. Pocock in 1982:

> As the American Revolution is the exception among the revolutions of the late eighteenth century, the Irish is the exception among those of the early and middle twentieth century. In no other country of Western Europe was a new state created by revolution in the aftermath of the First World War; yet, because this revolution was neither communist nor fascist, it does not interest intellectuals and has received little attention from historians. They may have missed an instructive case.[2]

This is a valid perspective given the climate of the 1930s and the widespread contempt shown for democracy and it is important to highlight how de Valera was determined to consolidate his hold on power democratically, but there is one weakness in Mair's argument. He rightly takes Joe Lee to task for making the claim that 'nothing so became Cosgrave in office as his manner of leaving it', which seems to imply that Cosgrave should be applauded for not staging a coup to prevent Fianna Fáil taking office in 1932. By the same token, Mair invites de Valera to be lauded for not becoming a dictator.

The virulence of de Valera's critics at home, notably Cumann na nGaedheal, was based on genuine and understandable fears, given that de Valera had come to power less than ten years after the end of the Civil War. John Regan summed up their concerns by noting that 'to the conservative Cumann na nGaedheal elite the scope of the changes de Valera wanted to bring about in what amounted to a second constitutional revolution seemed impracticable and ultimately ruinous'.[3] The *United Irishman* newspaper, as well as screaming accusatory headlines about Bolshevism and Trotskyism, claimed in the summer of 1932 that de Valera was encouraging the IRA's revival in order to establish a dictatorship, and the following year, after de Valera's electoral victory in 1933, still maintained that 'the government have not a record for respect for the national will or for the democratic rights of the people'.[4]

Contrast this dubious assessment with the actions of de Valera when facing the onslaught of the Army Comrades Association (Blueshirts) in the mid 1930s. Eoin O'Duffy revelled in the hysteria, disorder, violence, extremist rhetoric and megalomania that underpinned his leadership of the Blueshirts, but it is also important to acknowledge that de Valera's critics' fears, particularly regarding free speech, were genuine, especially when in March 1934 he introduced a bill to abolish the Senate. In an embarrassing setback for de Valera, the Senate had refused to approve The Wearing of Uniforms Bill, which was intended to prohibit the public wearing of uniforms, the use of military titles in political organisations and the carrying of weapons at meetings. According to Fearghal McGarry:

> The peremptory nature of this response illustrated why de Valera's commitment to democracy was genuinely doubted by the opposition. De Valera's actions may appear more defensible in hindsight, but to many contemporary observers it provided further evidence of his willingness to contravene the spirit of the constitution.[5]

In the early 1930s his opponents accused him of a blatant hypocrisy in continued toleration of the IRA and not of the Blueshirts, but in the long run such critics were proved wrong in their predictions of what power would do to him. De Valera was the main victor of the Blueshirt episode, enabling him to present Fianna Fáil as a firm defender of the state and protector of democracy, an identity it would need in relation to the IRA as well.[6] He was correct too, to take such a strong stance against the threat that Eoin O'Duffy represented, and de Valera showed innate decency in granting O'Duffy a state funeral in December 1944 and followed the cortege with most of his Cabinet to Glasnevin Cemetery.

But de Valera did not defeat the Blueshirts on his own. John Regan makes the important, and frequently overlooked point that it was the Gardaí keeping order at grass-root meetings that did much to ensure a resistance to Fascism in Ireland: 'They dispensed justice and blows with equanimity in 1934 and Irish democracy, and for that matter, de Valera's ascendancy, were all the safer for that'.[7]

It was also fortunate for de Valera that the total allegiance of the army to the state had been ensured at an early stage in the life of the Free State. Following the quelling of the army mutiny of 1924 any ambiguity concerning their allegiance was disposed of through the Defence Forces Act of that year, which established the army on a permanent legal and constitutional footing and prohibited membership of oath-bound societies.[8] This was to be of particular significance to de Valera in terms of resisting the threat from the IRA in the 1930s and 1940s.

Right from the foundation of the Fianna Fáil party, as pointed out by Richard English, de Valera emphasised inclusiveness, wanting to prize the 'national interest as a whole' and avoid the 'clashing' of various sections within the community, and this also involved an 'overlap with and repudiation of the party's revolutionary past'.[9] In June 1936 the government made an order under the Special Powers Act declaring the IRA an unlawful organisation, and like his counterpart in the North, James Craig, it has been suggested by Henry Patterson that 'de Valera proved much more successful in marginalizing challengers from the extremes than he did on delivering on the economic and social dimensions of his political project'.[10]

Those challengers included the IRA. As noted by Brian Hanley, despite de Valera's dependence on their support for his new party, and his release of republican prisoners after he came to power in 1932, as early as 1933 Fianna Fáil began to refer to the 'new IRA' sheltering behind the 'honoured name' of the older organisation. In 1934 the *Irish Press* insisted that it was a different organisation than it had been between 1919 and 1923 and was now a 'private army'.

In continuing with his rhetoric about inclusiveness, de Valera insisted the Old IRA had been an 'army of the nation … of the whole people' but had now become a group of instigators of 'sectional strife'. He answered accusations that IRA prisoners were being ill-treated by reminding a rally in Tralee, Co. Kerry, that he knew that prison 'was never easy' because he 'had been there', and that he and Kerry republican, Austin Stack, had endured far worse conditions in 1919 but 'we didn't grumble about it'.[11] De Valera's ripping up of the Treaty pages could hardly be opposed by the IRA, even though it had the potential to lessen their support base by reconciling many republicans to the Free State.

Fearghal McGarry points out that 'the IRA failed to depict Fianna Fáil as mere Free Staters, though not from want of trying. Its demise was hastened by schism and decline ... future support for the IRA would depend on partition and northern grievances rather than rejection of the southern state'.[12] Another nail in the IRA's partially closed coffin was the new Constitution of 1937, particularly Article 16.6.1: 'The right to raise and maintain military or armed forces is vested exclusively in the Oireachtas'. As Ronan Fanning pointed out, the introduction of the Treason Bill in the Dáil in 1939 also indicated that 'the moment the constitution was enacted by the people ... treason had a new meaning'.[13]

Seán MacBride's memoir of this time makes it clear that for him as a republican, the enactment of the Constitution was a watershed:

> I certainly took the viewpoint, that once the 1937 constitution was adopted, the whole position in the country was radically altered ... I decided some time before 1937 that, if the constitution was enacted, we should work through it. We should accept any constitution which invested sovereignty in the people of Ireland and work through it to achieve the rest of the independence of the country. As far as the constitution was concerned, I was quite prepared to accept it, and I said so publicly on a number of occasions. I also decided that I would terminate my connection with the IRA as from then.[14]

In that sense, some of de Valera's gestures were certainly bringing some republicans in from the wings, even if they were unhappy with the pace of change. Left-leaning republican, Sighle Humphreys, probably summed up this mindset in an interview she gave to Richard English in 1987 when he was researching the relationship between socialism and Irish republicans: 'There were a lot of people that thought [de Valera] was going slowly, but he was going somewhere—and they were happy with it'.[15]

In May 1940 in a radio broadcast following an IRA attack on two Gardaí, Detective-Sergeants Shannahan and MacSweeney, in which they were seriously wounded, de Valera suggested that the government 'for many years, has shown an extraordinary patience. I am afraid that I must say, now, an excessive patience towards these people. ... the policy of patience has failed and is over'.[16] During the Second World War a military tribunal, allowed for under the draconian public safety legislation originally introduced in 1931 and then repealed but subsequently revived by de Valera, 'acted as the state's last line of judicial defence against political crime, sentencing a number of IRA men to death for murder'.[17]

Six IRA men were executed by army firing squad during the war; Charlie Kerins was hanged in December 1944, three others were allowed to die on hunger-strike, while more than 500 were interned without trial and another 600 were committed under the Offences Against the State Act, which became law in June 1939. Backed by 'the steel' of Justice Minister Gerald Boland, the essential issue for de Valera was the legitimacy of the state, particularly because, in his own words, 'there were no longer any obstacles in the way of any section to utilising constitutional means'.[18]

UCDA, P150/623: De Valera talking with reporters outside Lincoln Jail, 1950. Black and white print given to de Valera by the *Sunday Telegraph* of his visit to the jail from which he escaped in 1919.

UCDA, P150/2949: De Valera and Frank Aiken pictured with Irish film star, Maureen O'Hara, 17 March 1948. Taken at the Ancient Order of Hibernians and Ladies Auxiliary Seventieth Annual St Patrick's Day banquet in Los Angeles.

► UCDA, P150/2590: Typescript of a radio broadcast given on 8 May 1940, in which de Valera condemned IRA activities following an armed attack on two detective officers of An Garda Síochana who were conveying post to the Department of External Affairs on the previous day.

I am speaking to you tonight for a few minutes to remind you of a duty which each of you owes to himself, to the community as a whole, and to Ireland.

This moment when small nations throughout Europe are devoting all their efforts to strengthening national unity in order, the better, to defend their independence is the moment that a group in this country has chosen to attempt to destroy our organised life.

In the last few years, as you know, every obstacle has been removed which could in any way be used to justify a recourse to violence. Today every party within this State is free to seek to achieve its political aims by peaceful means. The use of violence is therefore not only unjustifiable. It is a wanton attack upon the whole community engaged in with a cynical disregard of the vital need to keep our people strong and united in the face of universal danger.

The Government, for many years, has shown an extraordinary patience. (I am afraid that I must say, now, an excessive patience, towards these people.) Putting our hope in patience, we punished mildly and with reluctance and we forgave easily. I am glad to think that this policy was not altogether without fruit. For everybody now realises that we are not the people to go to extremes without grave and persistent cause. But as regards the men who are now in hiding and planning new crimes, the policy of patience has failed and is over.

Yesterday a dastardly attack was made on two Irish police officers escorting the Government mails. To achieve their purpose the assailants did not shrink from murder. The gallantry of Detective-Sergeants Shanahan and MacSweeney ~~saved the property~~ what had been entrusted to their keeping. Their conduct shows us all what nobility there can be in a simple devotion to duty, ~~and it was these two officers who,~~ though outnumbered and gravely wounded,

VIII

'Too trained in

English democracy

to sit down

under a dictatorship'

UCDA, P150/1984: Being conferred with the Supreme Cross of Christ by Pope John XXIII, 17 March 1962. This occurred during his official visit with Sinéad to Rome and the Vatican at the close of the Patrician year.

D e Valera's Constitution of 1937 has stood the test of time, and it is important to acknowledge that it was not just a document reflecting the concerns of the mid 1930s, but a reflection of values built up over the previous fifteen years, and that the general characteristics of the state were firmly entrenched before 1937. Nor was its creation possible without the contribution of civil servants like John Hearne, Philip O'Donoghue and Maurice Moynihan, chairman of the drafting committee, though Moynihan was emphatic 'about de Valera's ultimate responsibility for it'.[1] Overall, it can be seen, in the words of John Kelly's *The Irish Constitution* as 'a stabilising and reforming continuation of that of 1922', with some significant additions, including the principle of judicial review of legislation and constitutional criteria, and the 'very extended recitals of fundamental rights'.[2]

With the passage of time, it came to be seen as a significant human rights document, though Kelly was critical of the confused relationship between 'personal rights' and 'fundamental rights' and 'the tendency for concepts to proliferate needlessly and confusingly and the defective dogmatic groundwork for some departments of constitutional doctrine'.[3] In updating the work of Kelly in 1994, Gerard Hogan and Gerry Whyte drew attention to the ever increasing significance of the courts in constitutional adjudication, because so many issues of political controversy provided the spur for legal challenges, while in terms of personal rights, the more cases that were taken, the more the general clauses concerning 'fundamental concepts' were given depth and meaning.[4]

In a further update, Hogan and Whyte wrote in 2003 of 'the vibrancy of Irish constitutional law', attested by the 'explosion' in constitutional litigation and the increase in the number of constitutional amendments (since 1937 there have been 28 attempts to amend the Constitution, 21 were successful).[5] It was clear that the passage of time, and the deletion of provisions which were considered overly confessional and nationalistic, facilitated a better perception of the merits of the Constitution, and an appreciation of the 'true nature of the fundamental constitutional architecture: the separation of powers, the system of judicial review and in particular, the nature of fundamental rights protection', as well as 'the sophisticated legal thinking' of those who drafted it.[6]

In truth, Irish lawyers largely ignored it until the 1950s because most of them had been educated in the British tradition that emphasised the primacy of parliament over the law. This began to change when a Supreme Court judge, Cearbhall Ó Dálaigh, looked up from the Bench and commented that 'we have a constitution, but nobody knows what it means'. Ó Dálaigh, who became Chief Justice in 1961, and his Supreme Court colleague, Brian Walsh, began to interpret the Constitution in order to expand the rights of individuals under the law, and together they were responsible for a revolution in the interpretation of the Irish legal system.[7]

Framed when democracy was widely under threat in Europe, the Constitution was also necessary in the realm of practical politics to emphasise the exclusive legitimacy of the state. This was particularly important in view of the threat to the state from the IRA (there was a provision for the operation of special courts in Article 70) and the wider importance in the 1930s of symbolic change as an important part of de Valera's foreign policy. It was also necessary for de Valera to move with caution due to his need to win the popular vote regarding approval of the Constitution, and the degree to which he would be dependent on votes other than traditional Fianna Fáil votes. Because the Constitution was framed prior to the 1938 Anglo–Irish Agreement, and the outbreak of the Second World War, he especially needed agreement on the legitimacy of the state.[8]

Brian Farrell suggests that it needs to be acknowledged that de Valera had much contact with 'less strident' Catholics over its provisions, and that in framing Article 44, which deals with respect for religion and freedom of religious conscience and practice, de Valera exhibited 'a degree of subtlety, pragmatism and patience far removed from the image of a self-centred and dictatorial leader'.[9]

Much has been made of the contribution that John Charles McQuaid, Holy Ghost Father, headmaster of Blackrock College and Archbishop of Dublin from 1940, made to the text of the Constitution. There was certainly extensive consultation between the two men, and McQuaid undoubtedly influenced de Valera with regard to many aspects of it. It is no exaggeration to assert, as John Cooney has, that de Valera was 'bombarded' with letters from McQuaid from early 1937 concerning various sections of the Constitution.[10]

McQuaid became immersed in papal teachings on economic and social matters and church–state relations, and was 'indefatigable' in checking sources for de Valera. But McQuaid's tone was 'generally courteous and deferential'; de

Valera clearly valued his advice, but also had reservations about some of McQuaid's more extreme views on the primacy of the Catholic Church.[11] The tone of the correspondence between the two men in the spring of 1937 reveals the extent to which McQuaid helped him with the Constitution, but also that they did not always arrive at the same conclusions.

On 15 April 1937 McQuaid wrote to him revealing his preoccupation with the Constitution, which was on his mind during the saying of Mass:

> Kindly pardon my sending you another note. I fear my many notes and papers must have only bothered you the last ten days. But it occurred to me as I said mass this morning that last night, I may have so shown my disappointment as to seem wanting in courtesy. If I did in the least way, I am very sorry for it. ...
>
> P.S: I shall work at the Property Section today and if anything occurs to me, I shall send it across.[12]

A few weeks later he wrote again (addressing de Valera as 'My Dear President'): 'I have compared very carefully the draft and attach two notes. It reads very well'. But he added that he had concerns about the reference to 'other Christians': 'I have been thinking much about it. Of course, they claim the title, but as so very many in all these Churches deny the divinity of Christ, unlike their ancestors, they have truly ceased to be Christian. Very often they are only ethical. But—you may have already settled the question'.[13]

De Valera had indeed settled that question, by resisting the pressure to have Ireland declared a Catholic state. He also played a clever game of Vatican diplomacy, knowing that Pope Pius XI would be unhappy about the recognition which the Constitution gave to religions other than Catholicism. Joseph Walshe reported to de Valera from Rome in April 1937 about his meetings in the Vatican to seek approval for the Constitution. His mission needs to be understood in the context of the recognition, as Walshe expressed to Cardinal Eugenio Pacelli, the Cardinal Secretary of State, that de Valera:

> fully realised that the sections of the constitution under discussion did not correspond with the complete Catholic ideal. You would like to have the approval of the Vatican in so far as it could be given. At any rate you wished to have the satisfaction of having let the Card[inal] Sec[retar]y and the Holy Father see the sections relating to the Church before putting them before parliament. ... He said that he had had a preliminary chat with the Holy Father

... He felt however that the 'special position' given to the Catholic Church had no real value so long as there was not a formal acknowledgement of the R.C. Church as the Church founded by Christ. ... Ireland was *the* Catholic country of the World, and he thought we should have made a very special effort to give to the world a completely Catholic Constitution. I told him ... In our case the full Catholic framework would destroy absolutely the building which we desired to construct. We had to take the long view in order to conciliate the most hostile religious opinions, and to get all our people to work for our common country. ... The Cardinal told me with a smile but quite truthfully that according to the strict teaching of the Church we were heretics to recognise any church but the one true Church of Christ.[14]

The response of the Pope was '*Ni approvo ni non disapprovo; taceremo*' ('I do not approve, neither do I *not disapprove*; we shall maintain silence'). Walshe added, 'I tried to translate the evil out of this double negative but the Cardinal held me to the sense'. Neutrality and silence from the Vatican was actually a considerable coup for the heretical de Valera.

In terms of the function of the government, de Valera was happy with the strong centralised state, and historians have rightly been cynical of his creation of a new Senate, seeing it as largely cosmetic and something that would not impinge on parliamentary decision making. Joe Lee described it as 'simply a sop thrown to eager ecclesiastics preaching the importance of the principle of subsidiarity propounded in papal encyclicals', with a system of election designed not to disturb the existing system of party control.[15] (The Taoiseach could nominate eleven members to ensure control.) Tom Garvin referred to it as 'the sop de Valera had given to the Vocationalists ... like so many of de Valera's constitutional devices, Seánad Éireann was an ideological red herring, and clearly intended to be so'.[16]

But these assessments need to be balanced with the recognition that, given the provisions for referendums, and an independent supreme court, 'while maintaining a system that was highly centralised in a territorial sense, within that all powerful centre, it nevertheless created a framework for the dispersal of power across a number of autonomous institutions. It also established a variety of important limits to the exercise of executive power'.[17] Moreover, it could not be enacted without the approval of the electorate and it was put to the people with no guarantee of success; the electorate voted in favour by a margin of 685,000 to 527,000.

Throughout the 1930s and 1940s there was an interest shown by Irish Catholic intellectuals in vocationalism or corporatism, terms that were sometimes used interchangeably. Inevitably, their interest in such ideas led to disagreement as to the nature of the powers of the state, because many of them were distrustful of politicians and bureaucracy and the extent to which there could be a meaningful distribution of power in Ireland. De Valera agreed to a Commission on Vocational Organisation, which sat during the Second World War and met on 312 occasions.

In addressing the opening of the Commission, de Valera ironically hinted that their work might in fact not be that useful, reminding them that the post-war world would probably be strikingly different to the contemporary one that they were about to analyse. But he did acknowledge that tasks set for the government often became too overwhelming, and that he was in favour of as much decentralisation as possible ('the trouble is that when the state begins to interfere at all it begins to interfere more and more until it is driven by force of logic and circumstance to centralise').[18]

The truth was that most government members, including himself, were not firm believers in decentralisation, and de Valera won the battle with the church on this matter decisively, although vocational ideas continued to be promoted, due to the dexterity with which many educated Catholics revealed how they were practised in countries like Spain, Portugal and Austria.[19] But in reality, de Valera's government was not going to surrender even a fraction of its power. As far back as April 1933 a memorandum drawn up by the Department of Local Government and Public Health for the Department of the Taoiseach had questioned the usefulness or relevance of local government, which was 'defective and unsatisfactory' and any review of which 'would logically point to the complete abolition of local governing bodies and the merger of their functions with those of the central government'.[20] It treated the report of the Commission on Vocational Organisation, chaired by the Bishop of Galway, Michael Browne, with contempt because it had suggested a widescale reorganisation of the manner in which Irish society was structured, with a criticism of the prevailing government structures and the emphasis on power from below. It was a report that irritated the government (Lemass called it 'slovenly', while Seán MacEntee believed the Irish needed strong central government because they were too argumentative)[21] and left the church looking stubbornly idealistic.

Perhaps there is some truth in Joe Lee's assertion that the failure of the Catholic Church to counteract the power of bureaucratic centralisation represented 'one of the great lost opportunities of Irish intellectual endeavour'.[22] But this must be qualified by emphasising that the opponents of bureaucracy had more than met their match in the administrators and politicians who were determined to develop a strong central state at a time of international economic and political instability.

Bishop Browne, for example, had complained that departmental claims of immunity from releasing information on the grounds of state secrecy were inconsistent with de Valera's undertaking that the Commission would be accommodated in every way in its search for information.[23] The Department of Finance suggested 'that there would be a certain grim satisfaction in getting rid of the Bishop of Galway on the grounds of War economy',[24] an indication that Fianna Fáil was not going to allow itself to be bullied by one of the more formidable members of the Irish hierarchy.

De Valera kept his distance in relation to any suggestions regarding the desirability of distributing power more widely. As late as 1947 he suggested tentatively that his approval of the Commission's recommendations would be limited to those cases, 'in which the government was satisfied that the interests of the community were adequately safeguarded',[25] a meaningless reply indicating that like his colleagues, he was happy for the report to gather dust. J.H. Whyte expressed surprise that vocational ideas did not receive a more sympathetic hearing in Ireland 'because they had no ideological competitors'.[26] In truth, they did—those who believed in the strong state.

De Valera, who briefly served as Minister for Local Government in August 1941, (and also served briefly at other times as Minister for Education and Minister for Defence) preferred to confine his emphasis on 'decentralisation' to those aspects that would not directly challenge or threaten state power. He enthusiastically backed the rural self-help group Muintir na Tíre (People of the Country), seeing these voluntary efforts as being of more value than legislation.[27] The Local Government Bill of 1940 allowed for the creation of harmless parish councils, which could only execute functions delegated from the local authority. This was a convenient way of insisting that the true spirit of local government could not be created by an act of the Oireachtas, but had to come from the people themselves.

De Valera's critics may have been more worried about the creation of the office of president, but it did not become a politically powerful or controversial office during his lifetime. A day in his life as president included listening to the radio bulletins, dealing with correspondence, attending daily Mass in the Áras oratory, signing documents and messages to heads of state, receiving presentations of letters of credence, visiting 'friends in hospitals', chatting with the Taoiseach once a month, and occasionally walking in the grounds and attending cultural events in an official capacity.[28]

In February 1967 de Valera had an informal and often light-hearted chat with the British ambassador to Ireland, Sir Andrew Gilchrist, whose account of the conversation is held in the Gilchrist papers in the Churchill Archives Centre. When Gilchrist questioned de Valera about the Constitution, de Valera replied that when writing it:

> I remember hesitating for a long time over the American Presidential system. But it wouldn't have done—we were too trained in English democracy to sit down under a dictatorship, which is what the American system really is. ... Besides, I wanted to prepare a nice quiet job without too much work for my old age... Still, I admit I was tempted—look at the way de Gaulle rules France ... absolute rule ... very efficient.[29]

UCDA, P150/1985: President and Mrs Sinéad de Valera's visit to St
Patrick's Church, Rome, at the close of the Patrician year, 17 March 1962.

UCDA, P150/2224: Dr John Charles McQuaid, President of Blackrock College, Papal Nuncio Paschal Robinson and Taoiseach de Valera in the grounds of Blackrock College, 1932. Courtesy of the *Irish Times*.

UCDA, P150/2395: John Charles McQuaid to de Valera, 15 April 1937. McQuaid writes regarding the drafting of what became in the published version, Articles 40–5 of the Constitution. A Holy Ghost priest, McQuaid was president of Blackrock College 1931–9, and was appointed Archbishop of Dublin in 1940, the first time a priest from outside the ranks of the regular clergy had been appointed to this position since 1786. De Valera and Irish diplomats at the Vatican had urged for him to be appointed. He remained archbishop until 1972. Although initially close, the relationship between McQuaid and de Valera became progressively more fraught.

TELEPHONE
BLACKROCK 27.

FROM THE REV. PRESIDENT,
BLACKROCK COLLEGE,
BLACKROCK,
CO. DUBLIN.

15ᵗʰ April, 1937.

My dear President,

I beg to enclose some suggestions on work of last night, which I trust may prove useful in some way.

It was kind of you to 'phone and I am very grateful. At the time, I was surrounded by people and could not say more than I did, in a bald way.

I do not judge myself so indulgently as you have done. I was clearly at fault and I am sorry for it.

With kind regards,

I beg to remain,

Yours very respectfully,

J. McQuaid. C.S.Sp.

UCDA, P150/2395: John Charles
McQuaid to de Valera, *c.* April 1937.
McQuaid again writes relating to the
drafting of the Constitution.

TELEPHONE
BLACKROCK 27.

FROM THE REV. PRESIDENT,
BLACKROCK COLLEGE,
BLACKROCK,
CO. DUBLIN.

My dear President.

I have compared very carefully the

draft. and attach two notes.

It reads very well.

Have you in Art. 45. fixed yet the

form "other Christian"? I have been thinking much

about it. Of course, they claim the title, but as so very

many in all these Churches deny the divinity of Christ,

unlike their ancestors. They have truly ceased to be

Christian. Very often they are only ethical. But you

may have already settled the question.

I am sure you will be relieved to have it all

finished.

With kind regards.

I am,

Yours very respectfully,

✠ McQuaid, 6.5.56.

207

He promised to have long talk with the Holy Father and ~~to get the~~ obtain his blessing ~~for~~ ~~but~~ for having done ~~doing~~ so well in such difficult circumstances. It was clear when saying this that the Cardinal did not realise that the Holy Father was going to adopt ~~such a~~ the negative attitude which he made known to me the following day. Indeed he gave me the very clear impression that having said all he could say, he was going to get the ~~Holy~~ Pope to bless the ~~govt~~ ~~fut~~ for the effort they had made to meet the Catholic view point — without making any reference to the ~~"other than books."~~ ~~The Cardinal approved of the title of the Lord and~~ therefore I need hardly say that I was very disappointed ~~titled~~ when I received from the Cardinal yesterday The exact ~~text~~ text of the words used by the Holy Father. "Ni approvo ni nondisapprovo taceremo." And the Cardinal did not leave me any doubt as to the meaning. I had asked him to ensure at least that the H.F. would not disapprove. The answer was: "I do not approve, neither do I ~~not~~ disapprove. We shall maintain silence." I tried to translate the evil ~~of~~ out of this double negative but the Cardinal held me to the sense. He went on to show that the H.F. was doing quite a lot in saying that he would maintain silence.

UCDA, P150/2419: Handwritten report from Joseph Walshe to de Valera, 22 April 1937 (page 6 of which is reproduced here). This was an account of his visit to Rome to assess the attitude of Pope Pius XI to Article 45 of the new Irish Constitution, then being drafted. Walshe's report was mainly concerned with an interview with the Cardinal Secretary of State, Eugenio Pacelli.

S. 10677

Telephone: 92136.

ROINN AN TAOISIGH

28 EAN 1939

ÉIRE

ead to Taoiseach
psons.
2/2/39.

MILLTOWN PARK,
DUBLIN, S.4.

Friday: 26 : 1 : '39.

Dear Mr. de Valera,

I have to thank you for your kindness in forward-
ing the announcement of the appointment of the Commission
on functional organisation.

May I say that I think the Commission is a very
well selected one and gives promise of something tangible
being suggested in this matter? I have, of course, no hope
---nor indeed any desire, for I think it would be very unwise
---that any very revolutionary or far-reaching changes can
be immediately brought about.   But I do think that there
are one or two very fecund "organisational-seeds" that could
be planted and stakes provided for them, and then let grow
organically and slowly, adapting themselves, under the bene-
volent and vigilant eye of the Government, to our own concrete circumstances.   If we can get substantial agreement
from this very diverse personnel on these seeds and the way
they should be planted, the Commission will not have been a
failure.

Again thanking you for the honour of inviting
me to sit on this Commission,

Sincerely yours,   E. J. Coyne S. J.

Strongbow's Horse.

De Valera: You have a very fine residence in Dublin,
Mr. Ambassador, a very distinguished residence.

A.C.G.: Yes. One of the things that make it distinguishe[d]
is that the grounds contain the grave of a
famous horse — one that won the Kentucky Derby,
I believe.

De Valera: No, it won the English Derby, it was a first-cla[ss]
animal.

Aiken: That is wrong — I am sure it was the Irish Derby
that it won.

De Valera: But you also have buried there an even more famo[us]
animal — you will find at Glencairn the grave of
Strongbow's horse!

A.C.G.: I didn't even know Strongbow had a horse.

Aiken: This is all news to me. Where did your informat[ion]
come from, Mr. President? Where is the grave?

De Valera: It is either in or near Glencairn — it is spoken
about in old legends, recorded in some publicati[on]
of one of the Gaelic societies.

A.C.G.: I shall make every effort to follow this up. [I
very nearly said: "And when we do find the hors[e's]
grave, we'll ask for it to be dug up and returne[d to]
England in return for Casement": but I am growin[g]
discreet with advancing years]

Archive personal papers of Sir Andrew
Gilchrist (Churchill Archives Centre, Gilchrist
Papers, GILC 14B): Transcripts of informal
chats between de Valera, Sir Andrew Gilchrist,
British ambassador to Ireland, 1967–70 and
Frank Aiken, Minister for External Affairs and
Tánaiste, in which they discuss, amongst other
things, the Irish Constitution and sport in
Ireland, 27 February 1967. © Crown
copyright material is reproduced with the
permission of the Controller of HMSO and
Queen's Printer for Scotland.

/Football

Football.

A.G.G.: ..... disastrous day for Scotland in Edinburgh.

De Valera: Ah, we can always beat the Scots. I used to play myself in my young days, you know. /Resumé of his young days on the Rugby field, capped by my record of playing in an international match, Siam v. Indochina_/

A.G.G: And is Rugby the most popular form of football here? What about Soccer?

De Valera:)
Aiken: Soccer was the game of the British Army.

A.G.G.: I see. What about your Irish games?

De Valera: Well, hurling you probably know: it is very like your Scottish shinty, only much better.

A.G.G.: And Gaelic football? Is it like Rugby?

De Valera: No, not exactly. You see, at the time of the Irish revolution, Rugby was the game of .. of ..

A.G.G. The Ascendancy? Is that the right word?

De Valera: The very word - my, but you are making quick progress with your Irish, Mr. Ambassador. A very fine word, Ascendancy. So some of our people at that time preferred to play this so-called ancient game with a new name.

A.G.G.: You mean this Gaelic football was really a made-up sort of game, not really native?

De Valera: That is more or less right - the rules, anyhow. For my part I have always preferred Rugby.

Aiken:
(boiling slightly) This is not right, Mr. Ambassador. Gaelic football is not a made-up game - it was played a thousand years ago and more. It is a splendid game ...

De Valera: I know my position - I must not argue with a Minister!!!

/Irish Constitution.

Irish Constitution.

A.G.G.: I'm rather ignorant about the Irish constitution. Does the Cabinet write you a sort of Queen's spee[ch] for opening Parliament with?

De Valera: No, certainly not: I don't open Parliament, and [I] write my own speeches!

Aiken: /clarification of this statement_/

De Valera: Of course, I wrote most of the Constitution mysel[f]. I remember hesitating for a long time over the American Presidential system. But it wouldn't ha[ve] done - we were too trained in English democracy to sit down under a dictatorship, which is what t[he] American system really is - Ministers not respons[ible] to Parliament - that would never do. Besides, I wanted to prepare a nice quiet job without too mu[ch] work for my old age ... Still, I admit I was tempted - look at the way de Gaulle rules France[:] absolute rule ... very efficient.

Aiken: You're wrong there, Mr. President, quite wrong. You cannot have studied the present French positi[on.] De Gaulle's system may <u>look</u> like a dictatorship sometimes, but his Ministers very definitely <u>are</u> responsible to Parliament.

De Valera: Is that so? Then it sounds a very good political system: a powerful President with responsible Ministers. We in Ireland could live with that on[e.] Now, my friend, just get one of your young men from the Department to send out a copy of the French constitution this afternoon - I want to study it!

Aiken: My God!

/Gunmanship

Gunmanship.

De Valera: I have one other constitutional point to make –
mind, I'm not supposed to talk politics with
Cabinet Ministers, so I'm really talking to you,
Mr. Ambassador: this is understood.

Aiken: ⌊coughs⌋

De Valera: There is a growing tendency in this country to
disregard the political framework of the
constitution. ⌊ This was of course a reference to
the trouble with the farmers, scores of whom are
now behind bars for illegal action⌋ I feel that this
is a very dangerous symptom. If people begin to
go outside the constitution in pursuit of political
objectives, then we are moving towards the end of
the rule of law in Ireland. And what rule do we
have then? We shall be at the mercy of the man with
a gun in his hand; and so much for the Irish
experiment in democracy.

Aiken: ⌊Nods his head throughout⌋

....

IX

'A definite Liberalism

is always present.'

UCDA, P150/3855: President de Valera kissing the ring of Rev. Dr John Charles McQuaid, Archbishop of Dublin (1940–72), at the turning of the sod for the Science Building, UCD, 1962. Also in photo Michael Tierney (President of UCD), and Dr Patrick Hillery (Minister for Education, 1959–65). © Irish Press.

Winning the battle against the Catholic Church over centralisation was just one indication that de Valera's supposed deference and subservience to the church has been exaggerated, and the assertion that he 'easily outscored Cumann na nGaedheal in moral zealotry' is dubious.[1] There was considerable hostility directed towards him by individual bishops and priests during the Civil War period, a resentment that, in many instances, continued into the 1930s. When the High Court ordered the release of Eoin O'Duffy in 1933 on the grounds that he was being illegally detained, he received a telegram from the fanatically anti-de Valera Bishop of Achonry, Patrick Morrisroe: 'Congratulations on [the] victory of justice over shameless partisanship and contemptible tyranny'.[2]

De Valera's personal papers also include a Garda report on remarks reputedly made in 1933 by Fr Thomas Bowe, Parish Priest of Freshford, Co. Kilkenny, to the effect that 'there is not a shadow of a doubt that they [the government] incline towards communism ... let every voter say to himself. I voted against communism'.[3] The following year, de Valera wrote to Bishop Robert Browne of Cloyne, complaining about a speech made by Canon Browne, Parish Priest of Rathcormac, Co. Cork, in which the canon reportedly said that de Valera's government was 'depraved and tyrannical': 'Attacks of this character made by a priest cannot but inflict grave injury on the State, and, I am sure your Lordship will agree, on the Church also'.[4]

The portrayal of the state as demonstrating consistent deference to the Catholic Church is a simplification of the complex distribution of power in Ireland. It is worth reflecting on the assessment, made by Emmet Larkin, that if de Valera had 'done much to make the Irish state more confessional, he ... [had] also prevented it from becoming any more clerical'.[5] It is naïve to isolate individual letters or exchanges and brandish them as evidence that twentieth-century Ireland was, in all but name, a Catholic theocracy. Politicians frequently consulted members of *all* churches when legislating for so-called moral issues.

It is also the case that the term 'church/state clash' is often misleading. Those with a determination to oppose or impose change were frequently lay groups who brought the church on board, as happened with the Irish Medical Association during the controversy surrounding the Mother and Child Scheme in 1951 (and later with the Catholic lay lobbyists who pressed for a pro-life amendment to the Constitution in 1983). In both cases, powerful and unrepresentative lay organisations sought to highlight the supposed danger to Catholic morals if certain proposals were not adopted or were rejected. There are many other examples that could be given of this unofficial pro-Catholic lobbying, but there is also documentation revealing occasions when the church did not get its way, as with de Valera's 1937 Constitution.

Like many of his contemporaries, de Valera considered the priesthood when he was younger, and historians were later apt to depict him 'as a sort of lay cardinal, at one level expressing and symbolizing Ireland's interface between church and state ... a Church whose rule as a layman he dutifully followed in most aspects of his waking life'.[6] He also, according to Tim Pat Coogan, helped to create a 'political church–state monolith' and was 'primarily a Catholic head of government'.[7] But at times he was not Catholic enough for some, including Archbishop John Charles McQuaid. Although de Valera had consulted him regarding the Constitution and entertained his concerns about censorship, McQuaid grew completely disillusioned with de Valera, as this characteristically frank, but uncharacteristically detailed 1952 letter to the Apostolic Nuncio in Dublin, Reverend Gerald P. O'Hara, reveals. It gives a direct insight into McQuaid's view of Irish politicians and contains cutting criticisms of de Valera personally, and Fianna Fáil generally:

> To deal with Mr Costello's Cabinet [the coalition government 1948–51] was, with the exception of Dr Browne, Minister for Health, and Mr M[a]cBride, Minister for External Affairs, a very pleasant experience; for one met with a Premier who was not only an excellent Catholic, but also an educated Catholic, in immediate sympathy with the Church and the teaching of the Church. Nor was Mr Costello unduly worried about placating the Liberals and Freemasons of North or South. Neither was he anxious to remain in the position of being the political leader. ...
>
> To deal with Mr de Valera and his Ministers is indeed a different matter.

From Mr de Valera's re-assumption of political leadership, the chief element of note, as far as the church is concerned, is a policy of distance. That policy is seen in the failure to consult any Bishop on the provisions of a Health Scheme. All the present difficulty results from that failure.

It will be remembered that Mr de Valera had promised to give a Health Scheme based on 'the Constitution and Social Directives thereof'. It would not be in character for him to make any reference to the Hierarchy; such a reference would be felt to be inopportune in view of the Protestant support and the voting-power of the Liberal Independents on whom he has been obliged to lean for a continuance in office. Further, any consultation of the Hierarchy would, if later discovered, bitterly antagonise the North of Ireland Protestants, whom Mr de Valera always considers, in the hope of being able to remove partition.

Besides, in assessing the attitude of a Fianna Fáil government, one may never forget the Revolutionary past of that Party. On so many occasions, the Party was on the side opposed to Episcopal directions. While, then, the outward courtesies will be accorded, the inner spirit of sympathetic and open collaboration with the Hierarchy will be missing from a Fianna Fáil Government. Not that anti-Catholic measures may be expected from men who faithfully practice now the Faith, but, as I have said in my present *Quinquennial Relatio*, a definite Liberalism is always present.

In my opinion, that Liberalism must be incessantly watched.[8]

In 1952 De Valera, in McQuaid's eyes, was not a compliant Catholic but an utter pragmatist with a definite taste for liberalism. He had already provoked McQuaid's ire in a number of confrontations. An indication of de Valera's determination to resist McQuaid's interpretation of Ireland as exclusively Catholic had been revealed in his refusal to submit to dictates over the Commission on Youth Unemployment, which the archbishop chaired. In February 1944 McQuaid came into conflict with Seán Lemass over how to handle submissions to the commission from Protestants. He had made clear to Lemass that he would not accept answers from non-Catholic organisations to a questionnaire concerning the religious and spiritual welfare of their members, but that they should be sent to the government instead who could provide for the 'freedom of conscience of non-Catholics' in whatever decisions they subsequently made.[9]

Lemass's alternative solution—that the commission should exclude questions about people's spiritual and religious welfare—angered McQuaid who went over his head to deal directly with de Valera, whose response was defiant: 'The Commission itself is essentially a lay body, set up by the civil authority, and the fact that the Chairman of the Commission is at the same time the Catholic Archbishop of Dublin seems to me not to alter its fundamental character in this respect' and that the state could not be seen to endorse an action 'involving religious discrimination or to co-operate in any such action on the part of a body established by its authority'.[10]

This letter amounted to the waving of a red flag to McQuaid's bull. As noted by John Cooney, McQuaid sent a six page reply, complaining about the grave insult to his spiritual office, insisting that even as chairman he 'must always act in the person and capacity of authoritative teacher of Faith and Morals in this diocese'. As Cooney reveals, McQuaid's next move was to send a friend of his from the Knights of Saint Columbanus to call on de Valera to tell him that McQuaid had drafted a letter of resignation. De Valera was unfazed and reiterated his earlier position. McQuaid did not resign, but insisted that he intended as chairman to act in all matters 'in the person and capacity of the Archbishop of Dublin'.[11]

This episode revealed quite clearly that de Valera was well capable of withstanding the bullying tactics of the Archbishop of Dublin. The two men also disagreed over the question of a cathedral being built in Merrion Square, an irritated McQuaid finding de Valera's attitude 'elusive and shadowy'. They fell out again over McQuaid's increasing criticisms of aspects of the health and educational policies of de Valera's government, though relations between the two men seemed to have improved once de Valera was president, and out of active politics.[12]

De Valera's coolness in this regard was in stark contrast to some of his contemporaries who prided themselves on their republicanism, for example, Seán MacBride, the leader of Clann na Poblachta. When elected as TD for Dublin County in a by-election in October 1947, MacBride wrote to McQuaid that he would undertake 'as my first act, to pay my humble respects to Your Grace and to place myself at Your Grace's disposal'. He repeated these words after the general election of 1948 when Clann na Poblachta became part of the coalition government that replaced Fianna Fáil, adding that he would welcome any advice 'which your Grace may be good enough to give me'. McQuaid rather ominously replied, 'When the occasion arises, I will not hesitate to avail of your services'.[13]

But neither should the degree of de Valera's independence from the church be exaggerated; what was different about de Valera was his absolute determination to prevent divergence between the church and his government's attitudes from becoming public. Moreover, when this secrecy was threatened, and he felt, unlike the argument regarding the Constitution, that the battle was not worth fighting, he went to considerable effort to satisfy the demands of the church, as was evidenced in his decisive action over what became the 1953 Health Act.

De Valera was in Utrecht, Switzerland, for an eye operation when the bishops made clear their opposition to sections of the Health Act, and their belief that efforts were being made to 'socialise' the Irish health system. In April 1953 the bishops sent de Valera the text of a statement that they were planning to release to the newspapers outlining their belief that state responsibility for mother and child care would 'seriously weaken the moral fibre of the Irish people'.[14] De Valera acted with great haste to avoid a re-run of the controversy that led to the resignation of Noël Browne as Minister for Health in 1951. He contacted the president, Seán T. O'Kelly, to arrange a meeting with Cardinal John Francis D'Alton in Drogheda. (McQuaid was in Australia at the time.) He was accompanied to this meeting, in the presbytery of St Peter's Church in Drogheda, by Minister for Health, James Ryan, who told Brian Farrell in 1968 that prior to this meeting he had been prepared to resist pressure from the bishops.[15]

De Valera, however, had no intention of being confrontational. Although, as a precaution, he had sent some documents concerning the Health Act to Joseph Walshe, the Irish ambassador to the Holy See, in case it would be necessary to lobby the Vatican, what he wanted to avoid, above all else, was a public confrontation with the bishops, or in the words of Ronan Fanning, 'De Valera's concern, as always, was to remove the causes of contention—not to assert any abstract right on his government's behalf to frame their health policy independent of the Bishops' views'.[16]

What was arranged instead was an agreement that the bishops would not authorise the publication of their statement, and de Valera arranged for representatives of the government and the bishops to discuss the issue at Áras an Uachtaráin. His request for this meeting, and the president's agreement to host a lunch for the two sides, was completely inappropriate, given that the president, should the bill have been referred to him, could have been required to make a decision on whether to test the constitutionality of the bill by sending it to the Supreme Court. The result of that meeting was that the bishops got the amendments which they wanted in relation to the choice of doctor and hospital and a restricted eligibility for the Mother and Child Scheme, or according to Ronan Fanning, they 'in effect rewrote as much of the Bill as they wanted to rewrite'.[17]

This may be an exaggeration, but the claim that there was an 'easy resolution of the issues at the meetings held in 1953',[18] downplays the inappropriateness of what de Valera did to secure the agreement on 25 June of that year that ensured the hierarchy's protest would be withdrawn. He may have been astute in believing that 'the best interests of church–state relations were served in private',[19] but this was hardly in the best interests of democratic government. The fact that de Valera took personal control of this situation, from a bed in Utrecht, all the way to Drogheda and then to the Phoenix Park in Dublin, was also an indication that where he saw fit, he overrode the authority of his ministers and made crucial decisions, it seems, without prior consultation with his Cabinet.

Perhaps the truth was that de Valera chose his battles carefully. He was clearly uncomfortable with secretive Catholic organisations that continually tried to create the impression that Ireland was only one step away from a descent into paganism. At the Fianna Fáil Ard Fheis in 1943 he left no ambiguity as to why he was uncomfortable with the Knights of Saint Columbanus. After he had criticised the GAA's ban on its members playing 'foreign games', he continued: 'I think it is just as absurd to have that type of protection as to have here, where 93% of the people are Catholics, an organisation for the protection of Catholic interests. I think such organisations do harm to the very cause they are intended to defend'.[20] In this assessment, he was proven correct in the long term.

In his autobiography *Avowed intent*, published in 1994, Frank Pakenham devoted an entire chapter to Ireland and reiterated his belief that de Valera was the greatest statesman of his generation and elaborated on his perception of de Valera's attitude to religion:

> His only rival [for the title of greatest statesman] in my eyes would be Clement Attlee, whom I have described as an ethical giant, but Attlee's attitude to Christianity ... was distinctly cryptic. De Valera, when president, used to visit the Sacrament five times a day, but he was no bigot. His chaplain once told me that de Valera would have made an excellent Protestant.[21]

Todd Andrews recalled that de Valera was 'deeply religious but not evidently pious. He did not evangelise'.[22]

UCDA, P150/2261: De Valera's visit to Bobbio, Italy, 5–8 June 1933. A young priest requests an autograph as de Valera arrives at the Abbey of St Colombano at Bobbio.

UCDA, P150/3838: De Valera
walking in a cornfield with
two unidentified nuns, late
1940s/early 1950s.

UCDA, P150/829: De Valera and Matthew O'Connor Ford (far left),
Organiser and Secretary, Cuchulain Branch, Friends of Irish Freedom,
and a number of clerical supporters in Scranton, Pennsylvania,
September 1919. Given by James G. Ford to de Valera.

UCDA, P150/3140: En route to Lourdes to attend the Marian Congress, 13 September 1958. De Valera's party in Dublin Airport, prior to their departure to France; Frank Aiken, de Valera and his son, Major Vivion de Valera, walking across the tarmac at Dublin Airport.

Most Rev. Patrick Collier, D.D.,
Lord Bishop of Ossory,
Sion House,
KILKENNY.

My dear Lord Bishop,

I have been informed on what appears to be
very good authority that the Very Rev. Canon Bowe,
Parish Priest of Freshford in your diocese, has on at
least three occasions recently used the pulpit in his
church to make pronouncements very harmful to the cause
of order in the district and likely to bring the constituted civil authority and the administration of justic
into contempt.

It appears that on the 16th December in the
course of a sermon in the church, Canon Bowe, after some
references to the general election of 1933, spoke of
"Coercion" Acts and the arrest and alleged ill-treatment
of "innocent" men. On the following Sunday, 23rd Decembe
also speaking in the church, he said:

"I consider it my duty to protest in the
strongest possible manner against the arrest
of a young man from this parish while on his
way home from Mass on last Sunday morning.
Such things were not done even in the 'Black
and Tan' times. Even criminals should not be
treated in that way. Catholics should be
permitted to go to and return from the
practice of their religion without fear of
arrest."

He returned to the subject again on Christma
Day, when he said:-

"I never had less heart to wish the
people a happy Christmas. We have
certain patriots mar 'eadh in this parish
gloating over their neighbours' downfall.
We know now for a fact that there are people
in this parish prepared to make money by
spying on their neighbours."

I understand that the only persons recently
arrested in Freshford parish under Article 2 A. of the
Constitution (which is presumably the "Coercion" legislation to which Canon Bowe referred) were three men who
admitted having maliciously damaged public property.

If the remarks which I have quoted have been correctly attributed to the Very Rev. Canon Bowe, it appears to me that they cannot fail to be interpreted by his parishioners as a condonation of lawlessness and an attempt to discourage co-operation with the police in their duty. The use of the pulpit and of the priestly authority for such purposes is a very grave evil, and I am confident that once your Lordship's attention has been drawn to it it is not likely to recur in the diocese of Ossory.

I am,

my dear Lord Bishop,

Yours sincerely,

oc

UCDA, P150/2878: Correspondence with Dr Patrick Collier, Bishop of Ossory, concerning reported remarks made from the pulpit by Fr Thomas Bowe, Parish Priest of Freshford, condemning the Fianna Fáil government, 24 January 1935.

My Lord Bishop,

Some time ago my attention was directed to a report in the Cork Examiner (July 5th) of a meeting held in Rathcormac on the previous day. In the report the Very Rev. Canon Browne is represented as having characterised the present Government as "depraved and tyrannical". I do not know what element of truth there is in the report, but if Canon Browne used these words he made a most unworthy and subversive attack on the Government and on the State as representing the organised community. Attacks of this character made by a priest cannot but inflict grave injury on the State, and, I am sure your Lordship will agree, on the Church also. Words such as these tend to undermine all respect for authority, and if not a direct incentive to, be used at any rate to justify resistance and even deeds of violence against those who have been entrusted with the task of government.

I have been more than reluctant to write your Lordship this letter, but I feel I have a duty in the matter which I must perform. Your Lordship will recognise the gravity of the issue raised and take such action as may seem appropriate to ensure that no priest in your Lordship's diocese will follow the irresponsible lead which Canon Browne is reported as having given on the occasion referred to.

ARCHBISHOP'S HOUSE,

DUBLIN N. E. 3.

7th November , 1952.

Excellency ,

I beg to enclose a memorandum on the White Pater on new and extended Health Services , which we discussed some days ago.

The memorandum takes the form of my report to the Hierarchy , as Chairman of the special Episcopal Committee formed to deal with the situation. To this report I have added some notes on the position as it actually exists , with documents to illustrate the attitude of the Irish Medical Association.

It may be helpful at this stage to point out that the whole situation, in its origin and development , very usefully illustrates the profound difference that the Hierarchy must expect to find between the Government of Mr. de Valera and that of Mr. Costello.

To deal with Mr. Costello's Cabinet was , with the exception of Dr. Browne, Minister for Health , and Mr. McBride , Minister for External Affairs, a very pleasant experience; for one met with a Premier who was not only an excellent Catholic , but also an educated Catholic , in immediate sympathy with the Church and the teaching of the Church .Nor was Mr. Costello unduly worried about placating the Liberals and Freemasons of North or South. Neither was he anxious to remain in the position of being the political leader. Had he been a man of less integrity, he could have avoided many difficulties. When the crisis came in the Mother - and - Child Scheme of Dr. Browne , Mr. Costello immediately and , when the need for declaration arose, publicly , made his own the decision of the Hierarchy.

To deal with Mr. de Valera and his Ministers is indeed a differen matter.

From Mr. de Valera's re-assumption of political leadership , the element of note , as far as the Church is concerned , is a policy of distance. Th policy is seen in the failure to consult any Bishop on the provisions of a Health Scheme . All the present difficulty results from that failure.

It will be remembered that Mr. de Valera had promised to give a Health Scheme based on " the Constitution and Social Directives thereof ". It wou not be in character for him to make any reference to the Hierarchy ; such a reference would be felt to be inopportune in view of the Protestant support and t voting-power of the Liberal Independents on whom he has been obliged to lean for a continuance in office. Further , any consultation of the Hierarchy would, if later discovered, bitterly antagonise the North of Ireland Protestants , whom Mr. Valera always considers , in the hope of being able to remove Partition.

Besides , in assessing the attitude of a Fianna Fail Gove nment , may never forget the revolutionary past of that Party. On so many occasions , the Party was on the side opposed to Episcopal directions. While , them, the outward courtesies will be accorded , the inner spirit of sympathetic and open collaborat with the Hierarchy will be missing from a Fianna Fail Government. Not that anti-Catholic measures may be expected from men who faithfully practice now the Faith as I have said in my present Quinquennial Relatio, a definite Liberalism is alway present.

In my opinion , that Liberalism must be incessantly watched. And I particularly fear is the effect on the rising generation of an attitude which would successfully oppose the Hierarchy on the present Mother and Infant Scheme.

That there are definite signs of the younger people wishing to know
nd to assimilate a Catholic philosophy in things social and political , is one of the
st encouraging features of the present Irish Scene. But the presence of a Protestant
nority, with its focus of operations in Trinity College , powerful in finance and in
e professions and very firmly organised on a Masonic basis with strong affiliations in
ndon and Belfast , will always demand an unrelaxed vigilance on the part of the
urch, particularly in education.

Such are the features of the present situation which I think
ght to be presented to Your Excellency and the Holy See.

Your Excellency may rest assured that I will continue to do all
 my power to obtain from the Government the most favourable solution that is possible
 the present situation.

With sentiments of deep esteem, I beg to remain, Excellency,

Yours very devotedly in Christ,

+ John C. McQuaid,

Archbishop of Dublin,

etc.

is Excellency,

he Most Reverend Gerald P. O'Hara , D. D.,

Apostolic Nuncio,

Dublin.

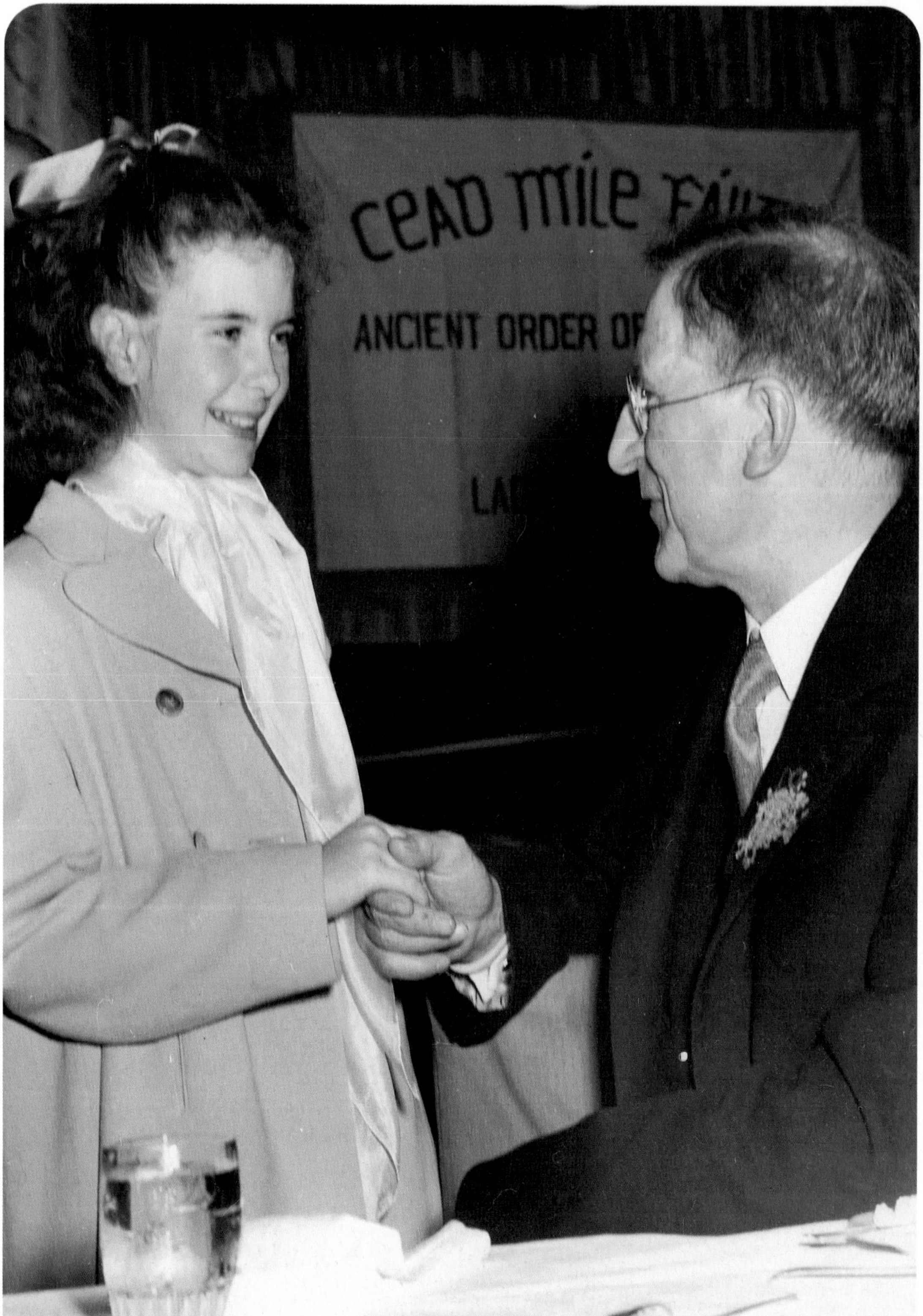
CEAD MILE
ANCIENT ORDER

X

'A fascist and

slave conception

of woman'

UCDA, P150/2949: De Valera shaking hands with Margaret O'Brien, 17 March 1948. O'Brien was a celebrated child actress who received a Special Academy Award in 1944, as the 'outstanding child actress' of the year.

Another aspect of the Constitution that generated controversy was the provisions relating to women. These provisions combined with marriage bars to women's employment, the 1936 Conditions of Employment Act (which limited women's participation in certain work) and the Criminal Law Amendment Act of 1935 outlawing the importation and sale of contraceptives, led to caustic judgements of de Valera's perceived paternalism and failure to acknowledge the full contribution that women made to Irish society. Todd Andrews' autobiography implies that de Valera had a limited commitment to female equality, a trait Andrews believed that de Valera shared with Seán Lemass. Referring to his wife, Mary, an active republican who, like many of her colleagues on the executive of Cumann na mBan, had been opposed to the creation of Fianna Fáil, Andrews wrote:

> I thought that Mary's stand was due more to her feminist principles than to her political convictions. She regarded Dev, and even more so Frank Aiken, as what nowadays would be called sexists; in this opinion I don't think she was far wrong. Had she known Seán Lemass, her misgivings about the attitude of the Fianna Fáil leadership to women's status would have been reinforced. Dev always commanded the devoted service of women, but I believed, and when I got to know him I told him so, that he never gave women sufficient recognition for their dedication.[1]

This was a view shared by Margaret MacEntee, wife of de Valera's colleague, Seán. Furious with the contents of the Constitution, she quarrelled bitterly with Seán over the provisions relating to women which she saw as 'compelling them back into the home, or at least as the thin end of that wedge ... she did not change her mind but she voted for it as the lesser of two evils'.[2]

Cumann na mBan members had been overwhelmingly against the terms of the Treaty, so much so that P.S. O'Hegarty had referred to them as, under the influence of de Valera, being largely responsible for the bitterness and ferocity of the Civil War, a contention that Tom Garvin in his book *1922: the birth of Irish democracy* did little to refute.[3] But as can be gleaned from his correspondence with Mary MacSwiney, one of the 'furies' that so annoyed the likes of O'Hegarty, de Valera found it difficult to accept their virulent opposition, while admitting to MacSwiney that 'I find I have written you a letter such as I have never before written to anybody'.[4] It was also the case that some of the female republicans felt a certain maternal instinct towards de Valera; Constance Markievicz, when writing to wish him well before his trip to the United States in 1919, signed herself 'Your adopted mother'.[5]

But they were not cowed or overawed by him. In 1926 Kathleen Clarke refused to withdraw from the senate election in favour of Margaret Pearse after de Valera informed her that 'the party would not support two women as they would only be able to elect five members … I could see no reason for the party refusing to support two women when women had played such a big part in the struggle for freedom'.[6] In 1935 Clarke and her Fianna Fáil senator colleague, Jennie Wyse Power, opposed Seán Lemass's proposed Conditions of Employment Bill, Section 16 of which empowered the Minister for Industry and Commerce to prohibit the employment of women in some areas, or to fix the proportion of women to men.

Writing in 2003 Catriona Clear suggested that 'it has got to the stage where only five words are needed for a shorthand history of women in twentieth century Ireland before the changes set in motion by the 1960s. The three words "De Valera's Ireland" are used to convey an oppressive, stagnant uncomfortable social environment for women. No elaboration is necessary, except perhaps to throw in the two words "comely maidens"'[7] (words used in de Valera's 1943 'Ireland which we dreamed of' speech).

Joe Lee's *Ireland 1912–1985* in general has little to say about the issues of the role and status of women in Ireland, but he does assert that 'de Valera's image of women was widely cherished in Ireland, not least by the women themselves', and that only 'a few educated women' repudiated the role allotted to them in the Constitution. This is an underestimation; opposition to de Valera in this regard was substantial and achieved considerable publicity; the women who were offended by the paternalistic and sexist articles of the Constitution were not silent. The most infamous of the offending sections was Article 40.1: 'The State recognises that by her life within the home, a woman gives to the State a support without which the common good cannot be achieved. The State shall therefore, endeavour to ensure that mothers shall not be obliged by economic necessity to engage in labour to the neglect of their duties within the home'.

While the Constitution acknowledged that 'all citizens shall, as human persons be held equal under the law' a qualification was added: 'This shall not be held to mean that the state shall not in its enactments have due regard to differences of capacity, physical and moral and of social function'. What was clear from these words was that de Valera envisaged equal rights for women to be confined to the *political* sphere.[8]

Nor was this a parochial squabble. Letters of protest concerning Articles 40 and 41 came from international organisations, including the International Alliance of Women for Suffrage and Equal Citizenship, and the Six Point Group in London who suggested that 'these clauses are based on a fascist and slave conception of woman as being a non-adult person who is very weak and whose place is in the home. Ireland's fight for freedom would not have been so successful if Irish women had obeyed these clauses'.[9] Louie Bennett of the Irish Women Workers Union was more circumspect, and asked de Valera, if he had to retain the offensive wording, to add a sentence to the effect that there was no intention to discriminate against any citizen on the sole grounds of sex or class: 'In country homes, the housewife often finds it necessary to keep the house door open, but it is usual then to put up a half door as a safeguard against unwelcome intrusions. If you must keep this particular door in the Constitution open, put up a guard against Fascist intrusions'.[10]

Lucy Kingston, honorary secretary of the National Council of Women of Ireland, expressed her association's opposition to Articles 40 and 41 on the grounds that the objectionable clauses were not 'in keeping with the spirit of the Republican Proclamation of 1916'.[11] The Joint Committee of Women's Societies and Social Workers objected to Articles 40, 41 and 45 of the Constitution, and also demanded a 50% representation in the new Senate, restoration of jury service to women, and the revoking of the objectionable clauses of the Conditions of Employment Act.[12]

A brief meeting between de Valera and the protestors in January 1937 achieved little, except the deletion of the phrase 'inadequate strength' in Article 45 which had outlined the state's intention to protect women and children from unsuitable 'avocations' because of their 'inadequate strength'.[13] As pointed out by Margaret O'Callaghan, despite the dropping of this phrase 'the substance remained the same. These clauses became essential to the Local Government Act of 1941 which enabled the Minister for Local Government to declare, as a qualification for a specified office, that the woman holding it be unmarried or widowed. This ensured that in teaching and the civil service women were obliged to resign from their positions if they married'. (This was not always the case with married primary teachers some of whom did work after marriage though with no holiday pay or pension entitlements.) But the women who opposed these Articles seem to have been more concerned about barriers to work rather than any dispute over the view that it was the primary duty of women to be in the home.[14] To this extent at least, Joe Lee was correct, and it is significant that the deletion of articles offensive to women was never suggested in the Dáil.

As Catriona Clear asserts, the proliferation of societies and organisations devoted to improving the political and social welfare of women in Ireland in the 1930s meant that 'there was a feminism to be against'. Such organisations included the Irish Country Women's Association, the Joint Committee of Women's Societies and Social Workers and the Irish Women Workers' Union. During this period there was an improvement in maternal mortality rates, and despite prejudice, discriminatory legislation and setbacks, there was a general improvement in the lives of women also.[15]

T.P. O'Neill suggested to Clear that the reason de Valera inserted the clauses was because he had been reading Ivy Pinchbeck's *Women and the Industrial Revolution* and had wanted to protect women from the ravages of industrial employment and associated ill health.[16] This seems far-fetched; for feminists, in any case, there was a much simpler reason. As Gertrude Gaffney wrote in the *Irish Independent* in May 1937, de Valera 'had always been a reactionary where women are concerned. He dislikes and distrusts us as a sex and his aim ever since he came into office has been to put us in what he considers our place and to keep us there'.[17]

De Valera's own response to the kind of anger outlined above was somewhat abstract and clumsy, as he informed the Dáil in May 1937: 'I myself was not conscious at any time of having deserved all these terrible things that I am told I am where women's rights are concerned'.[18] In reality, de Valera envisaged 'a single recognisable domestic sphere' and, according to Catriona Clear, he 'idealised it in an opportunistic way to justify having introduced some gender-specific legislation'.[19]

De Valera singled out particular women who wrote history that extolled the virtues of 'good' nationalist and Catholic women, such as the prolific Helena Concannon, who published extensively on the history of Irish women, providing historical and intellectual validity for the ideal of the republican mother. He nominated her to the Senate, and his support, argues Mary O'Dowd, 'thus integrated the biographical approach to women's history … into the national identity of the Irish Free State'. Concannon's books are still regarded as an important starting point for research on women in Irish history.[20]

De Valera's wife, Sinéad, was a successful and widely read children's author, who could recall poetry at will, and wrote plays and fairy tales in Irish, and four collections of short fairy tales in English. Deserving of her own biography, she was a strong, independent and talented woman who made a big impression on President John F. Kennedy. At the age of 95 she was able to recite the whole of Thomas Gray's poem 'Elegy Written in a Country Churchyard' from memory without a single prompt.[21] In this regard, the lines included in Brendan Kennelly's poem 'De Valera at 92', written following a meeting with de Valera six weeks before he died, and based on their conversation, are revealing:

My wife is dead. For sixty years

She stood by me, although I know,

She always kept a secret place in her heart

For herself. This I understood. There must always be

A secret place where one can go,

And brood on what cannot be thought about,

Where there is noise and men and women.[22]

Another author favoured by de Valera, Dorothy Macardle, despite being a public apologist for him in her writings on Irish history, was also angry with de Valera over the Constitution. Gerardine Meaney makes the point 'that the Gothic scenarios of Mc Ardle's [*sic*] fiction began to bear an uncanny likeness to the dark side of that Ireland', exploring themes such as the post-war fate of women who engage in violence and the repression that was a feature of socially approved sexual and family relations.[23]

UCDA, P150/3666: De Valera and Dorothy Macardle (historian and author of *The Irish Republic*) in conversation, 1930s. Note by Macardle on reverse 'Evidently taken at the Secretariat, after [a committee meeting]. Sep. 10'. Postcard stamped " 'Agreil' Genève 4" on reverse.

UCDA, P150/3136: De Valera taking tea with renowned soprano, Margaret
Burke-Sheridan (far right), and two unidentified ladies, 1930s/40s.

UCDA, P150/246: De Valera at his desk with Kathleen O'Connell, his personal secretary, *c.* 1944. This photograph was taken to commemorate Ms O'Connell serving in her position for 25 years, and stood in de Valera's study during his years as Taoiseach and president.

Dear Eamon

Just a line to wish you god speed
tell you that we are all going fine
in great hopes & spirits, & often
thinking of you. I saw your last
letter to Miss B. She is very hard at
work at home in the absence of her
mother. I have been on the run since
Dec. & have been very lucky. People are
so kind & stand by one so splendidly.
The clique are all well, but have
no where to gather just now. We all
look forward to seeing you again.
with love from
                        your adopted mother

PHONE 44929.

ULSTER BANK BUILDINGS,
3 LR. O'CONNELL STREET,
DUBLIN.

May 15th 37

My Dear President,

      I am sorry to observe that you are disposed to
take the clamour of those Sufferagettes so seriously. In this
attitude you are wholly misinterpreting the mind of the country.

No doubt you have concluded that the agitation has been worked up
by two or three women who are by no means disinterested in the
matter of political limelight. As one who has had some experience in
sensing the mind of the ordinary man or woman I can positively say
that the most popular thing you could do, as well also as the very
best thing nationally, would be to make it known that your
desire was to send women back to the home where they belong.

      That there is general regret if not resentment at the
intrusion of women in the spheres of men is not an exaggeration.

In Brazil, for instance, no women are permitted in industry except
such indispensable occupations as Stores stocking womens garments.
Even typists are males everywhere except in certain foreign
establishments with the result that there is no unemployment whatever.

      I would beg of you to take a strong stand in this matter
and you will have the support of the people. You will solve the
male unemployment problem at once if you direct that definite
occupations must employ men and men only. Meanwhile take those young
lads who now hang around the corners and put them into Labour Camps
under military
tutelage and make men of them. If they get the same conditions as
privates in the National Army I cant see where the grievance would
come in.

                       Mise Do Cara.

                       J Walsh

NAI, DT, S9880: Women and the 1937 Constitution, 15 May 1937. J. Walsh of
the Ulster Bank urges de Valera to stand firm and keep women in the home

THE SIX POINT GROUP

Telephone No.
I. 'TVIEW 1727.

31, BROOKFIELD,
WEST HILL,
LONDON, N.6.

Vice-Presidents.

VISCOUNTESS ASTOR, M.P.	MISS AGNES DAWSON, J.P. L.C.C.	MRS. JAMES O'HEA, C.B.E.
LADY BALFOUR OF BURLEIGH	MRS. BRUCE DICK	VISCOUNTESS RHONDDA
MISS VERA BRITTAIN	MR. ISAAC FOOT	SYBIL VISCOUNTESS RHONDDA, D.B.E.
CAPTAIN CAZALET, M.P.	MISS CICELY HAMILTON	DAME ETHEL SMYTH, D.B.E., MUS. DOC.
LADY VIOLET BONHAM CARTER	MR. E. L. MALLALIEU, M.P.	LORD STRABOLGI
PROF. WINIFRED CULLIS, C.B.E.	MISS WINIFRED MAYO	DR. JANE WALKER, M.D., J.P.
MISS CLEMENCE DANE	MISS EVA MOORE	MRS. CHALMERS WATSON, C.B.E.
ALDERMAN A. EMIL DAVIES, L.C.C.	MRS. FRANK OGLIVY	MRS. MARGARET WINTRINGHAM, J.P.

Executive Committee.

Chairman: BETTY ARCHDALE, LL.B.,
Barrister-at-law.

FLORA DRUMMOND	CLAIRE MADDEN
DOROTHY E. EVANS	ELSIE MAITLAND
MARION GRAHAM	CHARLOTTE A. L. MARSH
MARY GREW	AVABAI MEHTA
MILDRED HAY	MONICA WHATELY
ELSIE CLIFFORD JONES	LOTTE WHYTE
GERTRUDE LIEBEN	

Hon. Auditor: MISS L. M. HARRIS, A.C.A.
Hon. Solicitor: MRS. CROFTS, M.A., LL.B.
Hon. Treasurer: MISS E. M. HAY
Chairman Nationality Committee: MISS D. E. EVANS
    „   Social   „   MISS E. MAITLAND
Hon. Secretary: **MISS MONICA WHATELY,**
TO WHOM ALL COMMUNICATIONS SHOULD BE ADDRESSED.

14th June, 1937.

Dear Mr. de Valera,

I hope you will excuse the Six Point Group writing to you on a primarily Irish Free State matter, but as we have had such help from you in Geneva we felt we could not let this matter pass without approaching you. We also feel that inequalities to women concern all women wherever they may be.

When the I.F.S. adopted her 1923 Constitution women felt elated at the recognition of the equality of men and women in Art 3. For many years at Geneva the I.F.S. has been an invaluable supporter of the women in their efforts to raise the status of women by international means.

You can, therefore, imagine our sense of dismay at the clauses in the draft constitution, particularly clauses 40, 41 (2) and 45 (4) ii. These clauses are based on a fascist and slave conception of woman as being a non-adult person who is very weak and whose place is in the home. Ireland's fight for freedom would not have been so successful if Irish women had obeyed these clauses. You who have fought all your life for the freedom of your Country can surely not wish to deprive Irish women of the freedom for which they also have fought. If you would only help the women to be free instead of clamping these tyrannous restrictions on them you would be doing a great service to women and to Ireland.

Yours sincerely,

B. Archdale

Chairman.

Mr. de Valera,
The Dial,
Dublin, Ireland.

Kerry House,

28, Basil Street,

London. S.W.3.

21st May, 1937.

Dear President de Valéra,

I want to write to you personally rather than write a
length in the newspapers about the clauses on women.

Many of the attacks on these seem to me unreasonable,
but I find myself in absolute agreement with Miss Louie
Bennett's published letter to you.   The real crux is the
question of employment.   The language of certain clauses
suggests that the State may interfere to a great extent in
determining what opportunities shall be open or closed to
women, and there is no clause whatever to counterbalance t
suggestion or to safeguard women's rights in this respect.

If, as I trust you do, you wish to be fair to women i
the economic as well as in the political and civic spheres
I think that a clause could be inserted in Article 45 whic
would at least exercise a good directive influence.

I suggest:

45. 4. 3°.

"The State shall endeavour to secure that
neither in opportunities for employment
nor in conditions of employment shall women
suffer unfair discrimination on the sole
ground of sex."

The "unfair" spoils it from the point of view of ideal justice, but to omit that would require the abolition of parts of/recent Conditions of Employment Act and that is too much the to hope for, I know. This "unfair" permits the process of reform to be gradual and leaves the way open for the establishment of a tribunal or Court of Appeal.

The phrase "sole grounds of sex" permits discrimination on grounds of possession of other sources of income, functions and occupations (such as motherhood), and necessity for supporting dependants.

I think this should do something to satisfy the legitimate fears of both men and women for the moment, imperfect as the provision might be, and would leave the way open for advanced legislation.

As the Constitution stands, I do not see how anyone holding advanced views on the rights of women can support it, and that is a tragic dilemma for those who have been loyal and ardent workers in the national cause.

                    Is mise

                        le meas mór

NAI, DT, S9880: Women and the 1937 Constitution, 21 May 1937. In a personal letter to de Valera, Dorothy Macardle expresses her concerns about the Constitution. Macardle was an accomplished historian and the author of *The Irish Republic* (1937), a book sympathetic to de Valera's career and those who opposed the Anglo–Irish Treaty. A member of the first executive of the Fianna Fáil party, she was also vice-chairperson of the National Council of Women of Ireland which opposed Fianna Fáil legislation affecting women. She later served as president of the Irish Association of Civil Liberties. of the Irish Association of Civil Liberties.

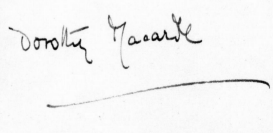

<u>XI</u>

'Is it smugness or insurgency

that makes them say

"Emergency"?'

UCDA, P150/2237: De Valera broadcasting to the US, 3 December 1932. Annotated on reverse as follows 'The new President of the Irish Free State speaks to his followers in America. Dublin, Ireland'.

Whatever about the political and social divisions in Ireland in the early decades of independence, historians until the end of the twentieth century generally agreed that de Valera's policy of neutrality was justified, necessary and the only realistic option. But this too has come under question in recent years. Unlike the situation in Austria, where permanent neutrality is written into its 1955 Constitution, there is no such provision in Ireland. One of the arguments against Irish neutrality by the end of the twentieth century was that it was too vague, was morally indefensible and that, in any case, rather than seeking to act independently, Irish governments followed the prevailing international wind with the main concern not to offend the USA, coupled with an insistence that military traffic through Ireland has no implications for Irish neutrality.

The attempt to make Ireland's neutrality during the Second World War appear dishonourable was apparent in 1999 when Robert Fisk suggested in a BBC documentary interview that de Valera was right to have refused the 1940 offer on unity because post-war Stormont approval would have to be obtained. This sequence was cut from the film: 'Dev was wrong was the documentary's message. Dev was small-minded. *Ireland's Hated Hero* was the title of the programme'.[1]

Neutrality and its legacy also provided opportunities to satirise the perceived self-satisfied and self-imposed isolation. In 2005 the Dublin theatre company, Rough Magic, staged an enthralling musical, *Improbable Frequency*. One of its songs was sung by curious Britons working in Dublin during the Second World War and included the lines:

> Is it smugness or insurgency
>
> that makes them say 'Emergency'?
>
> I feel it lacks the urgency
>
> Of World War II.[2]

The following year, Brian Girvin's *The Emergency: neutral Ireland, 1939–45*, suggested that there was both smugness and insurgency, but that plenty of other ingredients needed to be thrown into the mix, including stubbornness, insecurity, short-sightedness and a damaging self-interest that retarded Ireland's political and economic development, along with a moral ambiguity associated with Ireland's neutrality that has lasted to the present day.[3]

Girvin rode roughshod over the traditional interpretation of neutrality as representing de Valera's finest hour. 'Every state has the right to be neutral, but has it the right to be indifferent to outcome?' is the question posed. Girvin's stance is clear: Ireland should not have been neutral; could have joined the Allies after 1943 with relatively little cost; and a united Ireland could have been achieved in the process. Instead the government opted for a policy based on 'scepticism and indifference ... the safer Ireland became the more emphasis the government placed on its insecurity', and in doing so exercised an extreme and at times farcical censorship.[4]

Although Girvin acknowledges the complexity and ability of Fianna Fáil's Cabinet, de Valera is presented as stubborn, mean-spirited and strangely insecure. In meeting with de Valera, British officials and politicians were often under the illusion that they agreed on 'the facts as they were', only to discover this was not the case. Britain in 1940, it seems, was desperate enough for Irish military involvement to be flexible and Girvin suggests that a more coherent and generous response from Ireland could have yielded much, by forging a new relationship with Britain and Northern Ireland. There was, as the author acknowledges, a genuine fear in Ireland that Britain would seek to re-conquer the country. US president Franklin D. Roosevelt thought this was 'preposterous ... absurd nonsense'.[5]

The American representative in Dublin, David Gray, in musing on Irish demands for US arms to defend themselves, concluded that de Valera was frightened by the changing military situation 'but not prepared to cope with it'. Gray was appalled by the perceived hypocrisy of Ireland's dependence on British sailors risking their lives to bring supplies to the neutral country,[6] but Gray was not an unbiased, or indeed balanced, observer.

Girvin was quite right to broaden the debate about Ireland and the Second World War and focus attention on the forgotten Irish volunteers. Granted, there was much Irish hypocrisy and self-interest on display, but the tendency to interpret all Irish rhetoric negatively is accompanied by an unwise willingness to take most of the British and American rhetoric and political intentions at face value. For all his obduracy, de Valera was surely correct to bring the struggle for Irish independence to its logical conclusion by implementing an independent foreign policy. Why should he have agreed to promises (such as a united Ireland) when he had no guarantee that they would be honoured, and every reason to believe that they could not be? Girvin suggests that de Valera in his dealings with Churchill evaded any discussion on the rights or wrongs of Britain's war with Germany, and that this reflected the 'worst aspects of nationalism'.[7] This is a simplification, and underestimates just how important sovereignty was for de Valera; after all, he had devoted the previous decade of Anglo–Irish negotiations to this very cause. It is also a specious argument: why would Churchill have listened to de Valera's views?

It is difficult to accurately define Irish people's relationship with neutrality in the 1940s. During his victory broadcast at the end of the war, Churchill attacked the Irish position, and if the public reaction to de Valera's dignified response is anything to go by, there was a sense that neutrality was seen as something to be cherished and defended as the ultimate expression of Irish independence. The observations of the Irish novelist, Elizabeth Bowen, who compiled war-time reports for the British government, are also worth noting. In November 1940 she offered the following: 'It may be felt in England that Éire is making a fetish of her neutrality. But this assertion of her neutrality is Éire's first free self-assertion: as such alone it would mean a great deal to her. Éire (and I think rightly) sees her neutrality as positive, not merely negative'.[8] This was something that other contemporaries, and historians, despite their hostility to the policies of de Valera, also recognised.

The more information that has come to light about neutrality—most recently in Clair Wills' book *That neutral island*, published in 2007—the more one can appreciate and respect, in the words of Terence Brown, 'the way de Valera kept his nerve, when the fate of the country was an uncertain one and when he had great powers lined up against him'.[9] This could not have been done without paying a price, including countless accusations of treachery, the Irish response to which was 'strident and confused in equal parts' and a difficulty in holding 'the moral questions at bay'. As Seán O'Faoláin put it in the *Bell* in July 1945, 'We emerge, a little dulled, bewildered, deflated. There is a great leeway to make up, many lessons to be learnt, problems to be solved which, in those six years of silence we did not even allow ourselves to state'.[10]

But it is also the case that thousands of Irish-born people served in the Allied forces and the immigrant Irish made a significant contribution to the British war-time economy and health services. At least 60,000 southern Irish citizens served in the British forces, and Girvin makes the point that some of them returned to an Ireland that did not want to know: 'For many Irish men and women who joined the battle there was a sense of disappointment that the Irish neutrality which they often defended could be used to ignore what they had achieved'. Indeed, it was not until 1995 that there was public acknowledgement of them by the Irish government. Girvin makes the point that 'although men of Irish origin won 8 Victoria Crosses during the war, only one of these was a soldier in an Irish regiment. Of the total Irish dead of 4,543, those from Irish regiments accounted for 1,385, suggesting that the majority of Irish volunteers found themselves in non-Irish regiments'.[11]

Part of the problem of analysing concepts of allegiance is a tendency to impose an early twenty-first century debate about the morality of Ireland's neutrality on to the 1940s with a resulting judgemental approach to de Valera and his colleagues. But many contemporaries managed the apparent contradictions in their positions with relative ease, because they knew, as de Valera did, that there was no such thing as absolute neutrality. Englishman, Francis Bailey, who served with the Royal Engineers in Burma during the war, fought alongside a company of Enniskillen Fusiliers, 'the overwhelming majority of whom came from south of the Border'. He recalled that when asked why, as citizens of a neutral country, they were serving in the Allied services; the usual answer was 'we know whose side we are neutral on'.[12]

The successful maintenance of neutrality was also dependent on British and American restraint, and there was a gulf between public perception and actual practice during the war. De Valera mixed his public stubbornness with an informal pragmatism in relation to 'assisting' the Allies. In 1945 the British government admitted that neutral Ireland had not denied them co-operation when necessary and listed fourteen areas in which this was the case.[13] But that was only one aspect of the pragmatism that underlined the policy. The other was the determination to avoid divisions in the body politic.

Garret FitzGerald makes the point in relation to cross-party support for neutrality that an important factor was determination not to see the country split again as it had been only sixteen years previously during the Civil War. Although this was not something that was stated publicly, it would explain the support that existed for neutrality despite deep personal commitments to the Allied cause.[14] But there was a difference in emphasis between the two parties over the question of assistance from outside in the context of danger from attack. In July 1940 William Cosgrave wrote to de Valera concerning the possible abandonment of neutrality, asserting 'My colleagues and I would be prepared to give them our fullest support in such a change of policy'; eight days later he wrote specifically contending that 'our suggestion was and is that changing circumstances may conceivably make it in the best interests of the country to take that step before actual invasion'.[15]

De Valera responded to Cosgrave in July 1940 by stating that:

> there would appear to be little difference between our view and yours as to what is the paramount national issue at the moment. ... The difference between your views and those of the Government is in regard to the means by which these objectives can be achieved. The question which you raise is whether we should not immediately ask for military assistance from one belligerent to strengthen our defences against the danger of attack from the other. The Government view is what it has been since the beginning of the war, that the best hope of preserving the country from invasion and its consequences lies in maintaining our neutrality and giving no pretext to either side for violating our territory.[16]

There was also the question of Ireland's ability to be an active combatant. Eunan O'Halpin pointed out that:

> there simply was not the basis there for any organised successful defence, even with the expansion of the defence forces ... by 1942, the Chief of Staff reported that the army was, in his view, in a sense now militarily ready for an invasion, but it still didn't have any armoured vehicle worth the name, still didn't have any anti-aircraft artillery, still didn't have a long shopping list of elements that any modern defence force would have needed.[17]

In this sense, neutrality was also about survival and self-interest, which seemed, at a later stage, to be morally dubious, if not reprehensible to some, but for a country that had won significant concessions in Anglo–Irish relations and that was still raw from a Civil War, de Valera's stubbornness was necessary. There was a lot of hostility to de Valera personally, not just, most famously, in Churchill's attack at the end of the war, but also from David Gray, as mentioned earlier, and John Maffey (later Lord Rugby), the British representative in Dublin. Maffey initially thought that de Valera was vain, ambitious and petty with a memory that stretched back far too long (but he clearly changed his mind, given the warmth of their later correspondence).

Churchill's denunciations of Irish neutrality were also disingenuous given MI5's own account of its Irish activities. As revealed by Eunan O'Halpin, MI5 was more than happy for Ireland, as a neutral country, to have diplomatic relations with Germany, because it enabled British Intelligence to closely monitor the German legation as a result of the 'friendly and unofficial channel for co-operation' with Irish Army Intelligence.[18]

De Valera's response to Churchill's insulting broadcast at the end of the war was masterful and did much to secure his national 'father figure' status. Churchill contended that Britain had shown 'restraint and poise' in not invading an Ireland that had 'frolicked' with the Japanese. De Valera's reply to the bellicose Churchill was dignified and firm, and in his own words, delivered in a 'much quieter atmosphere'. In defending the Irish pursuit of independence and its neutrality, he queried whether, if Germany had invaded and partitioned England, Churchill would have led 'this partitioned England to join with Germany in a crusade? I do not think Mr Churchill would'. The sentiments expressed, and his demeanour, won applause across party-political divides. Tom Garvin observed: 'There is surviving newsreel footage of middle-class gents standing in bars and around fireplaces puffing their pipes and nodding to each other satisfiedly, "quite right—Dev stood up to him!". That's why they loved him. Even people who didn't support him admired him for that kind of behaviour'.[19]

Another aspect of the war years that continued to cause controversy was the relationship between neutral Ireland and the Nazis. In reality, the pro-Axis underground in Ireland during the war, was, in the words of R.M. Douglas 'numerically weak, poorly led and ideologically unsophisticated ... nevertheless, evidence suggests that a considerable number of Irishmen and women on both sides of the border shared its underlying objective of aligning Ireland with what they regarded as an emerging post-democratic world order'.[20] There were a number of groups relevant in this context, including the Irish Friends of Germany; Cumann Náisiúnta (National Club); the People's National Party, which had a tiny membership; and finally the most significant numerically, Craobh na hÁiséirghe (Branch of the Resurrection). Craobh na hÁiséirghe had perhaps 1,200 members by the end of 1941, an indication of a significant anti-democratic sentiment, but 'efforts to recruit a nationwide cadre of Pro-Axis agents ... proved a dismal failure'.[21] In one sense the very existence of this group was another reason for de Valera to hold firm.

In 2004 Tom Garvin commented that:

> there would have been a significant minority among the voters, and a significant minority among his [de Valera's] own people [who] were actively pro-German, not necessarily because they were Nazis, but because your enemy's enemy is your friend

basically, and also traditional sentiment in favour of Germany because of the First World War and the declaration of 1916— 'our gallant allies in Europe', and all that sort of thing. In other words, de Valera had to keep them on side.[22]

But Garvin also maintained that few were prepared to express publicly their pro-Allied feelings and argue that Ireland should join the Allies:

Perhaps 10% or 15% of the population who were actively pro-allies—make it 20%—I'm guessing. But I think most people were in favour of neutrality and the republicans were violently in favour of neutrality if you like, many of them pro-German, and the rest of the population were just non militarised, they just wanted nothing, they didn't want to hear about the war, the war was something that was going on over there, something very horrible: 'They've all gone mad *out there*'—said one Fianna Fáil senator in 1939 during the debate on neutrality. 'They've all gone mad *there* and we are *in here*'—Irish isolationism was a very powerful cultural sentiment at that time.[23]

Therefore, it may have been isolationism rather than a deep-rooted anti-Semitism that prompted the seeming indifference to the plight of Jewish refugees, as well as an empathy with the nationalism that produced puppet Nazis and a reluctance to follow instructions from Britain and the US.

In 1995 the Taoiseach, John Bruton, apologised on behalf of the government of the day for Ireland's restrictive policy in relation to the admission of Jewish refugees during and after the war. The Irish National Holocaust Memorial Day, however, was not instituted until 2003, at which point the Minister for Justice, Michael McDowell, suggested that Ireland had betrayed its own Constitution in failing to protect the Jews.

In 2005, when the sixtieth anniversary of the end of the Second World War was being widely commemorated, there were suggestions that the president of Ireland, Mary McAleese, should apologise for de Valera's visit to the German ambassador, Edouard Hempel, to express condolences on behalf of the Irish people following the suicide of Adolf Hitler in May 1945. It was also suggested that there was an onus on her to express shame at the failure to adequately respond to the humanitarian crisis created by Hitler's Germany by not allowing more Jewish refugees in to Ireland. It raised an obvious dilemma: should contemporary politicians have to apologise for the perceived sins of their political ancestors, or are those demanding the apologies simplifying the past in order to satisfy present-day political sensibilities? It was easy, it seemed, sixty years after the event, to suggest, even demand that a public apology should be made by Ireland's current head of state. President McAleese did suggest that Ireland should be ashamed that it did not take in more Jewish refugees, but fudged the question about de Valera's condolences by maintaining that it was impossible to find an apology 'to blot out that period of human history'.[24]

But had the inactivity of the Irish government amounted to evidence of an ingrained anti-Semitism? Undoubtedly, blind eyes were turned, and in relation to helping Jewish victims, it is difficult to refute the charge that de Valera (and the Department of Justice) should have done more, particularly, as according to Dermot Keogh, de Valera had been made aware of the Holocaust by Isaac Herzog, who had been the Chief Rabbi of the Irish–Jewish community in the 1930s.[25] It is also the case that a small number of pre- and post-war Irish government officials articulated anti-Semitic sentiments. Charles Bewley, Ireland's Minister to Germany from 1933 to 1939, was one who embraced wholeheartedly the Nazi ideology and vilification of Jews, becoming, in the words of Michael Kennedy, 'sucked into the vortex of Nazi racial theories'.[26]

But it is also interesting to see how he was sidelined and unpopular with his colleagues in the Department of External Affairs. His attempt to re-orientate Irish policy towards Germany according to his own preferences led to a falling out with Joseph Walshe, particularly as Bewley had gone on record in the German press to describe the supposedly enthusiastic support the Nazi administration had in Ireland, a view clearly at variance with his colleagues, and Irish government policy.

While it is true that the horrors of the Nazi Holocaust were beginning to emerge, and the *Irish Catholic* newspaper had been able to assert in 1937 that 'Hitler has many admirers among Irish Catholics',[27] it is also the case that the lifting of the strict censorship that had operated in Ireland since 1939 would not make Irish people, or their politicians, experts on foreign atrocities overnight. There was much that was not known, not only about the Holocaust, but also about Ireland's neutrality, and its various contradictions. What could not be disputed was the inflexibility of the Department of Justice in the pre-war period, and the existence of a refugee policy in the 1930s that was 'illiberal' and 'stubbornly restrictive'. More contentious is the assertion that the policy was influenced by 'the traditional European Christian anti-Semitism shared by politicians and society alike'.[28]

As Cormac Ó Gráda has pointed out in his recent book, *Jewish Ireland in the age of Joyce*, 'Irish anti-Semitism existed and traces doubtless still persist, but it was of a relatively mild variety'.[29] The Irish–Jewish community was small, but well-integrated and many of its members thrived in business, arts and education. Had there been a more pronounced anti-Semitism, it is difficult to see how such integration could have happened. Some boys from poorer Jewish households attended the Christian Brothers' schools in Dublin and did not experience anti-Semitism; they were exempted from prayers and allowed to leave early on Friday during the winter months.[30]

De Valera had singled out the Jewish community for special mention in the 1937 Constitution at a time when there were up to 27 Jewish grocery, bakery and general stores on Clanbrassil Street in Dublin, a number of kosher butcher shops and more than a dozen synagogues dotted around the South Circular Road (the Jewish population in Dublin in the 1940s was nearly 6,000); they had 'a vibrant and rich communal life' and made a disproportionate contribution to business and the social fabric of the capital.[31]

Reacting to the claim that Ireland provided refuge for only about 30 Jewish people during the Nazi era, Gisela Holfter of the Centre for Irish–German studies in Limerick maintained:

> We can estimate safely that around 250 to 300 victims of Nazi persecution lived in Ireland for some time between 1933 and 1945, obviously a painfully small number in the international context ... among them were the first and second directors of the Dublin Institute for Advanced Studies, Jewish entrepreneurs who set up and managed factories that provided employment for many Irish people, and many 'ordinary people', surviving by giving German classes or anything else that opened up to them and through the support of people from all religious backgrounds.[32]

Brian Girvin maintained that de Valera and his closest colleagues 'struck a public attitude amounting almost to disdain for the Holocaust and indifference to the actions of the Nazis'.[33] But as Dermot Keogh has pointed out, de Valera was not indifferent to the genocide of Jews and 'the world of diplomacy in Dublin during the Emergency was not a time of philosophical discussion between de Valera and the different foreign ambassadors. It was a world of shadow language and shape-shifting'.[34]

The reports of the Berlin legation headed by Con Cremin, who despised the Nazis, but who stayed in Berlin long after other diplomats had fled, because he believed that it was the correct thing for the representative of a neutral country to do, reveal that Joseph Walshe had inquired about exit visas for '200 Polish Jewish families ... and ... 500 Christian children'.[35] On 24 March 1944 Cremin telegraphed Dublin indicating that the German authorities were anxious to know what would happen to the Jews if they went to Ireland. According to the unidentified German official: 'If it was intended that these families should become Irish citizens the German authorities would, I was given to understand, *gladly save us the inconvenience of having so many Jews*"'. Cremin persisted in his inquiries, on instructions from de Valera. On 5 October 1944 a senior German Foreign Office official told him that an inquiry had been sent to the authorities of Oswiecim/Auschwitz (about the group of Jews) but that no reply was received from that source.[36] Dermot Keogh makes the point that de Valera 'actively sought to reverse' the illiberalism of Jewish policy during the war years. In 1946 he provided for the sending of kosher meat to Europe, providing work permits for Jewish butchers to travel from the Continent to conduct the slaughter of the animals; the meat was subsequently sent abroad for relief purposes.[37]

Undoubtedly, there was a difference of views within government and diplomatic circles, but Girvin exaggerates pro-German sympathy, and ignores figures like Con Cremin. While it is true that Joseph Walshe was sympathetic to Vichy France, Seán Murphy in Vichy was important in convincing the Irish government of the reality of the situation in France and in determining a more pro-Allied neutrality from late 1940, and Maurice Moynihan, an influential adviser, was certainly not someone ambivalent to the outcome of the war, as noted by Dermot Keogh.[38] Deirdre McMahon remarks that Moynihan's brother, Michael, had been killed in 1918, and even '80 years later the memory of the day the telegram arrived at the family home in Tralee was still a searing one for his brother'.[39]

In reacting to another controversial aspect of Irish neutrality, de Valera acknowledged in private that he could have made himself unavailable in May 1945 to avoid expressing his condolences to Hempel. The text of the letter he sent to Robert Brennan, Ireland's ambassador to the United States of America, made it clear that he knew what he was doing would be criticised, but he went ahead anyway, on the grounds that Ireland retained diplomatic relations with Germany and that the visit, in the circumstances, was correct protocol. It may have been perceived as foolhardy, but for him, it was a logical act, and the ability to act independently went to the core of his political project during the 1930s and 1940s:

I have noted that my call on the German Minister on the announcement of Hitler's death was played up to the utmost. I expected this. Gray could not fail to try his usual upon it. I could have had a diplomatic illness but as you know I would scorn that sort of thing. I acted very deliberately in this matter. So long as we retained our diplomatic relations with Germany to have failed to call upon the German representative would have been an act of unpardonable discourtesy to the German nation and to Dr Hempel himself ... It is of considerable importance that the formal acts of courtesy paid on such occasions as the death of the head of a State should not have attached to them any further special significance, such as connoting approval or disapproval of the policies of the State in question or of its head. It is important that it should never be inferred that these formal acts imply the passing of any judgement good or bad. I am anxious that you should know my mind on all this. I have carefully refrained from attempting to give any explanation in public. An explanation would have been interpreted as an excuse, and an excuse as a consciousness of having acted wrongly. I acted correctly and I feel certain wisely.

Brennan replied on 25 May: 'Personally I am glad you did the right thing concerning Hempel but the atmosphere created here because of that is still bad. For instance, not one of our old friends in Congress offered to put your speech in the Record'.[40]

One would imagine, given de Valera's visit to Hempel that the Irish–Jewish community would feel more aggrieved than any other group. But de Valera was regarded as a friend of the Jewish community. State papers released in 2005 reveal how, in the mid 1960s, the Irish–Jewish community funded the planting of a forest of 10,000 trees in Israel in honour of President de Valera, who only agreed to this tribute providing the fundraising received no publicity. In a letter to the committee which organised this honour, he expressed his thanks, but added: 'I feel I did nothing for the Jewish community except to express the general goodwill of our people towards them and what the constitution demands'.[41]

Another stir was caused by two programmes broadcast on RTÉ television in January 2007—*Ireland and the Nazis*—which set out to show how a number of ex-Nazis had made a home in Ireland after the war, which contrasted strongly with the reluctance to accept Jewish refugees. Words like 'embrace' and 'sanctuary' were liberally employed. The presenter, Cathal O'Shannon, made clear at the outset his personal anger at the fact that for people like him, who had served with the British forces (in his case the Royal Air Force), there was a refusal to acknowledge their service on their return to Ireland (O'Shannon returned in 1947).

This was indeed the case. But the contention that Ireland was a haven for Nazis was undermined by generalisations and a selective use of documentation, added to assertions like the following, made by O'Shannon during the pre-programme publicity: 'There was a huge, huge minority, maybe even a majority, of people in Ireland who were pro-German in the Second World War' and 'there was always an underlying anti-Semitic attitude in official Ireland'. During the programme, he asked why the state denied victims of the Holocaust asylum while 'embracing Nazi war criminals with open arms'.[42]

The two programmes were built around these assertions, but neither can withstand scrutiny. Undoubtedly, there was strong pro-German feeling in Ireland, but it is impossible to quantify it. The contention was also made that 'former Nazis played a leading role in the story of post-War Ireland', but only six such individuals were examined in the programme. These included Andrija Artukovic, Minister for the Interior in Nazi-occupied Croatia, and responsible for brutal murders of Serbs, Romanies and Jews; Breton nationalist Celestin Laine, founder of the Brezen Perpt nationalist movement, organised as the Waffen SS unit; and Dutch Nazi, Pieter Menten, involved in the extermination of Jews in Poland.

In truth, in the last decade, contemporary politics and selective history have combined to produce damning indictments that have ignored the context and the different layers of Ireland's relationship with the Jewish and Nazi communities. In an article in *History Ireland* in 2006, David O'Donoghue pointed out that Ireland's leading pre-war Nazi, Dr Adolf Mahr, Director of the National Museum, was refused reinstatement in his job after the war had ended: 'Under pressure from MI5 and opposition TD James Dillon, de Valera heeded the advice of his military intelligence chief Colonel Dan Bryan that allowing the return of such a "blatant Nazi" would be "unwise". Mahr was pensioned off against his wishes and never set foot on Irish soil again'.[43] Peter Berry, Secretary of the Department of Justice, was another who expressed anti-Semitic sentiments and argued trenchantly against the entry of Jews into Ireland in 1953, but significantly, his claim that there was 'fairly strong' anti-Semitic feeling throughout the state was disputed by his colleagues in the Department of External (later Foreign) Affairs.

Berry claimed in June 1953, as a result of requests from Robert Briscoe, a Fianna Fáil TD and leading member of the Irish–Jewish community, that Jews had refused to assimilate and appeared to have 'disproportionate wealth and influence'. Admitting them as refugees presented 'a special problem' and the law had always been administered 'less liberally' in their case:

> Although the Jewish community in Ireland is only 3,907 persons, according to the 1946 census, there is a fairly strong anti-Semitic feeling throughout the country based, perhaps, on historical reasons, the fact that the Jews have remained a separate community within the community and have not permitted themselves to be assimilated, and that for their numbers they appear to have disproportionate wealth and influence.

He continued:

> No reasons have been put forward why this Jewish group should take precedence over the thousands—even millions—of European refugees and stateless persons seeking admission to Western countries other than that a Jewish international society will guarantee their maintenance ... Is the fact that international Jewry is prepared to put up the money to guarantee the State against loss to be regarded as a good and sufficient reason for allowing these people to 'jump the queue'?[44]

A note from a civil servant in the Department of External Affairs expressed 'considerable disagreement' with Berry's views: 'I think we can, for the honour of our country, refute the suggestion of a "widespread anti-Semitism". I know of no such feeling except amongst a few fanatics. Moreover, our Constitution is so far as I know unique in giving specific recognition to the Jewish faith— surely a proof that anti-Semitism is not widespread'. A note in Irish, probably by the Minister for External Affairs, Frank Aiken, states: 'Aontuím' ('I agree'). It was agreed that five Jewish families should be admitted for a maximum stay of two years. However, no action was taken to admit the refugees and, on 22 June, Berry wrote to Thomas Commins at External Affairs, 'We have deliberately adopted a "go-slow" policy in this matter as we have reason to believe that the Jewish community in Ireland and the international organisation abroad have fallen out as to who should bear the costs'.[45]

In all this, it can be seen that contradictions abound. The lifting of censorship, the benefit of hindsight, and decades of research have all combined to ensure that most now have a certain view of the morality and immorality of various decisions made during the Second World War. In an interview with Robert Fisk, James Dillon, who urged an abandonment of Irish neutrality, stated his belief that de Valera 'never did anything which at the time of doing he believed to be wrong. When he acted, he would act ruthlessly and inflexibly and never look back'.[46] But these, of course, were the very traits that had enabled de Valera to implement an independent foreign policy, to prevent a split in his own party and probable considerable civil strife, and later on, facilitated a considerable role for Ireland in the United Nations and international peace-keeping.

Later, in 1956, when the question of the treatment of the 530 Hungarian refugees who had been admitted to Ireland was being discussed in the Dáil, while Donogh O'Malley was arguing that the protesting Hungarians needed to stop complaining and behave themselves 'in a reasonable manner', and one Fine Gael TD suggested that they were being overfed, it was de Valera who attempted to moderate the debate by reminding the Dáil that 'we have not passed through the trials which they have'.[47]

UCDA, P150/3051: De Valera shaking hands with Winston Churchill in Downing Street, 1953. F.H. Boland (Irish ambassador to Great Britain) and Frank Aiken in the background. © The Irish News Agency, Dublin.

UCDA, P150/2573: Frank
Aiken and de Valera (in
flying kit) with the American
aviator, Colonel Charles
Lindbergh (to de Valera's
left), at Baldonnel Airfield,
21 November 1936. This was
de Valera's first flight.

COPY/

July 13th, 1940

W.T. Cosgrave, Esq., T.D.,
Leinster House,
DUBLIN.

A Chara,

I received your letter of the 9th inst., and have
discussed it with my colleagues in the Government.

There would appear to be little difference between our
view and yours as to what is the paramount national issue
at the moment.   The aim of Government policy is to preserve
the national security and to provide that our independence
will remain unimpaired at the end of the war.   The difference
between your views and those of the Government is in regard
to the means by which these objectives can be achieved.
The question which you raise is whether we should not
immediately ask for military assistance from one belligerent
to strengthen our defences against the danger of attack from
the other.   The Government view is what it has been since
the beginning of the war, that the best hope of preserving
the country from invasion and its consequences lies in
maintaining our neutrality and giving no pretext to either
side for violating our territory.

We are fully aware that this policy does not guarantee
the country immunity from attack.   There is always the
possibility of attack should one side or the other decide,
during the progress of the war, that the circumstances are
such that the resultant advantages to its interests outweigh
the disadvantages.   The assumption that hostile invasion
need be feared from one side only is one which cannot in all
circumstances be relied upon.   But, so long as we are
neutral, there is a possibility that the danger of attack
may be averted;   whilst, if we invite military assistance
from one side, immediate attack by the other side, with all
its consequences, will be almost inevitable.   There are the
two alternatives: one, immediate entry into the war;   the
other, the maintenance of neutrality with dependance upon our
own resources in the first instance to meet an attack, should
such be made.   The Government are of opinion that the
national objectives, present security and the ultimate position
when the war ends, are more likely to be secured by choosing
the second alternative.

As you are aware, these matters have already been
discussed with your representatives on the Defence Conference
and the recent British proposals to which you refer were
outlined by me to two of these representatives who came to
see me.   They have been similarly outlined to the leader of
the Labour Party.

We have noted your view that the existing scope of the
discussions at the Defence Conference is not adequate for
the present needs.   I am prepared to arrange for further
discussions, in addition to those at the Conference, as to
the imminence and extent of the danger and the steps
necessary to defend the country.   We should be glad to have
such discussions with you and two or three of your colleagues,
and with one or two representatives of the Labour Party,
preferably in joint conference.   On hearing from you, I shall
have the necessary arrangements completed without delay.   The
ultimate decision as to any steps to be taken in the national
interest must, of course, rest with the Government in office.

Mise, le meas,

(Sgd.) EAMON DE VALÉRA

UCDA, P150/2597:
Correspondence
between de Valera and
William Cosgrave,
leader of Fine Gael,
on the subject of
neutrality and the
possibility of its
abandonment, 13–16
July 1940. Cosgrave
had been the first
president of the
Executive Council of
the Irish Free State,
and held this office
from 1922 to 1932.
Following electoral
defeat in 1932, he led
the opposition in Dáil
Éireann until his
retirement from
politics in 1945.

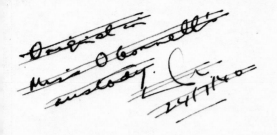

DÁIL ÉIREANN,

TIGH LAIGHEAN
(Leinster House

BAILE ÁTHA CLIATH.
(Dublin)

16th July, 1940.

A Chara,

I thank you for your letter of Saturday
last which has been considered by my colleagues and
myself.

On the question of the abandonment of
neutrality, our suggestion was and is that changing
circumstances may conceivably make it in the best
interests of the country to take that step before
actual invasion.   If the Government think it necessary
to take such a decision, we have indicated our view.

With regard to the suggestion in the last
paragraph of your letter, I would be glad if you would
arrange an appointment at which our representatives on
the Defence Conference may discuss with you the imminence
and the extent of the danger and the steps necessary to
defend the country.

(Sd.)   W.T. Cosgrave.

An Taoiseach, E.de Valera.

Written by hand.

Confidential of course

Whit Monday 1945.

Dear Bob,

A line to tell you how pleased we all were
with the work of our delegation to the Aviation

Conference and particularly with the American Agreement.

I am anticipating that your difficulties over th
with the press, etc.. will begin to lighten from now on.
I am sure you are keeping in the closest touch with our
friends and keeping them as fully informed as possible.

I have noted that my call on the German Minister
on the announcement of Hitler's death was played up to
the utmost. I expected this. Guy could not fail to try
his usual upon it. I could have had a diplomatic illness
but as you know I would scorn that sort of thing. I acte
very deliberatly in this matter. So long as we retained
our diplomatic relations with Germany to have failed to
call upon the German representative would have been an
act of unpardonable discourtesy to the German nation and
to Dr. Hempel himself. During the whole of the war
Dr. Hempel's conduct was irreproachable. He was always
friendly and invariably correct - in marked contrast with
G. I certainly was not going to add to his humiliation
in the hour of defeat. I had another reason. It would
establish a bad precedent. It is of considerable importa
that the formal acts of courtesy paid on such occasions a
the death of the head of a State should not have attached
to them any further special significance, such as connoti
approval or disapproval of the policies of the State in
question or of its head. It is important that it should
never be inferred that these formal acts imply the passing
of any judgment good or bad. I am anxious that you shoul
know my mind on all this. I have carefully refrained fro
attempting to give any explanation in public. An explanat
would have been interpreted as an excuse, and an excuse a
a consciousness of having acted wrongly. I acted correc
and I feel certain wisely.

I would like to write to you on two or three o
matters, e.g. Broadcasting and Partition. I have not the
time however and I shall ask Mr. Leydon to convey my views
orally instead.

Regards to Mrs. Brennan and the children. I hope
you are all very well.

Do chara,

Eamon de Valera

Mr. R. Brennan,
WASHINGTON.

éire

IRISH LEGATION
WASHINGTON, D.C.

25th May 45

Dear Chief,

Many thanks for your letter of what monday.

Personally I am glad you did the right thing concerning Hempel but the atmosphere created here because of that is still bad. For instance, not one of our old friends in Congress offered to put your speech in the Record. It would not be correct to say they are cool but they are wary because of the atmosphere I spoke of. The speech was inserted in the Record by a congressman from Ohio, a newcomer.

The reaction to the speech itself has been excellent & generally speaking here are indications that the hostile press barrage is easing up, thank God.

With kindest regards from all here.

Yours sincerely

Bob.

טקס הקדשת הי...
לכבו...
אימון דה ואליר...
נשיא מדינת אירל...

יום חמישי, ב' באלול תשכ"...
(18-8-1966)
בשעה 11 לפנה"צ...
ליד כפר כנא, נצרת...

DEDICATION CEREMONY
OF THE FOREST
IN HONOUR OF
EAMON DE VALERA
PRESIDENT OF THE
REPUBLIC OF IRELAND

THURSDAY, AUGUST 18th, 1966
AT 11 A.M.
NEAR KAFR KANNA
NAZARETH

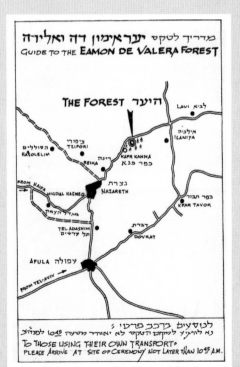

NAI, DT, 97/6/563: Guide to the Eamon de Valera forest, 1966. In the mid 1960s, the Irish–Jewish community funded the planting of an 'Eamon de Valera Forest' of 10,000 trees in Israel in honour of the Irish president. The forest was part of a series grown in honour of statesmen, including Winston Churchill and John F. Kennedy. The first sapling in the forest on government owned land was planted in August 1966. The ceremony took place on a hillside in central Galilee near Kafr Kana, an Arab-inherited village where it was reported Jesus performed his water and wine miracle. In April 1973 six pine trees, each two foot in height, were brought from the Eamon de Valera forest, quarantined in Dublin's Botanic Gardens for several weeks, and then replanted at a special ceremony in Áras an Uachtaráin.

XII

'One man shouldn't have

a vision like that

for all the people'

UCDA, P150/2102: De Valera working at his desk in government buildings, 1947/8.

As noted by Tom Garvin, in 1927 de Valera had articulated his economic philosophy in an interview with the *Manchester Guardian*, when he was questioned about self-sufficiency. By relying solely on native resources, would he be happy with a larger population but a lower standard of living? De Valera replied: 'You say "lower" when you ought to say a less costly standard of living. I think it quite possible that a less costly standard of living is desirable, and that it would prove, in fact, to be a higher standard of living. I am not satisfied that the standard of living and the mode of living in Western Europe is a right or proper one'.[1] According to Garvin, 'this strange anti-economic economics informed much of Fianna Fáil's thinking for a long time'.[2]

Undoubtedly, one of the appeals of Fianna Fáil in the early years was its commitment to economic protectionism and welfare policies; indeed, Seán Lemass throughout his career was fond of insisting that Fianna Fáil was the real Irish Labour party, and many high-profile members of Fianna Fáil down through the years may have found a more natural home in the Labour Party if the Civil War divisions had not tied them to de Valera and his successors. But how successfully did they deliver on the economic reform and welfare agenda?

When Fianna Fáil leader Charles Haughey unveiled a memorial to mark the one hundredth anniversary of the birth of de Valera in 1982, he spoke of Fianna Fáil in the 1930s, making the case for Fianna Fáil as the 'Welfare Party':

> These years were also years of enormous social advance. The first de Valera government took office in 1932 in the midst of a world-wide depression … It was a time when budget cuts were needed and they were made, but the new government did not narrow its initiatives to budget cuts alone. Within a few years of taking office the de Valera government succeeded in increasing industrial output by 44% and almost doubling the number of people in industrial employment. The Housing Act of 1932 began a great era of slum clearance, both urban and rural … In

the decade after 1932, almost a quarter of the population were re-housed. It was an epoch-making achievement ... unemployment assistance was introduced for the first time in Ireland, in 1933 old age pensions were immediately increased and widows' and orphans' pensions were initiated in 1935. If he had done nothing else in all his long lifetime of service, de Valera's social achievements in these first years of office would ensure that his name should live on in honour as that of a great social reformer.[3]

Is this a verdict that withstands historical scrutiny? The small amount paid under the Widows' and Orphans' Pensions Act of 1935 did not increase until 1942. David Fitzpatrick suggested that Fianna Fáil's appeal to the poor only lasted until 1938.[4] Notwithstanding, a commitment to an increase on social spending is revealed as social spending rose from 36% of the government's budget in 1929 to 40% in 1939.[5] Brian Girvin's account of Fianna Fáil's economic policy during these years makes the point that by 1939 approximately 50,000 new jobs had been created as a result of protection, a notable success at a time of international depression. The introduction of an unemployment assistance bill, although 'less radical and generous than originally proposed ... complied with Lemass's view that a minimum income should be available for the genuinely unemployed'.[6] In the 1930s the government also demonstrated a willingness to respond to trade union pressure, introducing the Workmen's Compensation Act in 1934 and the Conditions of Employment Act in 1936. These acts were introduced to improve working conditions, guarantee paid holidays and prevent exploitation of child labour. (Fianna Fáil also angered many in the labour movement with the 1941 Trade Union Act which limited the right of unions to negotiate and strike; received more positively was the Industrial Relations Act of 1946 which established the Labour Court.)

These various initiatives hardly amounted to a social revolution, but there were also significant reforms in the context of pensions, hospital care and the provision of labourers' cottages. There was a specific large-scale housing programme in the 1930s targeted at agricultural labourers. At key moments in his career, de Valera had made much of being a product of a labourer's cottage upbringing, telling the Dáil in January 1922, 'I was reared in a Labourer's cottage ... the first 15 years of my life that formed my character'.[7]

As well as using legislation to empower the Land Commission to expropriate land deemed suitable for redistribution among small farmers, Fianna Fáil increased the government subsidy for cottage-building from 36%

to 60% of the local authorities' loan repayments, and in 1936 the Labourers Act allowed for the sale of cottages to labourers. De Valera took a particular interest in this; over 16,000 cottages were built between 1932 and 1940 (Mary Daly cites a figure of 20,000)[8] and although their construction did not solve all the ills of rural Ireland, it went some way to giving meaning to the professed desire to achieve frugal contentment in cosy homesteads in rural Ireland. De Valera dealt rigorously with local government bodies attempting to obstruct his schemes and castigated the 'red tape' that slowed their construction.[9] Private individuals and public utility societies were responsible for the building of an additional 22,000 rural houses between 1932 and 1942.[10]

The urban housing programme initiated also yielded significant results, and economic historian, Cormac Ó Gráda, has identified it as one of Fianna Fáil's most impressive achievements in the 1930s.[11] As Mary Daly asserts, by 1931 there was an intensive publicity campaign to highlight conditions in city slums and, with the active intervention of the Department of Finance, between 1932 and 1942, local authorities built 29,000 urban houses and flats, while private individuals and public utility societies constructed 11,000 urban houses. There was also a high level of expenditure on grants for private houses that proved popular with the public, though it is questionable whether enough government assistance went to those most in need. Daly gives an approximate total of 82,000 houses (rural and urban) built in the decade 1932 to 1942.[12] This active housing programme, according to Joe Lee, combined social, economic and political motives 'in a nice blend from a Fianna Fáil perspective. It led to a genuine improvement in horrific housing conditions for families, provided employment for needy workers, profits for needy employers and in due course subscriptions to a needy party'.[13]

In 1931, 58% of all agricultural holdings were less than 30 acres in size.[14] In tandem with Fianna Fáil's economic manifestos and tillage policies of the 1930s, Article 45.2 of the Constitution contained the aspiration that 'there may be established on the land in economic security as many families as in the circumstances shall be practicable'. A measure of the gulf between de Valera's rhetoric and the reality was revealed in the same year that the Constitution was introduced, when a group of small farmers in west Cork, though themselves Fianna Fáil supporters, informed the government that 'in many of the so-called farms there is really no arable land at all' and that agricultural schemes were 'of no use to people of this kind'. Only twelve marriages had taken place in the parish of Bantry in 1935, housing was of a poor standard and the condition of roads pitiful. The farmers were demanding a marriage bounty for young men on holdings with a valuation of £5 and under.[15]

De Valera remained preoccupied with the issue of rural housing for much of his career. In December 1943 when addressing the Agricultural Science Society at UCD he proposed the erection of 'dower' or second houses on farms for farmer's sons who desired to marry while continuing to assist on their parents' farms. This was a proposal to counteract the reluctance of young farmers to marry as so many of the eldest sons were not inheriting the farm until relatively late in life. De Valera was surprised that his idea was 'so coldly received'[16]—worries about sub-division of farms and general resistance to changes in traditional land practices probably explained the reluctance—but at least he was proposing a solution, and some were taken aback by his forthright attitude.

The *Farmer's Gazette* welcomed it particularly because 'Mr De Valera does not often unbend in public'.[17] De Valera established an inter-departmental committee to look into the matter, but it never took off, though he continued to promote it. In the summer of 1947 the *Irish Times* referred to it as involving the Taoiseach displaying 'an unusual and welcome sense of reality', the plan being, the paper editorialised, 'a further revelation of Mr de Valera's resourceful and ingenious mind'.[18]

But de Valera did not have the same degree of success with his social and economic proposals as he did with his constitutional and political ideas, and his stubbornness was not enough to persuade defensive old men to share their land. In 1960 the *Irish Independent* noted that the problem was still in existence, that most farmers still wanted to remain in control of their farms until 'a ripe old age', and that 'any sort of coercion in so highly personal a matter as this would be undesirable and possibly disastrous'.[19]

In any case, even if de Valera's proposal had been put into practice it would have made little difference in overall terms. The real problem during these decades was the failure to invest in education. As Tom Garvin trenchantly argues, the failure to develop different types of education and open up educational opportunity to more people was one of the main factors retarding the Irish economy. The decision not to increase the school leaving age from fourteen to sixteen was taken by an interdepartmental committee in 1936; de Valera also left himself open to the notion that he was either sceptical or indifferent regarding the value of vocational training.[20]

Moreover, he supported, against the advice of a number of bishops, a ban on married women teachers in primary schools (not rescinded until 1958). De Valera was by no means the sole villain in the destructive lack of ambition and vision that plagued the Irish educational system; it had 'the tacit or even active assent of most of Irish society'; and when de Valera pressed for plans for 'educational reconstruction' in the aftermath of the Second World War, he received little in return from the Department of Education.[21]

A promise to achieve self-sufficiency had been significant in terms of electoral support for Fianna Fáil during the 1930s and 1940s, and protected industrialists and industrial workers had reason to be grateful to the government, and supported them accordingly, as did many small farmers. The Economic War of 1932–8, which occurred due to the withholding of land annuities, and the imposition of tariffs on Irish exports in response, did more damage to Irish cattle traders than any other group; it was eventually settled in 1938 and did not damage the overall popularity of Fianna Fáil. The irony of the overall economic policies, as observed by Garret FitzGerald, was that ultimately, the protectionist industries became dependent on imported raw materials for industrial processing and the industrial workers came to spend an increasing portion of their wages on imported goods; by 1950 the share of external trade in Ireland's economy had risen by almost one third. In effect, industrialisation was achieved 'with a reduction in self-sufficiency'.[22]

There was success in terms of semi-state companies such as the Industrial Credit Corporation, but despite nationalist rhetoric, Fianna Fáil governments allowed considerable monopoly powers to foreign companies, and, as Mary Daly has noted, while the policies resulted in a new economic elite, the existing elite did not suffer.[23] The poor performance of the Irish economy also explained the rise in the gap between British and Irish wages in the late 1930s and early 1940s, and a white paper on national income and expenditure for the years 1938–44 revealed that approximately the top 3,000 earners, took 5% of the income in 1943, suggesting little progress had been made in narrowing the gap between the poor and wealthy.[24]

Seán O'Faoláin penned a reassessment of de Valera in the June 1945 issue of the *Bell* and disputed the notion that Fianna Fáil was a party championing the poor, arguing that 'he is held in power by the conservative middle-part of the community'. He added that 'it is only in the thirteenth year of office that the present government introduces legislation to deal with tuberculosis … as for the poor and the unemployed we all know what has happened to the latter. The poor he has kept afloat by every kind of state charity; he has no constructive policy for either'.[25]

But Fianna Fáil continued to make the case for itself as a socially radical party. A summary of their achievements, as used by the party for electioneering, and held in the de Valera papers at UCD Archives, School of History and Archives (dating from the late 1940s) includes a section headed 'Social' and lists nine achievements—unemployment assistance and pensions; doubling the expenditure on old age pensions; aiding the building and reconstruction 'of 140,000 houses'; increased national health benefits; free fuel, food and clothes for the poor; more medical attention for those on low incomes; a TB scheme; increased hospital facilities; and 'brought the total spend on social services from £4½ millions in 1931–32 to £12,600,000 today'.[26]

Notable legislative developments in relation to health and child welfare included the National Health Insurance Act and the Public Hospitals Act, both in 1933, and the 1944 Children's Allowance Act, introduced 'after a long internal party struggle' and despite the opposition of Seán MacEntee who believed that such an allowance 'would drive the unfit into matrimony at the expense of the taxpayer'.[27] The possibility of a separate department of health had been discussed during the Second World War, and according to the *Irish Times*, was also necessary 'to disentangle the problems of health from those of "parish pump" politics'.[28] The new Department of Health was created in 1947 (health affairs had formerly been the responsibility of the Department of Local Government and Public Health). The 1947 Health Act, with its provisions regarding the health of mothers and children, was a response to growing concerns about the persistence of high levels of child and maternal mortality, and was an indication that the new Minister for Health, Dr James Ryan, 'lost no time in putting health at the centre of the government's agenda'.[29]

During the Second World War, de Valera established a Cabinet subcommittee on economic planning, comprising de Valera, Lemass and Seán T. O'Kelly, with a view to planning for the post-war period. Both Brian Farrell and Raymond James Raymond have made much of the fact that the creation of this subcommittee illustrated that de Valera was well aware of the problems facing Irish agriculture and industry and the need for economic planning in 'a recognizably modern sense'.[30] Farrell makes the point that the existence of the subcommittee and its priorities were very much at odds with the kind of rural idyll articulated in his 1943 'Ireland which we dreamed of' broadcast.[31] The 'classified list of main matters dealt with' included tourist development, housing, and afforestation. Arterial drainage of rivers featured prominently, as did the importance of 'village halls', the 'revival of athletics' and the need for 'youth organisation' as well as telephone development, rural electrification, electricity-planning and town-planning.[32]

With the instigation of this subcommittee, thoughts had turned to the future, allowing individuals like Seán Lemass, whose war-time Department of Supplies was amalgamated in 1945 with the Department of Industry and Commerce, to begin asking the difficult questions and proposing solutions. In the early years of Fianna Fáil, Lemass had envisaged the possibility of a free trade Europe, and during the Second World War he had called for the post-war expansion of technical education, bemoaned the dependence on trade with the UK and claimed that manufacturing rather than agriculture was the real future of the Irish economy; he remarked that 'we must make certain that we will participate in the general [international] recovery when it comes, and that is a matter mainly for ourselves'.[33]

Such ideas—and they were still only ideas—were of particular importance because the desire to 'root ... [Irish people] in the land' was not matched by an ability to prevent them from leaving in large numbers. Nearly 60,000 people emigrated from Ireland in the year 1957 alone, 25 years after de Valera had taken Fianna Fáil into government, and during a decade when half a million departed; by 1971, when de Valera was president, one in three people under the age of 30 in 1946 had emigrated.

In 1954 writer, Anthony Cronin, had suggested in the *Bell* that 'here, if ever was, is a climate for the death wish',[34] a sentiment that encapsulates the sense of doom that prevailed. For an issue so pervasive in Irish society, there was a curious reluctance to talk about emigration. De Valera, no more than any other Irish politician of his era, had no answers, and when he did get involved in what limited discussions there were, he angered emigrants with his contention that 'work is available at home, and in conditions infinitely better from the point of view of both health and morals. ... There is no doubt that many of those who emigrate could find employment at home at as good, or better, wages—and with living conditions far better—than they find in Britain'.[35]

These remarks, made at a Fianna Fáil function in Co. Galway in 1951, were not only controversial but were also inaccurate and included the accusation that emigrants were not only living in poor conditions, but were also leaving 'enterprises for the development of our own national resources without sufficient labour to enable progress to be made as rapidly as we would all desire'. De Valera had made the comments following a report on Irish emigrants compiled by the Young Christian Workers Association. The report suggested that poor housing conditions were only the tip of the iceberg; it hinted at moral degeneration (some Irish women were 'ill through too much dancing') and the loss to the Catholic Church of 'fifty thousand potential apostles' who had succumbed to the immoral individualism of English urban culture.[36]

The author of the report had spent more time talking to representatives of Catholic associations in Britain than to the emigrants themselves, and in the aftermath of de Valera's remarks, many were quick to intervene on their behalf. A telegram from Harry Weston, Mayor of the City of Coventry, read: 'Astounded at such remarks because obviously you are not aware of

Coventry[']s conditions. It seems a pity for you to have caused unhappiness amongst your Irish nationals who are working so hard here'. When he realised the anger his comments had caused, de Valera stubbornly stood over his comments and issued an arrogant statement, to the effect that 'I made this statement because I believed that a public statement was the quickest and most effective way of getting proper attention paid to the situation and of ensuring that a remedy will be provided'.[37]

In a caustic letter to the *Irish Press*, veteran republican socialist, Peadar O'Donnell, suggested that the real focus should be on conditions in Ireland, noting that 'it has become fashionable to look on emigration as a sort of mental weakness in our people'.[38] The following week de Valera received a large number of telegrams from England, most of which were critical of his handling of the issue. Many emigrants also wrote to the Irish newspapers, their general attitudes reflected in a letter to the *Irish Independent* from a female emigrant in Birmingham, asking the government to 'leave us alone and not make it difficult and embarrassing for us over here'.[39]

De Valera's approach, although no doubt motivated by genuine concern, was also somewhat disingenuous, since, in private, his government had made it clear that they were going to leave this issue to the Catholic Church. His government rejected an appeal from the Irish Community Trust, a group with church-backing, for state funds. In dismissing their request, the Department of External Affairs drafted a letter, noting that 'the Irish government would of course, be only too happy to look after them if they came home'. Significantly, de Valera ordered that this sentence be deleted.[40]

De Valera found it more politically astute to actually travel to talk to emigrants, rather than commit his government to financial contributions, as when he met emigrants in London in March 1954. The Irish Community Trust had more success with the organisation of a national collection under the auspices of the Catholic Church. De Valera's intervention in the emigration debate had also come at a time when more Irish women than men were emigrating (between 1946 and 1951, for every 1,000 Irish men who emigrated, there were 1,365 Irish women). In September 1951 Louie Bennett challenged what she saw as the government's failure to acknowledge the reasons for such emigration.

She suggested that much emigration was as a result of the selective role envisaged for Irish women in the domestic sphere. 'All our male politicians, philosophers, councillors and social experts prescribe domestic science as the be-all and end-all of the girl's life'.[41] Bennett wrote to the Department of the Taoiseach requesting a meeting with de Valera on the subject of women emigrating. The letter was passed on to the Department of Social Welfare, where a handwritten note revealed that the Tánaiste had no particular views on the subject, and that it would 'amuse' the Taoiseach to listen to such a deputation.[42]

Of course, it would be specious to blame de Valera personally for the country's economic failings; but what is striking is how he *was* personally blamed, probably because he was the best known Irish politician of the era, because he was in power for so long and because he devoted much of his rhetoric to the idea of 'rooting' Irish people to the land. One of the emigrants interviewed by Catherine Dunne for her book on Irish emigrants in London, *An unconsidered people*, published in 2003, was Joe Dunne. In his mid-seventies, he had spent 30 years in London, and when asked did he blame anyone for the fact that he had to emigrate in the 1950s, he was unequivocal:

> I blame de Valera. My mother was a de Valera woman, but I blame him for everything. He had a vision of what Ireland should be—his vision, only *his* vision. One man shouldn't have a vision like that for all the people ... I went to Inchicore School here, and I was starving. I used to go down the canal to school, no shoes on my feet. I couldn't speak English in the yard. I was made, forced, to speak Irish. Had I been a Galway man, I wouldn't have been able to speak English at all. I had to emigrate. If I'd listened to De Valera and my teachers—all from the west of Ireland, by the way—I wouldn't have been able to speak a word when I went away ... He's no hero.

Lemass, on the other hand, was perceived as the Saviour: 'Seán Lemass, now, he was a great man. That was the man that started it all here. That was the man that brought me home. He did everything right'.[43]

This tendency towards personal condemnation did much to fuel hostile assessments of de Valera. Tim Pat Coogan's 1993 biography, in particular, was controversial because of the perceived degree of personal animus. In the years since its publication, he has been accused by Martin Mansergh of being de Valera's 'most virulent critic'.[44] At the Douglas Hyde Conference in Roscommon in 2000, historian John Regan accused Coogan of contributing to 'the demonisation of de Valera'.[45]

What is significant perhaps, is the extent to which Tim Pat Coogan's dislike of de Valera *is* personal, as he revealed in an interview in *History Ireland* in 2004, during which he suggested that de Valera, when he was young:

> comes across as being quite a nice guy, but somewhere along the line he decided to put aside the things of childhood and the nice

guy stuff and do whatever was necessary for power. If it meant being arrogant, if it meant denaturing himself and if it meant letting a generation slip into emigration then he would do it and he did it. I feel very bitter, I'm a product of the '50s and both in my family and amongst my generation I saw terrible damage, people emigrating to dead end jobs without proper education and falling into alcoholism and so on.[46]

UCDA, P150/1972: Listening to an after-dinner speech, 17 March 1954. Frank Aiken, Dr J. Howlett and de Valera listening to Cardinal Bernard Griffin, Archbishop of Westminster, at a St Patrick's Day banquet. © Illustrated.

UCDA, P150/2181: 'Police keeping back crowds when
Mr. de Valera arrives in Downing Street', 15 July 1932.

UCDA, P150/3842: De Valera amidst a
crowd of supporters, possibly a Cumann
meeting, 1950s. © Irish Press.

22adh Mí na Nodlag, 1943.

A Chara,

        The Taoiseach has received your letter and
read it very carefully. He is glad to know that
you, as a farmer, and also the writer in the
"Farmers' Gazette", are interested in the scheme
of a second house on the farm which he mentioned
at the recent meeting of the Agricultural Science
Society, University College, Dublin. Although
he was aware of certain drawbacks and difficulties
which the scheme presented he has always been
surprised that farmers seemed to care for it so
little. The matter is being re-considered.

        In accordance with your request the cutting
from the "Farmers' Gazette" which you enclosed
is returned herewith.

                            Mise, le meas,

                            PRIVATE SECRETARY.

Mr. D. Glavin,
Kenilworth,
Youghal,
CO.CORK.

NAI, DT, S13413A: A reply to the letter of D. Glavin, a farmer in
Youghal, Co. Cork with a large family who wrote to express his support
for de Valera's proposed 'dower house' scheme, 22 December 1943.
Earlier that month, when addressing the Agricultural Science Society at
UCD, de Valera proposed the erection of 'dower' or second houses on
farms for farmers' sons who desired to marry while continuing to assist on
their parents' farms. He believed this was necessary to counteract the
reluctance of young farmers to marry, as so many of the eldest sons were
not inheriting the farm until relatively late in life. De Valera was surprised
his idea did not generate more enthusiasm.

FIANNA FAIL'S ACHIEVEMENTS

NATIONAL AND POLITICAL

1. Ended the Civil War disunion among the rank and file.

2. Gave Ireland a national organisation enabling all sect ions to resume the progress towards independence broken by the "Treaty"

3. Secured the abolition of the Oath.

4. Released the Irish Courts from the handcuffs of the British Privy Council.

5. Repealed all the Articles of the Free +State Constitution dictated in London which had created such frustration and dissension among the people.

6. Abolished the office of Governor General in which was embodied the inferior status imposed on Ireland by the "Treaty".

7. Suspended the unjustifiable payments of Land Annuities and other moneys to a total of £5 millions a year to Britain thus saving, to date, £75 millions.

8. Replaced the imposed Constitution with a Constitution wholly free from subordination to any outside Power. That Constitution, founded on principles acceptable to the whole people was first considered by the Dail and then made law by the direct vote of the people.

9. Secured British agreement to the repeal of the two internationally most dangerous articles of the "Treaty", those which gave Britain the right to use and occupy +Irish territory in war time.

10. Recovered for the Irish people, in time to make the national policy of neutrality effective, the ports occupied by the British since 1921.

11. Isolated Partition for mass attack by all groups in the country, by concluding agreement with Britain settling all lesser questions.

12. Directed successfully the national determination against involvment in the late ruinous war.

ECONOMIC

1. Established 100 new industries: *900 factories and workshops.*

2. Provided employment and increased earnings for 74,000 workers.

3. Made the country self sufficient in many groups of consumer goods.

4. Revolutionised agriculture by encouraging against intense opposition the growth of wheat, and of beet for manufacture into sugar -- two crops which since 1932 have been worth £65 millions to the farmers.

4½. *Doubled the agricultural grant*

5. Extended the tillage area by 1,000,000 acres

6. Divided in 51,099 farms 658,000 acres of land

7. Planted 78,413 acres of forest.

8. Reduced emigration from a yearly average of ~~27~~
27,494 in the seven years before 1932 to 8,043
a year in the seven years after 1932, until the
approach of war disrupted the national economy.

9. Initiated and encouraged as well as great industrial
projects such as sugar manufacture, cement manufacture, the making of our boots, clothes, flour etc
great electrical development through the Shannon *(expanding*
scheme, the Liffey scheme, the Erne scheme now in
course of construction and the project of using
turf to generate 200 million units at Clonsast
and Brosna .

10. Planned the £99 millions building an construction
programme outlined in the White Paper *and now being operated*

11. Initiated the turf scheme which supplied Irish
homes with fuel during the war years and since, *and the
Rural electrification scheme which will bring power and
light to the farms.*

SOCIAL

1. Established, *entirely* new services such as Unemployment Assistance: Widows and Orphans Pensions: Childrens' Allowances
:Food Subsidies.

2. Doubled the expenditure on Old Age Pensions and increased the number, ~~of pensioners@xxxxPensionarsxx xfrom~~
getting the full pension from 77,800 to 124,000 in *1945-6.*
in 1931

3. Aided the building and reconstruction of 140,000
houses.

4. Increased National Health Benefits and Unemployment
Insurance Benefits substantially.

5. Provided free bread, butter, milk, free footwear and
free fuel for the poor.

6. Initiated or enlarged such schemes as free milk for
needy children, medical attention for those of low incomes, hospital treatment, child welfare, school meals.

7. Initiated an important series of schemes in aid of
T.B. sufferers and their dependents.

8. Increased substantially hospital facilities and
public health services in all parts of the country.

9. Brought the total spent on social services from £4½
millions in 1931-32 to £12,600,000 today.

EDUCATIONAL AND CULTURAL

1. Provided this year £7,141,000 for education --
£4,610,000 in 1931-2

2. Built and reconstruction more than 1,000 ~~xxx~~ *primary* schools

3. Plans the building of 100 more Vocational ~~Schools.~~

and Post Primary schools *@* which have increased from 77
in 1931 to 203 in 1946 with an increase in the number
of teachers of 600 *and of pupils an increase of 3,500*

4.   Increased the salaries of/primary teachers *13,000*

5.   Aided in the increase, *in number* of children at Secondary *t@*
     Schools from 30,004 in 1931 to 42,730 in 1946.

6.   Helped to make university education available to
     fffff 6,360 in 1946 as compared with 4,311 in 1931.

7.   Instituted many new University Scholarships and education
     -al prizes.

8.   Founded the Institute of Advanced Studies

9.   Aided the revival of Irish by such practical help as
     grants for the production of plays, pantomimes, journals,
     books; by university scholarships and special prizes; by
     the great £2 -- now the £5 -- scheme; by grants for the
     Gaelic Oireachtas and for other bodies encouraging Irish;
     by special economic schemes and industries for the Gael-
     tacht and by preference for native speakers in public
     employment.

10. Made substantial increases in the grants to *xxx* uni-
     sities.

GENERAL

1.   Efficient rationing

2.   Price Control.

3.   Reorganisation of tansport

4.   Foundation of a Merchantile Marine.

5.   Improvement of the status, pay and amenities of the
     Army.

6.   Improved ~~conditions and~~ pay for the Garda and
     Civil Servants.

7.   Improved ~~great~~ Ireland's international position, as
     witness ~~increase representation with~~ increased diplomatic/ *(representation*

8.   Extended adult suffrage to local elections

9.   Established new Ministries of Social Welfare and Health.

10. *Established the Labour Court*

11. *Reorganised Irish Insurance,*

CABINET COMMITTEE ON ECONOMIC PLANNING.

Classified list of main matters dealt with.

A. Agriculture, Land Division, Fisheries, etc.

1. Land Commission Operations
2. Afforestation
3. Arterial Drainage
4. Sea and Inland Fisheries
5. Sundry Agricultural Schemes

B. Constructional Works.

1. General Planning of Building Activities
2. Housing
3. Derelict sites
4. Village Halls
5. Construction and repair of Courthouses
6. Hospital Works.
7. Houses for National Teachers and married members of the Gárda Síochána.
8. Married quarters for officers of the Defence Forces.
9. Provision of skilled labour in the building industry.
10. Ports and Harbours
11. Tourist Development
12. Construction of State Buildings.
13. National School Accommodation.
14. Army Works and Buildings.
15. Local Authorities - improvement of urban areas.

C. Education.

1. Revival of Athletics
2. National Theatre
3. Vocational Education
4. Houses for National teachers
5. Training of skilled labour in Building Industry.
6. Educational films
7. Youth organisation
8. National School accommodation.
9. Accommodation for National Museum, etc.
10. Village Halls.

D. Transport, Communications, etc.

1. Civil Aviation
2. Road and Rail Transport.
3. Road Works
4. Telephone Development.

Over/

CDA, P150/2648: Cabinet committee on economic planning, 11 May 1944. The members of this committee were de Valera; Seán T. O'Kelly, Minister for Finance; and Seán Lemass, Minister for Industry and Commerce (and, during the war years, Minister for Supplies). Their task was to begin planning for post-war economic development.

Telegrafa an poist.

Ni mór an fuirm seo vo cur le h-aon fiafruí a véanfar mar geall ar an telegram so.

(This form must accompany any enquiry respecting this telegram.)

C. or B. | Táille le n-íoc | s. d.

C — 103

Oifig Tosnuíte agus Treoraca Seirbíse

46

146 10/7 AM COVENTRY T 87

= MR DEVALERA PRIME MINISTER OF EIRE DUBLIN =

HAVE READ WITH CONSIDERABLE SURPRISE WHAT IS PURPORTI
TO BE A SPEECH RECENTLY MADE BY YOU CRITISING THE LIVI
CONDITIONS IN COVENTRY STOP ASTOUNDED AT SUCH REMARKS
BECAUSE OBVIOUSLY YOU ARE NOT WAWARE OF COVENTRYS
CONDITIONS STOP IT SEEMS A PITY FOR YOU TO HAVE CAUSES
UNHAPPINESS AMONGST YOUR IRISH NATIONALS WHO ARE WORKI
SO HARD HERE. IN SPITE OF DIFFICULT CONDITIONS STOP I
REQUEST YOU WITHDRAW YOUR REMARKS AS THEY EFFECT THIS

Telegrafa an poist.

Ni mór an fuirm seo vo cur le h-aon fiafruí a véanfar mar geall ar an telegram so.

(This form must accompany any enquiry respecting this telegram.)

C. or B. | Táille le n-íoc | s. d.

Oifig Tosnuíte agus Treoraca Seirbíse

4

Mr DeValera Prime Minister of Eire

CITY =

NAI, DT, S11582C: Emigration speech and controversy, August 1951. De Valera delivered speech (the first two pages of which are reproduced on the following pages) at a Fianna Fá function in Galway, after being made aware of a damning report compiled by a social worke Maurice Foley, on the conditions on which Irish emigrants were living in Birmingham. Befor delivering the speech, de Valera informed the Catholic hierarchy that he had instructed the Iris ambassador in London 'to make suitable representations to the British Government' on th matter. During the speech, de Valera singled out the cities of Birmingham, Wolverhampton an Coventry. Many emigrants found his intervention embarrassing and hypocritical. The Mayor c Coventry, Harry Weston, sent this telegram in protest on 30 August 1951.

HARRY WESTON MAYOR CITY OF COVENTRY +

J.5983. Wt.1877—15,000,000. 1/51. muinntir Dollard.

At the Jubilee dinner of the Fianna Fáil Organisation
in Galway last night, Mr. de Valéra, in returning thanks for the
set of volumes of the reproduction of the Book of Kells which
was presented to him, referred to the splendid work
accomplished by Fianna Fáil in the twenty-five years since the
Organisation was founded.   What was of greatest importance
now, however, he said, was not the work already done but the
work that remained to be done in the future.   There was no
reason why, in the next twenty-five years, Fianna Fáil should
not have an even greater record of achievement.

The Taoiseach went on to speak of Ireland's distinctive
national culture and of the artistic and spiritual gifts of
the nation in the golden age when it contributed so much to
western-Euroepan civilisation.   He said that Ireland's aim
today ought to be to work in the same spiritual field and to
win distinction in that field rather than in the material one.
The material side, of course, could not be neglected, but the
current of their aspirations should be directed towards the
spiritual side.   If they were to do this effectively, the fount
would have to be kept pure by the preservation and the
restoration and development of their own language.   Galway and
the western parts of the country had a particular part to play
in this.   Galway, which had been called the capital of the
Gaeltacht, should endeavour in every way to make itself worthy
of that title.

With enthusiasm and effort, Irish could quickly become
once more the language spoken in Galway's streets and the
language of ordinary commerce.

It was the aim of the Government to try to strengthen the
Irish-speaking districts so that the native speakers who were
brought up there might be preserved for the nation, instead of

being compelled to emigrate to find a living.   Material
development was necessary for that, and every department of
State would be pressed to co-operate in the work.

Emigration should be recognised by everybody as having
reached alarming dimensions.   "I have been at some pains", he
said, "to secure the most reliable estimates indicating the
trends in recent years.   The best figures which I have been
able to get indicate that net emigration, which was estimated as
having been 10,000 in the year 1947, went up to 28,000 in the
year 1948, reached 34,000 in the year 1949, and was not less
than 40,000 in the year 1950.   The rate of emigration per
thousand of the population is now more than 50% over what it
was in the period between 1936 and 1946, which includes the war
years."

Continuing, the Taoiseach said: "The saddest part of all
this is that work is available at home, and in conditions
infinitely better from the point of view of both health and
morals.   In many occupations, the rates of wages are higher
at home than they are in Britian.   It is true that, in some
cases, an Irish worker's total earnings in Britain are high,
but this is often due to the fact that the conditions in which
he finds himself obliged to live are so unattractive that he
prefers unduly long hours of overtime to a leisure which he
cannot enjoy.   There is no doubt that many of those who emigrate
could find employment at home at as good, or better, wages - and
with living conditions far better - than they find in Britain.
Moreover, not only do they fail to improve their own circumstances by going abroad, but they leave enterprises for the
development of our own national resources without sufficient
labour to enable progress to be made as rapidly as we would all
desire.

"ᵹuala le ᵹualainn ní claoiᵹean sinn."
" Each for all: All for each"

Cumann ban-Oibre Éireann

IRISH WOMEN WORKERS' UNION

Affiliated to :
The Irish Trade Union Congress,
The Dublin Trades Union Council,
The Labour Party.

Secretaries—
MISS LOUIE BENNETT
MISS HELEN CHENEVIX

Treasurers—
MISS M. CULLEN
MISS E. CROSS

48, FLEET STREET,

DUBLIN.

7th September, 1951.

An Taoiseach,
Leinster House,
Dublin.

A Chara,

My Committee would greatly appreciate an opportunity to put
before you their point of view on certain aspects of the problem
of emigration as it affects women.   They have instructed me to beg
that you will be so good as to receive a deputation representing
our organisation at some convenient date.   They make this request
because they believe that sufficient attention is not given to the
outlook of women upon social and economic affairs and that consequently
the community as a whole is at a disadvantage.

Mise, le meas,

Louie Bennett

Runai.

NAI, DT, S11582D: Louie Bennett to de Valera, 7 September 1951. Bennett seeks a
meeting to discuss the issue of female emigration. Bennett was a labour leader and
suffragist and general secretary of the Irish Women Workers' Union as well as the first
woman to hold the position of president of the Irish Congress of Trade Unions.

'I regret the

modern overwhelming

invasion of science'

UCDA, P150/156: Ever the maths teacher, April 1967. Personal photograph of de Valera with his eldest grandchild, Eamon, in his study at Áras an Uachtaráin. Originally found in an envelope annotated 'The Chief teaching maths to Eamon Viv'.

De Valera had been steeped in the cultural revival of the late nineteenth and early twentieth centuries and its attendant emphasis on the Irish language. In an interview published in the *New York Journal* in October 1957, he was asked by the interviewer which event he thought would have the most profound effect on Ireland's progress during the years ahead. He answered, 'Restoration of Irish as the ordinary spoken language. The Irish language was the bond which effectively preserved us as a distinct nation through all the vicissitudes of the past and is its best guarantee of preservation in the future'.[1] He also stated, on a number of occasions, that the aim of restoring the Irish language as a spoken language would, if it were necessary to make a choice, take precedence over the policy of reunification.

The focus on the language sometimes caused resentment, anger and derision. An uncomfortable relationship with the Irish language was even reflected in Sinéad de Valera's description of how their marriage ceremony was performed in Irish by a priest who was clearly incompetent in the language, as a result of which 'he married us three or four times before he got the words right'.[2]

When in power, de Valera put considerable pressure on UCD to facilitate Irish-language lectures. Fianna Fáil governments were building on a state Irish language policy in the 1920s that 'did little to elevate Irish but much to demean education',[3] and Thomas Derrig, Minister for Education from 1932 until 1948 (with the exception of 1939–40 when de Valera briefly held the position), 'bitterly and successfully resisted demands for an inquiry, even from the teachers themselves, into the effectiveness of the official approach'. Whatever about his personal devotion, de Valera was unable to bring his ministers with him by getting them to speak Irish regularly.[4] According to Todd Andrews, de Valera also suffered from a lack of confidence about his own command of Irish.[5] A crisis overtook the language movement in the 1940s and Terence Brown has suggested that 'the revivalists were right to detect in Mr de Valera a lack of immediate zeal'.[6]

In 1966 when de Valera was president and visited Cape Clear Island, off Baltimore in Co. Cork, the island priest complained bitterly that the Gardaí on duty did not speak Irish: 'They had not as much as one word of Irish between them, nor did they speak it while they were there. Not only that, but they were actually opposing Irish and poking fun at those who were speaking it'. Adding insult to injury, they reputedly told the locals: 'You are only speaking Irish for today'. Their bad behaviour, he contended, was 'a source of scandal and shame'. Suggesting that the Minister for Justice, Brian Lenihan, should send a letter to the Garda Depot, he added that 'you had better translate it into English for them, because apparently it is unlikely they will understand Irish'.[7] The letter led to a two month Garda investigation and the interviewing of the accused Gardaí who denied the allegations. The priest subsequently withdrew most of his allegations, but he had hardly created his smoke without a fair degree of fire.

Brian Fallon's account of Irish culture from the 1930s to the 1960s—in his book *An age of innocence*—disputes the idea of the country as a cultural wasteland, highlights an impressive range of artistic vibrancy and dismisses the image of Ireland as 'a chauvinistic statelet shutting its doors and windows on international currents'.[8] But de Valera's critics over the years have castigated his narrow intellectual priorities, often in a quite personal way. Writing about the Irish short story craft in the 1930s and 1940s—as practised by Frank O'Connor, Mary Lavin and Seán O'Faoláin—Terence Brown presents their concerns as a direct counterpoint to de Valera's vision: 'Instead of de Valera's Gaelic Eden and the uncomplicated satisfactions of Ireland free, the writers revealed a mediocre, dishevelled, often neurotic and depressed petit-bourgeois society that atrophied for want of a liberating idea'.[9]

The novelist, John Banville, wrote of what he saw as a mean-spirited time, referring to the Ireland that de Valera presided over as:

> a demilitarised totalitarian state in which the lives of the citizens were to be controlled not by a system of coercive force and secret policing, but by a kind of applied spiritual paralysis maintained by an unofficial federation between the Catholic clergy, the Judiciary and the civil service. Essential to this enterprise in social engineering was the policy of intellectual isolationism which de Valera imposed on the country ... as far as the de Valeran state is concerned, there are no adults.[10]

This impression of de Valera being largely responsible for imposing censorship cannot withstand scrutiny, particularly given that the main censorship legislation dated from the 1920s, and was supported by politicians generally. Peter Martin noted in relation to the censorship of publications legislation being debated in 1928 that 'at this time Fianna Fáil had no time in gaining the gratitude of intellectuals ... by supporting measures such as censorship, the party made it harder for Cosgrave to pose as the champion of the Catholic nation'.[11]

Perhaps this was also the reason why de Valera in 1930 unwisely backed the campaign to insist on a Catholic librarian in Mayo during the infamous row over the Mayo Library Committee's refusal to appoint Letitia Dunbar Harrison, a Protestant—'an unguarded reaction from the normally cautious de Valera'.[12] In contrast, by the time of the Fethard-on-Sea boycott in 1957, when Protestant businesses were targeted because the Protestant wife of a Catholic man refused to send their children to the local Catholic school, he showed courage, when in July he dismissed the boycott and left no ambiguity as to where he stood on the matter:

> I can only say, from what has appeared in public, that I regard this boycott as ill-conceived, ill-considered and futile for the achievement of the purpose for which it seems to have been intended; that I regard it as unjust and cruel to confound the innocent with the guilty; that I repudiate any suggestion that this boycott is typical of the attitude or conduct of our people.[13]

De Valera had also resisted pressure, when drafting the Constitution, to make the circulation of 'offensive' material unconstitutional, as demanded by the Jesuit priest, Fr Edward Cahill, though the article concerning civil liberties (Article 40.6) maintained that civil liberties could only be guaranteed 'subject to public order and morality',[14] which de Valera envisaged would be decided by the Oireachtas rather than by judicial review. The qualifications were intended, probably, to ensure that the courts would not overrule the state.

The issue of censorship for de Valera seems to have been one of practical politics and managing the various lobbies and critics. While it is true that a motion was proposed at the Fianna Fáil Ard Fheis in 1932 that 'steps be taken to prevent the spread of anti-Irish and anglicising propaganda through the medium of the foreign daily papers', which was adopted by the national executive, the following year, after meeting a delegation headed by the Fr Cahill, de Valera questioned the practicality of a stricter censorship scheme and told him pointedly that Roman Catholics were not united on the issue of censorship.[15]

In 1937 rather than meeting a delegation headed by another Jesuit priest, Fr Richard Devane, seeking a government inquiry on cinema to alter film censorship, he instead set up an interdepartmental inquiry into the viability of a National Film Institute 'which would encourage, educate and help fund large-scale productions on standard film'.[16] He was also far-sighted in his use of the radio—or as Clair Wills put it 'alert to the potential of the medium'—and in 1932 was able to broadcast to the Irish diaspora for the first time as a result of the new more powerful transmitters, the use of which he had encouraged. He made the annual St Patrick's Day broadcast his own and this did much to keep his profile high in the United States, in particular, as he sought to maintain the sympathy of the diaspora 'as well as putting the Irish point of view to the American public at large'.[17]

De Valera also brought to fruition the Irish Folklore Commission in 1935, which grew to be a substantial archive of written, oral and visual material. The folk stories gathered by voluntary collectors were numbered and arranged in chronological order, and by the 1970s there were almost 1,900 volumes in the folklore archives at UCD. One of the largest and richest collections in the world, it houses folk-tales in both Irish and English the equivalent of which have been lost in many other countries.[18]

The Dublin Institute for Advanced Studies (DIAS), established in 1940, was regarded as 'a landmark of its kind'[19] where Erwin Schrödinger became Director of the School of Theoretical Physics. It was also a result of de Valera using office to promote his favourite subjects, and its School of Theoretical Physics was established despite the opposition of Fine Gael TDs who believed that it would have a negative impact on the universities. But it also came into existence as a result of de Valera's disappointment that many postgraduates in Celtic studies were disappearing into the civil service or private businesses rather than furthering their research, which was why the DIAS, on the suggestion of the Irish Studies Committee of the Royal Irish Academy, incorporated a School of Celtic Studies.[20]

De Valera took his post as Chancellor of the National University of Ireland (NUI), a position he held from 1921 to 1975, very seriously and his attendance at the NUI senate meetings was exemplary; he attended, for example, all nine meetings that were held in 1935 despite pressure of government business. He was also well-disposed towards Trinity College Dublin, and gave money for the repair of the college's historic buildings. Donal McCartney's tribute to de Valera in relation to his attitude to third-level education was fulsome; he did not allow party politics to interfere with matters academic, and 'he set aside pennies from a poor state and an impoverished people for the cultivation of things of the mind'.[21] Such a conclusion, arguably, was true in relation to his individual pet projects at third level, but may be regarded as an exaggeration in general terms.

In terms of the media, the *Irish Press* newspaper, which he established in 1931, became a forum for many outstanding journalists. When researching his study of *De Valera and the Ulster question*, in the absence of a body of archival material, John Bowman observed: 'I feel a special debt to the political reporters on Irish newspapers for their accurate and fair-minded chronicling of Irish politics. This is especially noteworthy in the case of the *Irish Press*— founded after all by de Valera—and so often pilloried as the "kept paper" of the Fianna Fáil party'.[22]

It would be an exaggeration, however, to see de Valera as a great patron of the arts and culture; he was biased towards his own interests, particularly mathematics, Irish language and history, and the classics. A fascination with mathematics, which had provided him with his initial income as a teacher in Carysfort and elsewhere, clearly never left him, and was put to use in his politics as well. His problem-solving approach probably also contributed to his patience and stubbornness in negotiating.

He did take an interest in the Arts Council after its formation in 1951, and was influenced in particular by the Minister for Posts and Telegraphs, P.J. Little. De Valera drafted the guidelines for the council in its early years and wanted to see visual arts and industrial art championed rather than music and drama; he was not a regular visitor to the Abbey Theatre or the National Gallery.[23] He was more likely to be found peering into a bog than admiring a painting; in the 1930s he approved funding to the Royal Irish Academy for the first proper palaeobotanical study of how the peatlands developed, and came to peer into the excavations in Ballybetagh Bog, south of Dublin; his son Ruairí became an archaeologist and an expert on Neolithic tombs, while his daughter Máirín became a botanist.[24]

De Valera was quite stubborn about what constituted Irish culture; Gearóid Ó Crualaoich has highlighted 'the centrality of ancient tradition in official cultural ideology' during his time in power, and he argued that the concomitant emphasis on folk tradition served to 'mask and mute' the actual cultural history of Ireland.[25] In the early 1940s de Valera commissioned a history of the Famine with a grant of £1,500 offered by the government to prominent historians working on the project. It eventually appeared in 1956, but de Valera was unhappy with it 'presumably because it seemed to downplay those aspects of the tragedy that had been etched in his own memory' and indeed, the stories he had been told by his grandmother about the Famine.[26] The folk-memory, he seemed to believe, had been usurped by the viewpoint of the administration and those seeking to deal with the Famine 'from above'.

In May 1960 de Valera drafted a reply to Professor William Bedell Stanford, regarding the professor's inquiry as to whether he had ever turned to classical literature for moral strength in times of trouble. He replied that he:

> was not a good enough Classical scholar for that. I cannot now remember any occasion on which any such passages came consciously before my mind or had any such direct influence as is suggested in your question, except one. It was this.

> One evening in Dartmore [*sic*], my fellow prisoners and I were being marched from the workshop to our cells. ...

> As I was about to mount the iron stairs leading to the overhanging corridors, unto which our cells opened, the phrase, '*forsan et haec olim meminisse juvabit*' flashed in some extraordinary way across my mind. How it came I have never been able to understand, for I had not been at all thinking of the Classics, even remotely. My studies in prison had been Irish and Mathematics. The effect of the phrase, however, was magical. Before I reached the top of the stairs it was as if I had been changed into another person. I was completely renewed in energy and spirit. Looking back I have always regarded this experience as one of the most extraordinary happenings in my life.

> It is not, however, in exceptional incidents like this that the influence of the Classics is to be sought. Rather is it that they leave a lasting impression, moulding the outlook and character of those who study them. ...

> I regret the modern overwhelming invasion of science accordingly. The classics and science together helped to make the all-round man. Science alone will, I fear, leave us lop-sided, until time, once more, brings a true balance.[27]

If an issue was raised that attracted his interest, de Valera seemed to spend time pondering and researching it, and went to some lengths to seek an answer, suggesting a lively and curious intellect. Two letters, for example, discovered in 2000 in the Mountmellick Parish archives, contain the inner thoughts of de Valera on the morality of taxation, as he responded to a query from a Portarlington priest, Fr Thomas Burbage. (Burbage had served as chaplain to republican prisoners at the British internment camp at Ballykinlar, Co. Down, during the War of Independence.) In 1942 he wrote to de Valera questioning the morality of paying income tax, as it was 'a penal measure'. In July 1942 de Valera promised that he would spend time investigating the question: 'As I am by no means a theologian, I will have the whole question looked into'.

The following year, his homework on this subject completed, he replied, referring to the four volumes of Davis's *Moral and pastoral theology*:[28] 'I have read Davis's treatment and I am afraid he has not dealt specifically with the point you made. After reading him, and some reflection of my own on the matter I see no reason to change the general view which I expressed'. De Valera's view was that:

> just laws passed by a legitimate government in the interest of the community, i.e. for the common good, had behind them, quite irrespective of any intention of the legislator in that regard, a moral sanction. …
>
> Personally, I dislike the idea of the human legislator being able to add by express intent, and possibly, arbitrarily, a moral sanction over and above whatever sanction follows implicitly from the natural or the Divine law.[29]

He also devoted time and thought to leisure and sport. Although the product of the era that spawned the Gaelic Athletic Association (GAA), de Valera's preference was for rugby rather than Gaelic football, and he showed courage during his career in relation to the GAA's ban on 'foreign games', a prohibition he thought unnecessary and counterproductive. He caused considerable controversy in April 1957 by criticising the ban, nearly fifteen years before the GAA eventually scrapped Rule 27 in 1971.

At the beginning of his last term as Taoiseach, he addressed the fourth annual dinner of the Southern Branch of Blackrock College Past Pupils Union held in Shannon Airport. As reported in the *Irish Independent*, in the presence of about 70 guests, de Valera left no room for ambiguity, having acknowledged that he had not been at a rugby match since 1913 because he did not want it to be raised as a political matter, but he contended that 'for Irishmen there is no football game to match rugby and if all our young men played rugby not only would we beat England and Wales, but France and the whole lot of them together'.[30] The *Irish Press*, however, gave an account of the meeting without disclosing his comments.[31]

Nonetheless, it was taken up by a few journalists; the *Manchester Guardian*, which referred to de Valera furtively listening to radio broadcasts of rugby matches in the privacy of his own home, wondered if:

> now as an elder statesman who has won decisively what probably is his last election he has rebelled. Is it too much to hope that such an intelligent patriot in his last years will now, having taken the first step, do service to his countrymen by exposing a lot more nonsense which still is, for political reasons, considered by too many part of the basic creed of all true Irishmen?[32]

Inevitably, the GAA was asked to respond to the Taoiseach's remarks and the GAA president Seamus McFerran responded by 'noting with satisfaction' that de Valera had not been at a rugby game since 1913. He insisted that it was well-known that de Valera 'rates hurling supreme among all games', and criticised the media for not making more of the remarks that de Valera had made on the same night expressing regret that hurling was no longer being played at Blackrock College. The Blackrock College Union also released a statement insisting the same, but on his journey back to Dublin, the Taoiseach had stopped at Nenagh where he was thanked for his comments by the Nenagh Ormond Rugby team.[33] The *Gaelic Weekly* took de Valera to task, stating that his views had 'shocked and affronted' members of the GAA: 'Apart from its excellence as a sport, our national game *should not* be discredited in this manner—by innuendo, or otherwise—by any Irishman, particularly by any national leader'.[34]

De Valera felt obliged to clarify his comments in a personal letter to Padraig Ó Caoimh, the general secretary of the GAA:

> My views are very simple. I am in favour of all outdoor games. I think they make for the health and vigour of our young people. ...
>
> The one thing that is wrong, in my opinion, is that the GAA should continue to maintain the ban. ...
>
> ... If Ireland is to match herself in football and play with the national teams from England, Wales, Scotland and from France it must be in rugby or soccer, as at present. ...
>
> I do not think that under present conditions there need be any fear that the national spirit of the GAA players who would

also play rugby would be lessened by contact with those who played rugby alone. …

P.S. As regards my remark about refraining from attending a rugby match, my reason for doing so was that I did not think my assertion of my personal right to do so would be worth the fuss, the misrepresentation, and the necessary explanations to which it would give rise.[35]

Ten years later, when, with Frank Aiken, he was in conversation with the British ambassador Andrew Gilchrist, he told him, 'For my part I have always preferred Rugby' despite Frank Aiken making the case for Gaelic football being the best field game.[36]

UCDA, P150/2743: De Valera listening to an address of welcome from a crowd of Aran Islanders, July 1947. Labelled on reverse 'Aran 1947. On right Mrs Gerald Bartley [wife of Gerald Bartley, Fianna Fáil TD for Galway West, 1932–61]'.

UCDA, P150/93: Appointment as National University Chancellor, 20 November 1921. De Valera arriving for the ceremony with individuals identified on reverse as Prof. William F.P. Stockley (Professor of English, University College Cork); Rev. Prof. Timothy J. Corcoran S.J. (Professor of Education, UCD); Prof. Henry N. Walsh (Professor of Civil Engineering, UCC); and Prof. Matthew J. Conran (Professor of Mathematics, UCC).

UCDA, P150/3409: Irish Aer Corps aerial photograph of crowds awaiting de Valera's arrival at Cape Clear Island, 24 July 1966. De Valera visited the island (Oileán Chléire) to open a new Irish College. The president travelled on an Aer Lingus flight to Cork and took an Aer Corps helicopter to the island.

Not issued state to
President Stanford 23/5/60
Prof. Stanford gave substance
and gave substance
of this letter
over the phone
to him.

BAILE ÁTHA CLIATH
(DUBLIN)

22nd May, 1960

Dear Professor Stanford,

Miss O'Kelly has told you that I received your letter.

I was very sorry that I did not have an opportunity of a chat with you after dinner on Thursday, the 12th instant. I wanted to thank you for your presentation address. The Latin was much admired by many who could be regarded as competent critics, and as for the substance, I can only say that everyone must agree that the terms in which you referred to me were more than generous, and I thank you.

As regards the passages from Horace: I met them first when studying the texts prescribed for the Middle and Senior grades of the old "Intermediate" examinations, and, later, those for the Undergraduate courses in the Royal University. I brushed them up again, in preparation for the orals of the Trinity Freshmen Examinations. My examiners were, I think, Professors Culverwell and Alton, the late Provost. I had committed to memory the passages, to which you refer, as an easy way of identifying certain Horatian meters. I would like to think now that this was not the only reason!

Your question, whether recollection of passages from the Greek or Latin authors were "a source of strength or encouragement" to me "in times of danger or crisis": I am afraid I was not a good enough Classical scholar for that. I cannot now remember any occasion on which any such passages came consciously before my mind or had any such direct influence as is suggested in your question, except one. It was this.

One evening in Dartmore, my fellow prisoners and I were being marched from the workshop to our cells. The weather was warm, and after some hours spent in the routine monotonous work of stitching mail-bags I felt unusually tired and weary in spirit. I was sure that many of my companions were also very weary.

As I was about to mount the iron stairs leading to the overhanging corridors, unto which our cells opened, the phrase, "forsan et haec olim meminisse juvabit" flashed in some extraordinary way across my mind. How it came I have never been able to understand, for I had not been at all thinking of the Classics, even remotely. My studies in prison had been Irish and Mathematics. The effect of the phrase, however, was magical. Before I reached the top of the stairs it was as if I had been changed into another person. I was completely renewed in energy and spirit. Looking back I have always regarded this experience as one of the most extraordinary happenings in my life.

It is not, however, in exceptional incidents like this that the influence of the Classics is to be sought.

P.T.O.

(2)

Rather is it that they leave a lasting impression,
moulding the outlook and character of those who study
them.   Young minds are affected far more than is
generally appreciated, I believe, when they come upon
noble thoughts suitably expressed.   The old headline
copy-books, even, were valuable in this way.   The
maxims they contained persisted as guides of conduct
through life.   It is here that the teacher, particularly
the Classical teacher,has his opportunity, if he is
enthusiastic and avails of it.

There is no doubt that the teacher of
Latin and Greek have great opportunities.   At one
period I had a wonderful teacher of Greek.   I still
remember vividly how inspiring he made the drama, as
given in the Phaedo, of Socrates' death.

I regret the modern overwhelming invasion
of science accordingly.   The Classics and science
together helped to make the all-round man.   Science
alone will, I fear, leave us lop-sided, until time, once
more, brings a true balance.

Now that I have dictated all this I think
the subject is one I should talk to you about, not write
about, and so, instead of sending this letter to you,
I will turn to the phone.

A Phádhraic, a chara,

In view of your uniform courtesy at Croke Park
and on many other occasions I would not like you to misunderstand
my reported remarks at the recent Blackrock Union Dinner.

My views are very simple.   I am in ffavour of all out-
door games.   I think they make for the health and vigour of our young
people.   They provide enjoyable recreation and brighten country life.
Team games are the most valuable of all.   Without damping individual
initiative they teach the value of and give practice in combined
effort for agreed objectives.

If I had my way I would have a sports club with a
sports field established in every parish.   The work that the G.A.A. has
done and ix doing in this respect, apart from what it has done to
encourage a true national spirit, is beyond praise.   The one thing
that is wrong, in my opinion, is that the G.A.A., should continue to
maintain the ban.   There was reason for this at the time when ascendancy
influence and a certain tendency towards   had to be
countered.   I do not think that that is necessary today, particularly
in this part of the country.   Moreover, the supremacy of the G.A.A.
is so well established that the protection it might have needed in its
infancy is no longer required.

Aptitudes for particular games and the consequent
enthusiasm and likings for special games vary with the individual.
Anything that tends to restrict individuals from playing games for which
they feel themselves specially fitted or which they like particularly
should, if possible, be avoided, and such a thing as bans taboo.

For a number of reasons rugby is a favourite game with
some of our secondary boarding schools.   In some of them it has been
established by a long tradition,and generation after generation of students
engage in the game with enthusiasm, and follow the fortunes of their
team during the season with constant interest.   I think it a pity when
the season is over that such students should be debarred from turning

over to hurling as their summer game.

The ban has this other consequence to which I was referring
when I spoke at the Blackrock Dinner .   With soccar and rugby
established in the international field I think it unlikely that we
can succeed in getting hurling and Gaelic football into that field,
except where our own are established, as for example in some of the
cities of Britain and the United States.   If Ireland is to match
herself in football and play with the national teams from England,
Wales, Scotland and from France it must be in rugby or soccar, as at
present.   We are a relatively small nation in numbers, some four and
one third millions,in comparison with countries with a population of
twenty, thirty millions and so on.   We have, therefore, much fewer to
pick from, and we ought not to do anything which tends to restrict the
field.   Many who play Gaelic football would, if the ban did not prevent
them, be inclined to play rugby also.   And, I have not the slightest
doubt that if this were permitted our successes in the international
field would be outstanding, and our prestige abroad enhanced.

I do not think that under present conditions there
need be any fear that the national spirit of the G.A.A. players who
would also play rugby would be lessened by contact with those who played
rugby alone.   I would imagine that instead the introduction of the
Gaelic players would bring a strong national spirit to the rugby ranks.
I know that in the Partitioned area one could not be so sure of this,
but I think that even there the result would be beneficial.

As you know, I played Gaelic and hurling as a boy.   I
have no feeling of antagonism against Gaelic football, and as for hurling
I think it one of the ~~xxxxxxxxxxxxxxxxx~~ finest of the manly games.
It is distinctively our national game, and I have never seen a visitor
from other countries who ~~xxxx~~ was not thrilled at watching a good match.
I do not hide from myself that I may be somewhat prejudiced.   My
enthusiasm for rugby which was developed during my time in Rockwell

and Blackrock.   But these are my views and I simply give them to you
as such.   They are, of course, purely personal and, as I indicated at the
Decent Dinner, without any wider significance.

Sincerely yours,

P.S., As regards my remark about refraining from attending a rugby
match, my reason for doing so was that I did not think my assertion
of my personal right to do so would be worth the fuss, the misrepresentation,
and the necessary explanations to which it would give rise.

XIV

'I have had all the things

that in a human way

make for happiness.'

UCDA, P150/136: As a young couple in the US, 1920. De Valera and Sinéad in Plattsburg, New York, taken during his 1919–20 mission to the US when he was visited by his wife in August and September 1920.

M ore intimate material from his own and other archives has also provided an opportunity to view de Valera as a lover, a husband, a father, a grandfather and a colleague of humour and warmth. He and Sinéad had seven children together: Vivion, Máirín, Eamonn, Brian, Ruairí, Emer and Terry, the youngest, born in 1922. There is only one photograph of the entire family, taken at Cross Avenue, Blackrock, in July 1935. Tragically, the following year, Brian was killed in a horse-riding accident at the Phoenix Park in Dublin. Although an inconsolable Sinéad could never bring herself to visit his grave at Glasnevin, de Valera visited it every Sunday for a number of years thereafter.[1]

In December 2000 Gardaí seized 24 love letters from de Valera to his wife Sinéad, which were being advertised for auction, it being understood that they were stolen in the mid 1970s from the de Valera family home. The owners, who had bought them in England some years previously in an effort to ensure their return to Ireland, were unaware that they had been stolen. De Valera wrote the letters between 1911 and 1920 from Mountjoy Jail, Lincoln Jail, from the US during his mission there from 1919–20, and five letters were written from Tawin Island, off the coast of Galway where he ran a Gaelic League college during the summers 1911–13.[2] The letters, in which he often appears vulnerable and regretful about the impact of his absences on the intimacy between them, include references to his acute physical longing for Sinéad; the desire to press his wife close to his body and heart; and the frustration caused by their separation.

The publicity surrounding the uncovering of the letters caused quite a stir because they seemed to offer a previously unopened window to the private de Valera, for many, 'the epitome of joyless rectitude'; journalist Cian Ó hÉigeartaigh noted wryly, 'Just when we were getting used to the idea that our parents had sex and enjoyed it, a further imaginative effort is called for'.[3]

Here we see de Valera as a young husband, (he and Sinéad were married in 1910) struggling with aspects of his personality and his public life that made it difficult for him to be the husband he would like to have been. In January 1917, writing from Lewes Jail, he promised if he and Sinéad were reunited that he would make her happier than she had been before, acknowledging that she had suffered emotionally due to his unconscious selfishness. When away at political functions he also wrote to her apologetically about complaints he had made over inconsequential issues when at home, which he tended to regret subsequently. He also frankly acknowledged that in the early years of their marriage he sometimes struggled with emotional intimacy. When they were apart he stored up countless things to say to her, but when re-united with Sinéad he found it difficult to articulate these feelings, and wondered if she understood his dilemma in this regard.[4]

Sinéad probably did understand; their marriage endured almost 65 years, but the letters raised intriguing questions about the contrast between the private man and the public figure. The diary entries of Harry Boland, when in the United States with de Valera, as recounted by David Fitzpatrick, also bear witness to his constant sadness at being parted from his family, and being 'very lonely for home and children'.[5]

De Valera's personal correspondence was often warm and sensitive, and the personal material in his archives is at odds with the common perception of him as a public figure whose domination was expressed 'through aloofness rather than bonhomie'.[6] He was devastated by the death of Harry Boland in August 1922 during the Civil War, and referred to him as the 'dearest friend I had on earth'.[7] The papers of his personal secretary, Kathleen O'Connell, at UCD Archives, School of History and Archives, include a pocket diary recording certain events during the Civil War, which included an entry for 4 August 1922: 'Kathy [a sister of Kevin Barry] told him of H's death. He felt it terribly—crushed and broken. He lost his most faithful friend. We travelled in silence all the way to Clonmel'.[8]

His correspondence with Kathleen O'Connell was warm and sensitive (handwritten notes were to 'Dear K'); her assistance to de Valera was invaluable in his early years, and even more so later, as 'even in the most secret and confidential matters, she had become his eyesight'.[9] When in Utrecht for an eye operation in October 1952 he wrote her a letter which indicated that he was aware of the illness that was to result in her death a few years later, and perhaps, was conscious of his own health problems:

> You know how I wish you every happiness. We have been a third of a century now working together—no short spell. It is too much to hope that the partnership will not be severed before the

half-century could come around. Our spells of life are usually not given for such long periods. We can rejoice at what we have seen done at the heart of which you can feel that you have played no small part.[10]

His feelings about her death and his human situation generally were recorded as follows in April 1956, making a particular mention of his grandchildren, with whom he had an affectionate and close relationship:

> I have had a wonderful life. At the outset I want to thank God for it. I have not achieved the things I would have wished to achieve, but I have achieved more than I ever would have dreamed of—dared to dream of—as a boy or as a youth. I have had all the things that in a human way make for happiness. Good health, strength, the best woman in the world as wife; children of whom I can be justly proud and grandchildren a daily source of joy in my advancing years. And a firm belief in the life to come … In my life I have had as co-workers some of the finest people that God has made—noble, devoted, loyal. I am writing this a few days after we have laid to rest one who has worked with me for more than a third of a century. One who has shared I had almost said my most intimate thoughts, so far as they were concerned with public affairs.[11]

O'Connell's niece, Marie O'Kelly, became de Valera's new personal secretary.

Any perusal of de Valera's personal correspondence reveals a wealth of detail on a man who stirred very strong feelings of affection in people; someone who was capable of great charm and empathy and who commanded the loyalty of colleagues with whom he could often disagree. In a letter from Seán MacEntee to Marie O'Kelly, a few days after de Valera's death in 1975, the grieving MacEntee wrote simply: 'He set a standard in public conduct and private behaviour that those around him were led by his example to emulate. And with it all, he was so simple, so human, so merry and full of fun. … a human being who was infinitely loveable'.[12]

In 2004 Michael Fitzgerald, Professor of Child and Adolescent Psychiatry at Trinity College Dublin, claimed that de Valera suffered from the neurobiological disorder, Asperger's syndrome. This condition is a particular form of autism characterised by poor social skills, a lack of empathy, narrow or obsessive interests and an unusual sense of humour, eccentricity, childishness, but in some cases, genius or decidedly above-average intelligence.

The book he co-authored with Antoinette Walker, *Unstoppable brilliance*, claimed that:

> as with all Asperger geniuses, however, de Valera was unmistakably flawed. He could be both innovative and archly conservative, sincere and devious, sensitive yet lacking in empathy, erratic and consistent, pontifical and provincial, pragmatic and absolutist. His innate dignity was matched with toughness; asceticism with materialism; charisma with coldness.[13]

The difficulty with this list is that it could be applied to many electorally successful politicians. The authors continued: 'The sum of these contradictions led many to conclude that de Valera was either mad or a genius. Indeed, the Irish peer Lord Granard declared that de Valera was "on the borderline between genius and insanity": a typical assessment of an Asperger genius'[14] (or maybe the typical assessment of an Irish peer!).

As evidence of the condition, the authors offered a number of examples of his personal traits and mannerisms, including 'flashing eyes', 'a lurching gait', his preoccupation with mathematics, reading of detective novels, his exceptional capacity for concentration, outstanding leadership skills (including 'absolute conviction and inflexibility') and 'his narrow mindedness and stringent personal moral code'.

They also mentioned his repetitive use of language; in meetings with Lloyd George, he constantly returned to 'the same few dominating notions' (surely this, too, was clever politics, rather than being 'classically autistic'?!), but the authors also acknowledged that at times 'his message came across as direct, simple and burningly sincere'.[15]

The authors also maintain that he 'often took only a passive interest in his family'. Surely, again, this often came with the territory of being Taoiseach? As Garret FitzGerald, son of Desmond, a government minister in the 1920s with Cumann na nGaedheal, recalled in 2004, 'Because of the change of government in 1932, however Terry [de Valera's son] saw less of his father in childhood and I saw more of mine'.[16] Despite this fact, Terry's memoir records a father who was good-natured and humorous, who enjoyed laughter and playful banter with his wife.[17]

While the authors of *Unstoppable brilliance* acknowledge that de Valera was often humorous, with a close-knit group of friends, they maintain that he 'could not understand the motivations or perspectives of others'. This portrait of de Valera, while interesting from a psychological point of view, is too inconsistent and too heavily qualified to be convincing, and the impression is created that the authors, working only from secondary-published work, with no reference to his personal papers or intimate correspondence, are too keen to fit de Valera into an already decided category.

References to 'his degree of autistic aggression' could just as well be the description of a man single-minded in his preoccupation with politics, and perhaps one of the most glaring qualifications is the following: 'Although ... people with Asperger's syndrome rarely compromise, de Valera was forced to do so in order to avoid the end to his political career'.[18] They also acknowledge that 'as de Valera grew in international stature, he came to handle criticism more adroitly'.

The conclusion of the authors hardly bolsters their case:

> It is impossible to paint a single picture of de Valera because his personality was multi-faceted and he was different things to different people. In essence, he exhibited the kind of identity diffusion found in those with Asperger's syndrome. There is strong evidence to suggest that he lacked a coherent sense of self and was obsessed with matters of self, race and place throughout his life—much like Joyce. Inevitably, this was underpinned by a combination of insecurity and egotism.[19]

Again the problem with this description is that it could read, not as an assessment of Asperger's syndrome, but as an assessment of a revolutionary generation who sought to forge a degree of independence, and having achieved it, to keep it.

Interestingly, the authors also quote a damning and oft-cited judgment from W.B. Yeats (another person they identify with Asperger's syndrome) to the effect that de Valera was 'all propaganda, no human life ... He will fail through not having enough human life to judge the human life in others'.[20] But the truth was that Yeats, like many others, had an abstract view of de Valera, but then changed his mind when he met him. In August 2004 Oxford academic, John Kelly, reminded the audience at the Yeats International Summer School that Yeats and de Valera met for the first time in 1933 to discuss Yeats's concern about the Fianna Fáil government's intentions towards the Abbey Theatre in terms of censorship and control.

They chatted for an hour and afterwards Yeats admitted in a letter to Olivia Shakespear that he had been pleasantly surprised: 'I had never met him before and I was impressed by his simplicity and honesty though we differed throughout. It was a curious experience, each recognised the other's point of view so completely. I had gone there full of suspicion, but my suspicion vanished at once'. De Valera assured him that the government would not interfere with the Abbey Theatre.[21]

Yeats had in fact spoken supportively of de Valera's policies when in America at the end of 1932, as commented by Roy Foster, particularly in the context of de Valera's conduct of Anglo–Irish relations, and he articulated sympathy for him that also conveyed pride. In an address to an American audience, Yeats compared de Valera to Jonathan Swift, as representing a nation's 'turbulent self-assertion', as good a summary as any. Yeats's perception of Fianna Fáil as a welcome breath of fresh air in Irish politics is reinforced by a note in his journal in the summer of 1933: 'What I have seen of the present government I get a sense of vigour and sincerity, very unlike the old government party in the Senate, who left upon the mind an impression of something warm, damp and soiled, middle class democracy at its worst'.[22]

But for others, 'middle-class democracy at its worst' was precisely what de Valera came to represent, the longer that he was in power. Seán O'Faoláin's portrait of him in 1945 acknowledged that he was a realist ('if to be a shrewd politician is to be a realist he is one'), but criticised his procrastinations and slowness in making political decisions, his lack of sophistication ('a tendency to think along the simplest traditional lines'), and his use of 'meaningless clichés' in relation to partition.[23]

In terms of the wider perception of de Valera, the British government discovered relatively quickly in the 1930s that de Valera was a man that they could do business with, but suspicions in other quarters lingered, as did the tendency to depict him as a dictator-in-waiting. As revealed by Eunan O'Halpin, the British security service opened a personal file on de Valera in 1917 and maintained it until 1975, their first specifically Irish file. The file includes a report compiled in 1943 by the Secret Intelligence Service's man in Ireland, Captain C.S. Collinson, the head of the British Travel Permit Office in Dublin:

> The legendary Eamon de Valera desires to appear a Simon Pure Patriot with a single idea. He is conceived of as a twentieth century democratic leader whose record has never been spoiled by deviation from first principles. Fanatical but honest is another view. So skilfully has this fiction been fostered that to many it would be considered a travesty of the ideal to hold him up as he really is—a peculiarly astute politician with a strict economy of truth who by no stretch of the imagination is a democrat.[24]

Undoubtedly, he often bored his antagonists, including David Lloyd George, James Craig, and J.H. Thomas, the British dominions secretary, with his long accounts of the grievances of Irish history. But over the course of his career, there were many others who found that their initial trepidations about de Valera disappeared once they had actually met him in person, including Ian MacLennan who became British ambassador to Ireland in 1960. MacLennan was, after he met him, in his own words 'completely taken by him as a personality'.[25] According to Frank Pakenham, even Winston Churchill began to show him 'respectful attention' and got 'quite excited' about receiving him in Downing Street in 1953. Pakenham's own admiration for him was based on the impression that he always expressed 'an inflexible sense of universal values rather than any narrow nationalism'.[26]

UCDA, P150/147: Sixtieth wedding anniversary, January 1970. Official black and white press photograph of Eamon and Sinéad de Valera on their diamond wedding anniversary. © Irish Press.

UCDA, P150/145: Three generations of de Valeras, October 1970. De Valera, Sinéad, their children and grandchildren, outside Áras an Uachtaráin. Taken to celebrate his eightieth birthday. Autographed by de Valera and Sinéad. © Irish Press.

Sinead de Valera

n de Valera.

UCDA, P150/75: De Valera with boatmen on the beach at Tawin Island, 1911/12. De Valera was director of the Irish language summer school on the island in Co. Galway, between 1910 and 1912.

Utrecht,
Thursday 2/10/52

Dear Kathleen,

When I came here first
I thought I might be home for the 5th As
that is not now possible the only way I
can give you my good wishes is through
this. You know how I wish you every
happiness. We have been a third of
a century now working together — no short spell.
It is too much to hope that the partnership
will not be revised before the half-century
could come round. Our spells of life are
usually not given for such long periods.
We can rejoice at what we have seen done
at the heart of which you can feel that
you have played no small part.

You know that I always had a

UCDA, P155/103: Dictated letter from de Valera to Kathleen O'Connell, 2 October 1952. At the time, de Valera was in hospital in Utrecht undergoing eye operations.

UCDA, P150/249: An evaluation of his life, written by de Valera a few days after the death in 1956 of Kathleen O'Connell, his personal secretary for 37 years, 7 April 1956. O'Connell was a native of Co. Kerry who trained as a secretary in the United States and subsequently worked for Clan na Gael. When de Valera went to the US in 1919 she was assigned as his personal secretary and returned to Ireland with him in 1920.

I am writing this

a few days   after

we have laid to rest

one who has worked

with me for more

than a third of a century

one who has
shared   I had almost
said my most intimate
thoughts so far as they
were concerned with
public affairs.

Utrecht 27/9/52.

Dear Kathleen,

I'm afraid I will not be ho[me]
as soon as I had hoped. I had a third spea[k]
yesterday. I didn't tell anybody because I
didn't want to make the family or any of
anxious before it was over, and I particularly
didn't want Eamon to know lest he shou[ld]
be tempted to come over. He can do more
at home for his own patients than he can
for me. You know I am not depreciating [his]
goodness. I would like also if you could
replace him as a general source of infor[mation]
about me. I know he is absent from hi[s]
Office a good deal, and it wouldn't be [well]
if a large number of inquiries were being sen[t]
to him. I will, therefore, write to you, and
you can give out the news to home, Fran[k]
Aiken, the Tánaiste and the other Ministers, th[e]
Farnan's, etc.

If Frank Gallagher requires information
for the newspapers as regards my present situat[ion]
this is what the Professor suggested might be sa[id]
'Certain complications need a further operation

...essary, that was performed on Friday last. The
immediate results are statisfying but it will take
me further weeks before the final results can be
determined.

Continue to pray but don't worry. The days
pass here quickly enough; the nights are rather long.
The papers and the Radio keep me in touch with
general affairs. I would like, naturally, to be
back at home again and in the Office but I
can't hasten things. Dr. & Mrs Farnan are Lawson are
really were, I think, thinking of going to Lourdes this year.
Had they been going and were I at home I would have
tried to accompany them. I do not know what
they propose to do now. The suitable period for
going is coming to an end. I am delighted
to know that Dr. Farnan has completely recovered
from his accident.

McHugo and Seán read for me generally and of
course give me any Government information that is sent
along. The doctor does not want me to do anything
heavy, however, and thinks I should confine myself
to listening to light reading. Tell Lawson not to send
me any more books; I have quite a library
already.

I hope you yourself are keeping well and
that Dr. McHugo's absence has not thrown too
much work upon you. Maurice will see to this.

(Dictated) Éamon de Valera

UCDA, P155/101: Dictated letter from
de Valera to Kathleen O'Connell, 27
September 1952. This was sent from
Utrecht where he was in hospital for an
eye operation.

MONTROSE, 69244
30, TRIMLESTON AVENUE,
BOOTERSTOWN, Co. DUBLIN

3 September, 197

Dear Marie,

Now that the public obsequies are over and the who Irish Nati
here at home and wherever its children are to be found, has paid its trib
to the unique man who devoted his life to its service, I must write to
you who tended him so devotedly in his better later years. No pr
no earthly reward would be an adequate recognition of your kind
and goodness to him who is now among the saints in Heaven. One
certainty is that, even there, he has not forgotten you and all that y
did for him on earth.

I firmly believe that our Chief was among the best +
godliest of men. I cannot recall one unjust thing, nor even an unk
one that he consciously did. He was rectitude and integrity persony
and he evoked, though maybe not in an equal intensity, those qualiti
in others. He set a standard in public conduct and private behavio
that those around him were led by his example to emulate. And wit
all, he was so simple, so human, so merry and full of fun.

It must have been a wonderful experience to have been
so close to him as you were, to know his little mannerisms,
peculiarities and caprices, the things he liked and the things he didn
You must record them all, so that posterity may know of him, not
just as a historic figure, as a patriot and a statesman, but as a
human being who was infinitely loveable. This is a 'geasa'

I put upon you. It is the sacred obligation of the Gael; so fail me not or fail me at your peril.

Now, too, that De V. is at rest, you must give some thought to yourself. The stress upon you of your devoted service must have been intense and the toll it has taken in energy and vitality correspondingly great. I trust that you will find it possible to relax and recuperate. Try to take a long holiday; and, when it is over, start at once to put down for posterity your memories of the greatest Irishman, not just of his time but of the ages. It would be the culmination of all that you did for him to whom you were such a stay and a comfort while he was living.

Dear Marie, please accept this note as an expression of gratitude for all that you did for De V. Your devotion to him, your care for him, the solicitude you showered on him are things I shall never forget.

Deeply sincerely yours

Seán MacEntee

UCDA, P150/3559: Letter from Seán MacEntee to Marie O'Kelly, 3 September 1975. A few days after de Valera's death, MacEntee outlines the personal impact de Valera made on those who worked with him. Marie O'Kelly was a niece of Kathleen O'Connell and replaced her as de Valera's personal secretary.

XV

'Tough as teak'

UCDA, P150/3806: De Valera reading his notes while he waits to speak at an election rally, 1940s/50s.

D e Valera's departure from the office of Taoiseach in 1959 was overshadowed by question marks over the extent to which he and his family had benefited from the *Irish Press* titles while he was a serving minister. He failed to adequately answer in the Dáil the probing questions of Noël Browne and others who had raised the issue. Tim Pat Coogan has strongly argued the notion that de Valera's involvement in the *Irish Press* titles was fuelled by personal enrichment, stating that Terry de Valera, de Valera's son, ceded control of his voting shares to his nephew, Eamon de Valera, in the 1980s for £225,000.[1]

The demise of the *Irish Press* in 1995 caused considerable distress and recrimination; at their height the three titles (the *Irish Press*, the *Evening Press* and the *Sunday Press*) had employed 1,100 people. Initially, the *Irish Press* enjoyed huge success, and two further titles appeared: the *Sunday Press* in 1949 and the *Evening Press* in 1954. Getting the paper off the ground was a remarkable fund-raising feat in the 1930s. De Valera skilfully managed to persuade holders of bonds sold by the first Dáil to transfer their investment to the *Irish Press*. Within five years, circulation of the paper had reached 100,000, a significant achievement given the fact that this was a new readership, and that the newspaper was not dependent on winning readers from its rivals.[2]

The *Irish Press* evolved into a high-quality newspaper, but the issue of shareholdings for the 'men of no property' was more complex. Noël Browne insisted on raising the issue in the Dáil in 1958 and demanded to know who exactly was benefiting from the company shares. Browne insisted that the paper 'was funded by one pound notes collected from rank and file republican supporters of the party. It was the intention that it should become a national newspaper and certainly not the political play thing and enormous financial asset of the de Valera family which it later became'.[3] In effect, Browne had publicised the financial structure of the company; having received a present of two shares, he exercised his right to examine the company records.

In his autobiography, Browne recalled:

It became clear that de Valera had systematically over a period of years become a majority shareholder of *Irish Press* newspapers. Although he was controlling director of the newspapers, the share prices were not quoted publicly. The price paid by the de Valera family to shareholders was nominal. It was clear that de Valera was now a very wealthy newspaper tycoon.[4]

He alleged that since 1929, de Valera and his son Vivion had bought over 90,000 shares in the company.

Browne eventually managed to table a motion in the Dáil in December 1958 on the inappropriateness of de Valera holding both positions and accused him of hypocrisy, given that he had previously suggested that the holding of paid company directorships was incompatible with ministerial office. De Valera's reply was that his position was merely 'a fiduciary one'; that he had not made any money from the newspaper, and that profits had been used to expand and improve the newspaper.[5] As noted by John Horgan, this was 'a defence that sat uneasily beside the undisputed fact that his shareholding, in what was then a reasonably profitable enterprise, was itself worth a very large sum of money'.[6]

In any case, de Valera's decision to seek presidential office knocked the story off the front pages, and accusations that he had compromised the office of Taoiseach by continuing to hold his post as controlling director of the *Irish Press* were not enough to cause his resignation. De Valera subsequently passed his *Irish Press* shares and the post of controlling director to his son, Vivion.

But he failed to adequately answer what was a legitimate query—was it not inappropriate for him to hold the shares and the position of controlling editor of a commercial enterprise, when he had specifically suggested that holding paid company directorships was incompatible with ministerial office? Unusually, in December 1958, de Valera left the Dáil chamber shortly after the debate on Browne's motion began, leaving Seán MacEntee to make the case for the defence. Browne quite rightly threw words that de Valera had uttered the previous summer back at him. On 5 June 1957, in reply to a question on ministers holding company directorships, de Valera had declared that 'no Minister should engage in any activities whatsoever that could reasonably be regarded as interfering or being incompatible with the full and proper discharge by him of the duties of his office, for example acting in a position such as a company directorship carrying remuneration'.[7]

De Valera returned later to the Dáil chamber, reiterated that he had made no money from the paper, that his position was no secret, acknowledged that he had guided the editorial ethos of the papers but that he was just 'one of a board'. He acknowledged that he had always held a degree of 'moral trusteeship' regarding the control of the paper, but that no action of his was 'inconsistent with the dignity of the office of Taoiseach'.[8] It was an unconvincing defence.

The vote on Browne's motion was delayed until January 1959, when Browne maintained that the company was worth almost £1 million and reeked of corruption and nepotism. Fine Gael's Oliver J. Flanagan went further, and, taking advantage of parliamentary privilege, made accusations about the 'robbing of shareholders' before being expelled from the chamber. De Valera left the chamber before the vote was taken, and the Fianna Fáil majority ensured its defeat.[9]

Given the seemingly unanimous view that de Valera stayed in power for too long, would it have made any difference to Fianna Fáil, to the country or to the significance of his legacy if he had gone at an earlier stage? Garret FitzGerald argued in his *Irish Times* column in September 2006 that de Valera should have retired in 1952 because 'total economic stagnation marked de Valera's last seven years as leader of his party because all the chickens of his disastrous commitment to an inward looking policy of self-sufficiency were coming home to roost'.[10] This was challenged by his grandson, also named Eamon de Valera, who pointed out that Fianna Fáil was in office for only three of the nine years from 1948 to 1957 and the white paper 'Programme for economic expansion' was published in November 1958, during de Valera's last term as Taoiseach.[11]

There were plenty of de Valera's colleagues who were in a similar position in politics in the 1950s as 1916 veterans, and they too were seemingly bereft of new ideas as to how to improve the economy. The employment of (often deserved) purple prose to describe his successor, Seán Lemass, has been interpreted in a way which implies that anything that had gone before was staid and lethargic. But even if Lemass had taken over as Taoiseach earlier, in 1948, for example, it should not be assumed that the embrace of free trade would have happened then; T.K. Whitaker was not appointed secretary of the Department of Finance until 1956, and Lemass himself acknowledged that he and his party did not get to grips with the need for completely novel thinking about the economy until the mid to late 1950s.[12]

The constant use of the words 'restless' and 'vigour' alongside the name of Seán Lemass imply that he was a Fianna Fáil dam waiting to burst throughout the 1950s, and that de Valera was being unusually stubborn in not relinquishing control of his party. But the reality was that, in all political parties, those prominent in the 1920s and 1930s had significant staying power.

351   'Tough as teak'

Richard Mulcahy did not give up the leadership of Fine Gael until 1959 and William Norton did not step down as leader of the Labour Party until 1960. De Valera also sought in the 1950s to introduce younger members to the Fianna Fáil Cabinet, including, in 1957, Neil Blaney, Jack Lynch and Kevin Boland, then aged 40, 35 and 35 respectively.

While it is true that Lemass was seventeen years younger than de Valera, he was still a 1916 veteran; more crucial, perhaps, was the perception that although he had this lineage, he did in some respects seem to belong to another generation, and clearly, there were temperamental and psychological differences between the two men.[13] But it should not be assumed that there were countless, restless Fianna Fáilers queuing up impatiently to take over the mantle as leader of the party. Surely if there had been such pressure, de Valera would have gone sooner?

Lemass was in some respects a reluctant Taoiseach; clearly, whatever about de Valera overstaying his welcome in the context of the failure of economic policies, he still had a political appetite, endurance and skill that were unique. Shortly after he became Taoiseach, Lemass wrote to de Valera, 'Since I took over as Taoiseach, I have not ceased to wonder how you carried the burden for so long without showing the strain. You are a wonderful man and surely tough as teak'.[14] In an interview with Brian Farrell in the 1960s, Lemass admitted how apprehensive he was about taking up the post of leader of Fianna Fáil, given that the charisma of de Valera was now something which the party could no longer rely on.[15]

But the longer that de Valera remained in the public eye, particularly as president in the 1960s, the more likely it was that he would provide a focus for public criticism, particularly as older disillusioned republicans and a new generation of political activists sought to portray his party as having abandoned the 'men of no property'.

When he addressed the joint houses of the Oireachtas in January 1969 to mark the fiftieth anniversary of the founding of the first Dáil, there were protests and scuffles both inside and outside the Mansion House. Inside the building, a member of the 'distinguished audience' was Joseph Clarke, a veteran republican who had fought in 1916. De Valera had barely commenced when Clarke, leaning on his crutches, interjected the following, breaking not only with decorum, but the Irish language-only rule: 'The programme of the old Dáil has never been implemented! This is a mockery! There are people on hunger strike in Mountjoy. The housing of the people …'. Clarke could not finish his protest, as the ushers forcibly removed him. Ironically, Clarke had served as an usher at the meeting of the first Dáil in 1919. De Valera, it was subsequently reported, did not seem to hear the protest (he certainly would not have seen it, being virtually blind).[16]

Clarke's protest was a reference to the housing crisis in Dublin in the 1960s that had prompted increasingly militant action by the Dublin Housing Action Committee (DHAC), a socialist and republican protest group. On the same day, others protested against the failure of the government to protect and promote the Irish language. Up to 2,000 students from Democratic Action also protested in Dublin that day, demanding free education for all, and held aloft placards that included '50th ANNIVERSARY OF HOMELESS FAMILIES AND ENFORCED DIVORCE (EMIGRATION)' and 'CLASSLESS SOCIETY? BALLYFERMOT, FOXROCK'.

Later the same day, de Valera met the British ambassador to Ireland, Sir Andrew Gilchrist. They shook hands, and the ambassador said, 'Mr President, I want you to realise that this time the British are with you'. According to Liam Mac Gabhann, a contemporary *Irish Times* journalist, this comment took on an added resonance, given that clearly 'some of the Irish without the walls were not'.[17]

As he faced his final days in public office, membership of the European Economic Community (EEC) beckoned, but de Valera's attitude to this, it seems, was hostile. In his January 1969 Mansion House speech, while articulating the need to work closely with other countries, he also asserted: 'A great deal is said about internationalism and so on, and some people think that the small nations have nothing to look forward to except to be brushed aside or absorbed by great powers. I do not at all agree with that opinion'.[18] He had similar reservations about the EEC specifically. His son, Terry, recorded:

> I remember well speaking to him at the time of entry to the EEC. While he acknowledged that entry was inevitable, he accepted this with very strong reservation regarding loss of sovereignty. He agreed fully with the concept of the development of trade and commerce and the more desirable aspects of culture from the continent of Europe. Political union or the diminution or loss of sovereignty was quite a different matter in which he felt the smaller nations would fare worst.[19]

Bearing this in mind, it is not unlikely that de Valera voted against Ireland's entry to the EEC, and scepticism about the powers of what evolved into the European Union (EU) remained with the de Valera family. His two grandchildren in Irish politics at the end of the twentieth century—Eamon O'Cuív and Síle de Valera—were both publicly critical of the union. As a government minister, O'Cuív declared his intention to vote against the Nice referendum in May 2001, and Síle de Valera, in 2000, expressed her concern about the influence of the EU on Irish affairs, commenting that 'directives and regulations agreed in Brussels can often seriously impinge on our identity, culture and traditions' and that 'the Brussels bureaucracy' does not always 'respect the complexities and sensitivities of member states'.[20] One of the ironies of de Valera's hostility to the EU is that, as with Ireland's relationship with internationalism generally, 'his greatest claim to fame may be the paradoxical one that without him it might never have been possible at all'.[21]

UCDA, P150/2812: De Valera and four unidentified men outdoors at leisure, 1938. Found in an envelope labelled 'Miss Kathleen O'Connell, Some snaps of Annecy (Geneva 1938) with best wishes for a speedy recovery and a return to the good old times! M.R., 7.4.55'.

UCDA, P150/194: De Valera relaxing with an unidentified family, horse riding, 1930s/40s. The photo is annotated 'The President reviews his Mayo Troop with General Woods in the rear'.

UCDA, P150/162: Four generations, 28 July 1971. De Valera with greatgrandson, Eamon Annraoi; the infant's father, Eamon de Valera; and the president's son, Professor Eamonn de Valera, on the occasion of Eamon Annraoi's baptism. Autographed by de Valera. © Lensmen Press & P.R. Agency.

July 15 11

A Uachtaráin, a chara.

Thanks sincerely for your kind
greetings and good wishes. It
was very kind of you to remember
the occasion. Every milestone
passed marks so much of life's
journey completed and reduces
the number still ahead — but
two score more, notwithstanding
your wish, is an intimidating

prospect if I had to try to
fill each unforgiving minute
with sixty seconds worth of
distance run".

Since I took over as Taoiseach,
I have not ceased to wonder
how you carried this burden for
so long without showing the strain.
You are a wonderful man and
surely tough as teak

with kindest regards and
all good wishes

XVI

'One of the last
of the great Victorians'?

UCDA, P150/194: Anyone for tennis?, 1930s/40s.

nother factor that has influenced the interpretation of de Valera, and
frequently caused his name to be invoked, is the Celtic Tiger
economy and the extraordinary wealth produced in Ireland in the
last decade of the twentieth century, and into the first years of the
twenty-first century. In this context, direct and indirect references to de Valera's
unambiguous anti-materialism have become common. In 2003 P.J. Drudy, of
the housing agency Threshold, told an Oireachtas committee on the
Constitution and property rights that Eamon de Valera would turn in his grave
if he knew that landowners were getting unearned 'windfall' gains purely as a
result of land rezoning.[1]

This concern about venal materialism also provided an opportunity to ask
whether the much derided 'Ireland which we dreamed of' speech in 1943 was
really that bad? This speech was the most famous broadcast of any Irish
politician of the twentieth century; de Valera used it to mark the fiftieth
anniversary of the foundation of the Gaelic League, and it included the lines:

> The Ireland which we dreamed of would be the home of a people
> who valued material wealth only as a basis of right living, of a
> people who were satisfied with frugal comfort and devoted their
> lives to things of the spirit—a land whose countryside would be
> bright with cosy homesteads, whose fields and villages would be
> joyous with the sounds of industry, with the romping of sturdy
> children, the contests of athletic youths and the laughter of
> comely maidens, whose firesides would be forums for the wisdom
> of serene old age.[2]

With the passage of time, it came to be lazily sneered at as the 'comely
maidens' speech, but it contained much that was positive, particularly when set
against the excessive consumerism and unbridled materialism of Ireland over the
last decade. In November 1998 Fr Harry Bohan, chairman of the Céifin Centre
for Values-Led Change, organised a conference on the theme 'Are we forgetting

something? Our society in the new millennium' in which he invited speakers to reflect on the idea that 'even in the short period of the Celtic Tiger it was becoming increasingly obvious that Irish society, as distinct from the economy, is beginning to pay a high and unacceptable price for the material prosperity'.[3]

One of the contributors, Joe Lee, suggested a re-examination of de Valera's 'Ireland which we dreamed of' speech, by first of all purging it 'of the archaism of the de Valera lexicon—his vocabulary was, after all, that of one of the last of the great Victorians—and translate it into language more familiar today'. What he concluded was that, while de Valera's focus was on a rural rather than an urban Ireland, it amounted to a desire to see a well-populated country, with full employment, good housing, healthy children, an interest in sport, respect for the elderly and that 'de Valera's model emphasised the essential links between the generations as he identified his ideal for the dependent ages in society—childhood, youth and old age. Giving was as important as taking, service as important as wealth. It was a society in which rights were balanced by responsibilities'.[4] A message it seems, that is very relevant to any civilised society.

Another factor that has influenced the interpretation of de Valera's legacy in the last decade has been the revelations concerning some of the generation that came after him in Fianna Fáil, most obviously Charles Haughey, the extent of whose corruption was exposed in great detail by the Moriarty Report in December 2006. The report exposed the scale of his corruption and the countless payments made to him, the equivalent of €45 million today, which 'particularly during difficult economic times nationally, can only be said to have devalued the quality of a national democracy'.[5]

As a result, interesting questions arose: was there a gulf in standards between the Civil War generation of Irish political leaders and those who followed them? And if there was, when did the rot set in? In contrast to Haughey, de Valera's lack of personal wealth was causing him distress at the end of his life. A document in the National Archives, released as part of the state paper release in 2003, relates to the personal difficulties of de Valera. It revealed that when nearing the end of his second term as president, in January 1973, his doctor, Bryan Alton, wrote to the Taoiseach, Jack Lynch, about his patient's state of mind. While commenting on his relatively good physical health, he expressed concern that 'mentally, he is tending to develop a depression. The main basis for the matter appears to be financial'.

De Valera was due to retire from public life in June, and Alton wrote that the president was worried that his pension would be 'very small and inadequate. ... Many elderly people get depressed and feel they are going to end their days in poverty. On the other hand, Mrs de Valera is now a complete invalid and the President has the worry that she will need constant care. His fears may be totally unfounded but he speaks of them very rationally and convincingly'.[6]

Lynch, who visited de Valera the next day, made the point that a few years previously, de Valera had refused to accept an increase in his allowance when the salaries of Oireachtas ministers were increased: 'He specifically requested me not to include provision for such in the appropriate legislation and this notwithstanding pressure from me'. A few months later, the Minister for Finance sent a memorandum to the government proposing an increase in the president's pay and pension, and the Dáil subsequently passed a new bill, increasing the personal pay of the president from £5,000 to just over £11,000.[7]

In looking at these documents, there seems something appropriate about the president of a republic being worried about the same issues that would affect so many of its citizens. It is also a reminder of how debased Irish politics has become over the years through its association with personal enrichment.

His successor as leader of Fianna Fáil, Seán Lemass, was cut from the same cloth when it came to the issue of personal enrichment as a by-product of holding high political office. As pointed out by his biographer, John Horgan, while a minister, Lemass was adamant that his official car would not under any circumstances be used for transporting his wife or children to or from social engagements. During the Second World War, when rationing of essential foodstuffs was in operation, well-wishers sent packets of tea to the Lemass family, which were promptly repacked and returned. On trips abroad, Lemass did not claim his daily allowance unless he had actually spent the money. When paid fees for articles that he had written, he followed the practice which was established by de Valera and donated the money to the Red Cross.[8] When he died, his estate consisted of today's equivalent of a modest dwelling in a Dublin suburb.[9]

In her memoir, *Same age as the state*, the poet Máire Mhac an tSaoi, daughter of Fianna Fáil minister for finance, Seán MacEntee, recalls one Christmas Eve when a beautiful dinner service arrived from the new Arklow Pottery Company. Her father told her when he came home to 'put it back in the boxes', and it was returned, as 'my father could not even appear to be influenced in his decisions by gifts'.[10]

Nuala O'Faoláin, writing in the aftermath of the publication of the Moriarty Report, suggested: 'They were all like that. Then'. She also lamented the fact that there were so few expressions of regret from contemporary Fianna Fáil ministers:

> I sincerely wish there had been even one word of regret from Fianna Fáil for what it allowed itself to become in the Haughey era, because that would lay a ghost and move us all on ... but there was nothing—nothing but denial and bravado. The nearest

anyone came to expressing shock was Eamon O'Cuív. But then, he's a de Valera, and de Valera's impeccable personal probity was a prime value in Máire Cruise O'Brien's parents['] generation. Those, oh those, were the days.[11]

In writing the foreword to a new edition of the second volume of his father, Todd Andrew's, autobiography, *Man of no property*, Niall Andrews recalled that his father was 'genuinely a man of no property' and 'would never allow anyone to travel in the Bord na Móna or CIÉ- supplied car unless he was in it ... he insisted that "the company car" belonged to the state and was purely for his use'.[12]

Lest the use of these anecdotes be seen as simplistic sentimentalism, and a celebration of anti-materialism, it is also the case that some historians have depicted de Valera, not as the preventer of modernisation and prosperity, but as the one whose policies ultimately paved the way for it. In 2006 John A. Murphy, in reflecting on de Valera's foreign policy in the 1930s, suggested that 'the devotees of the Celtic Tiger would do well to realise that, for all the economic bleakness of earlier decades, our present prosperity would never have come about without a sovereign state, of which de Valera was the principal architect during those years'.[13]

No one would suggest that the social and economic depression of the 1950s was in any way positive, but in an age of vulgar wealth and consumption, and declining civic responsibility and participation, it is time, while acknowledging his mistakes and misjudgements, to reconsider the positive aspects of the de Valera legacy, and to be more broadminded when judging Dev.

Several of those positive aspects stand out immediately upon examination of the extensive archival and published material relating to de Valera. Too many accounts to date of his career and impact have sailed too close to hagiography or defamation. Much of the scapegoating of de Valera, and the preponderance of the 'dreary de Valera's Ireland' syndrome is born of an intellectual laziness, and it is legitimate to see it as a product of the critics' frustrations rather than any real engagement with the long and complex career of the man that they are determined to dismiss and belittle.

The abundance of archival material now allows for a substantial engage-ment, and highlights why it is necessary to deconstruct much of the negative symbolism associated with de Valera. In the modern era he has too often been automatically equated with ruralism, backwardness, stagnation, division and isolationism. Such negative conclusions do not involve a realistic assessment of what was and was not possible between the 1930s and the 1950s.

Prosperous modern Ireland often asks why prosperity did not come sooner and analyses the 1930s and 1940s from that perspective, as opposed to looking at the real and lasting achievements of an exceptionally talented state-builder, who viewed his task in realistic terms, while successfully attempting to give it some international significance. De Valera was careful about many things; language, aims, limits, authority, and the winning and exercising of power. This was particularly the case after the divisions of the Civil War era, when he adopted a clever and defiant but also a careful strategy to maximise independent Ireland's sovereignty and to invest that sovereignty with dignity. It could not be achieved without compromise and difficulties, and sometimes mistakes. But by and large it worked, and it invoked pride and a strong sense of nationhood, while at the same time producing an exceptionally stable democracy and a political party that managed, electorally, to become unique in its longevity and appeal to all Irish social classes. It did not become a party of a particular region or interest group while de Valera was at the helm. He managed to achieve consensus while in government by containing diverse and conflicting personalities within his Cabinets, but he was also fortunate to be surrounded by strong, talented and independent-minded ministers.

De Valera may have miscalculated in 1921 by believing at that time that his alternative strategy to the Treaty could have yielded greater independence, but he learnt from his mistakes in a way that benefited the country. The legislative record of Fianna Fáil in the 1930s and 1940s is impressive, not just in the context of foreign policy, but also in the areas of housing, health and welfare provision. De Valera also shared many of the failures of his contemporaries, particularly when it came to understanding and realistically assessing the impact of emigration, and his political longevity inevitably led to a degree of arrogance.

Where he stood out was in his leadership, his astuteness and sense of timing and most crucially, his ability to communicate his political ideas effectively in an era before marketing, spin doctors, focus groups and paid advisors. Elections were fought and won through mass meetings and often courageous initiatives, such as the 1937 Constitution, and in becoming adept at this, de Valera managed to project himself as an indispensable 'father figure' in Irish politics, despite the Civil War legacy.

The caricature of him as stern, remote and technocratic is a myth, as revealed by his personal correspondence and the affection and loyalty that he inspired in so many. He also displayed exceptional physical and mental stamina and endurance; nobody would have predicted that the politically and physically isolated figure in Arbour Hill Prison in 1923, would, 50 years later, be near the end of his second term as president of Ireland, having served as Taoiseach for 20 years. That 50-year journey was made by a unique politician, and a noble one.

UCDA, P150/2129: De Valera signing autographs on the deck of a ship, 1927. 'Fred H. Mann. News and Commercial Photographer United States Lines' stamped on reverse.

UCDA, P150/142: Postcard photograph of Eamon and Sinéad de Valera on their wedding day, 8 January 1910. Autographed by de Valera. 'President and Mrs Eamon de Valera after their wedding, 8/1/1910' typed on reverse.

38, UPPER FITZWILLIAM STREET,
DUBLIN, 2.

2nd. January, 1973.

An Taoiseach,
Government Buildings,
DUBLIN, 2.

Dear Taoiseach,

As you probably know, I have looked after the President
for nearly 20 years.

At the present time, physically, he is in quite good health
for his age. Mentally, he is tending to develop a depression.

The main basis for the matter appears to be financial. He
is worrying that his pension will be very small and inadequate - he keeps
talking about the 1937 Act. Many elderly people get depressed and feel
they are going to end their days in poverty. On the other hand, Mrs. de
Valera is now a complete invalid and the President has the worry that she
will need constant care. His fears may be totally unfounded but he speaks
of them very rationally and convincingly.

So much so that I thought I would have to discuss the matter
with somebody and you were the only one I felt I could mention it to without causing him embarrassment. I do not know whether he is right or
wrong in his notions. If he is right, I felt you should know the problem
exists. If he is wrong, it would be of the greatest possible help for me
to be aware of this so that I could treat him accordingly.

I should have preferred to discuss this matter with you but,
unfortunately, I shall be away on your return.

With kindest regards and all good wishes,

I, DT, 2004/21/65: Bryan Alton to Jack
ch, 2 January 1973. De Valera's doctor
lines his concern for the president's
ntal health, as he approaches the end of
second term as president. Taoiseach Jack
ch moved quickly to increase the
sident's salary.

Yours sincerely,

UCDA, P150/2968: De Valera and Frank Aiken leaving
Earlestown Town Hall, 9 October 1948. In a photo
album 'Presented to Mr Eamon de Valera by the Irish
National Club to Commemorate his Visit to Earlestown
Newton-le-Willows, Lancs. October 9th, 1948'.

Endnotes

Chapter I

[1] T.P. O'Neill and Lord Longford, *Eamon de Valera* (Dublin, 1970), 463.

[2] Quoted in *Irish Times*, 28 August 2005.

[3] Alexis FitzGerald, 'Eamon de Valera', *Studies* Lxiv (64) (Autumn 1975), 207–15.

[4] See *Irish Times*, 1 September 1975 and *New York Times*, 31 August 1975.

[5] John A. Murphy, 'The achievement of de Valera', in John P. O'Carroll and John A. Murphy (eds), *De Valera and his times* (Cork, 1983), 1–17.

[6] Tim Pat Coogan, *De Valera, long fellow, long shadow* (London, 1993), 693–705.

[7] Dermot Keogh, 'Eamon de Valera and the Civil War in Ireland', in Dermot Keogh and Gabriel Doherty (eds), *De Valera's Irelands* (Cork, 2003), 45–74.

[8] Pauric Travers, *Eamon de Valera (life and times)* (Dundalk, 1994), 5.

[9] National Archives of Ireland (NAI), Office of the Secretary to the President (PRES), 2003/18/62.

[10] Peter Mair, 'De Valera and democracy', in Tom Garvin, Maurice Manning and Richard Sinnott (eds), *Dissecting Irish politics: essays in honour of Brian Farrell* (Dublin, 2004), 31–48.

[11] Mair, 'De Valera and democracy', 32–4.

[12] *Irish Times*, 25 September 2004.

[13] Paul Durcan, *A snail in my prime: new and selected poems* (London, 1993), 41.

[14] See Declan Kiberd, 'Dev: the image and the achievement', in Philip Hannon and Jackie Gallagher (eds), *Taking the long view: seventy years of Fianna Fáil* (Dublin, 1996), 23.

[15] Fintan O'Toole, *The Irish Times book of the century* (Dublin, 2000), 205.

[16] Luke Gibbons, 'Engendering the state: narrative, allegory and Michael Collins', *Éire-Ireland* v.xxxi (4–5) (Winter 1996), 261–70.

[17] See Catriona Crowe *et al.* (eds), *Documents on Irish foreign policy: volume IV 1932–1936* (Dublin, 2004) and Catriona Crowe *et al.* (eds), *Documents on Irish foreign policy: volume V 1937–1939* (Dublin, 2006).

[18] F.S.L. Lyons, 'De Valera revisited', *Magill* (March 1981), 59–61.

[19] See Coogan, *De Valera*, 674–7.

[20] Seán O'Faoláin, 'Eamon de Valera', *The Bell* 10 (1) (April 1945), 1–18.

[21] Joe Lee, *Ireland 1912–1985: politics and society* (Cambridge, 1989), 331.

[22] Lee, *Ireland 1912–1985*, 333–5.

[23] Lee, *Ireland 1912–1985*, 340–1.

[24] Seán O'Faoláin, *De Valera* (London, 1939), 40.

[25] NAI, PRES, 2003/18/64.

[26] Tom Garvin, *Preventing the future: why was Ireland so poor for so long?* (Dublin, 2004), 38–45.

[27] F.S.L. Lyons, 'De Valera revisited', 61.

[28] F.S.L. Lyons, 'De Valera revisited', 61.

[29] John Bowman, *De Valera and the Ulster question, 1917–1973* (London, 1989 edn), 2.

[30] John Bowman, 'Eamon de Valera: seven lives', in John P. O'Carroll and John A. Murphy (eds), *De Valera and his times* (Cork, 1983), 182–195.

[31] Patrick Murray, 'Obsessive historian: Eamon de Valera and the policing of his reputation', *Proceedings of the Royal Irish Academy* 101C (2001), 37–65.

[32] University College Dublin Archives (UCDA), P150 (Papers of Eamon de Valera)/1698, 22 June 1923.

[33] Murray, 'Obsessive historian', 37–65.

[34] Murray, 'Obsessive historian', 60.

[35] Irish Military Archives (IMA), 'Files of those who did not give witness statements', S.429, 'Eamon de Valera'. McDunphy's account of a conversation with de Valera, 6 July 1949.

[36] IMA, S.429, 'Eamon de Valera', 11 July 1957.

[37] Diarmaid Ferriter, '"In such deadly earnest": the Bureau of Military History', *The Dublin Review* 12 (August 2003), 36–65.

[38] Murray, 'Obsessive historian', 43.

[39] Murray, 'Obsessive historian', 43.

[40] UCDA, P150/2013, 17 April 1926.

[41] Murray, 'Obsessive historian', 53.

[42] Murray, 'Obsessive historian', 65.

[43] Deirdre McMahon, '"A worthy monument to a great man" Piaras Béaslaí's life of Michael Collins', *Bullán* 2 (Winter/Spring 1996), 55–67.

[44] McMahon, 'Piaras Béaslaí's life of Michael Collins', 55–67.

[45] See Frank Pakenham, *Peace by ordeal: an account, from first-hand sources, of the negotiation and signature of the Anglo-Irish Treaty, 1921* (Dublin, 1935); Ernie O'Malley, *On another man's wound* (London and Dublin, 1936); Desmond Ryan, *Unique dictator: a study of de Valera* (London, 1936); Frank O'Connor, *The big fellow: Michael Collins and the Irish revolution* (London, 1937); Dorothy Macardle, *The Irish Republic* (London, 1937); and Piaras Béaslaí, *Michael Collins and the making of a new Ireland* (2 edn, Dublin, 1937).

[46] Tim Pat Coogan, *Michael Collins: a biography* (London, 1990), 422.

[47] Peter Hart, *Mick: the real Michael Collins* (London, 2005), 413–27.

Chapter II

[1] Travers, *Eamon de Valera*, 8.

[2] Quoted in Donal McCartney, *The NUI and Eamon de Valera* (Dublin, 1983), 21.

[3] UCDA, P122 (Papers of Maurice Moynihan)/113, 22 February 1950.

[4] Charles Townshend, *Easter 1916: the Irish rebellion* (London, 2005), 175, 261.

[5] Townshend, *Easter 1916*, 199–200; Max Caulfield, *The Easter rebellion* (Dublin, 1963); and Coogan, *De Valera*, 69.

[6] Coogan, *De Valera*, 201.

[7] NAI, Bureau of Military History (BMH), Witness statement (WS) of Simon Donnelly.

[8] Townshend, *Easter 1916*, 257.

[9] NAI, BMH, WS of Patrick Ward.

[10] David Fitzpatrick, '"Decidedly a personality": de Valera's performance as a convict, 1916–17', *History Ireland* 10 (2) (Summer 2002), 40–7.

[11] Thank you to Deirdre McMahon for this information.

[12] UCDA, P150/506, Item 6, G.F. McKay to de Valera, 27 June 1959 and de Valera's response, 4 October 1959.

[13] Townshend, *Easter 1916*, 283.

[14] Terry de Valera, *A memoir* (Dublin, 2005), 121ff.

[15] De Valera, *Memoir,* 124.

[16] UCDA, P150/524, 3 July 1969.

[17] UCDA, P150/528, 18 July 1916.

[18] Leon O'Broin, *W.E. Wylie and the Irish revolution 1916–21* (Dublin, 1989), 32–5.

[19] Owen Dudley Edwards, 'The American identity of Eamon de Valera' in Dermot Keogh and Gabriel Doherty (eds), *De Valera's Irelands* (Cork, 2003), 11–29.

[20] Fitzpatrick, '"Decidedly a personality"', 40–7.

[21] Fitzpatrick, '"Decidedly a personality"', 40–7.

[22] UCDA, P150/529, De Valera to Simon Donnelly, 23 April 1917.

[23] Townshend, *Easter 1916,* 324–31.

[24] Michael Laffan, *The resurrection of Ireland: the Sinn Féin party 1916–1923* (Cambridge, 1999), 108.

[25] David Fitzpatrick, *The two Irelands 1912–39* (Oxford, 1998), 196–7.

[26] Laffan, *Resurrection of Ireland,* 113.

[27] Townshend, *Easter 1916,* 324, 331, 335.

[28] Laffan, *Resurrection of Ireland,* 82.

[29] Laffan, *Resurrection of Ireland,* 97.

[30] Laffan, *Resurrection of Ireland,* 112.

[31] Laffan, *Resurrection of Ireland,* 139.

[32] Travers, *Eamon de Valera,* 14.

[33] Travers, *Eamon de Valera,* 15.

[34] Rachel Donnelly, 'Irish defence bike "cavalry" proposed by de Valera', *Irish Times,* 5 July 2001.

[35] NAI, BMH, WS 797, Michael O'Laoghaire, 40.

[36] Laffan, *Resurrection of Ireland,* 319.

[37] David Fitzpatrick, *Harry Boland's Irish revolution* (Cork, 2003), 123–6.

[38] NAI, Archives of Dáil Éireann (DE) 2/36, 'Instructions on precautions against enemy raids', *c.* May 1921.

[39] Fitzpatrick, *Harry Boland,* 125–32.

[40] Fitzpatrick, *Harry Boland,* 174.

[41] UCDA, P150/727, De Valera to Arthur Griffith, 9 July 1919.

[42] Owen Dudley Edwards, *Eamon de Valera* (Cardiff, 1987), 85–91.

[43] UCDA, P150/728, Griffith to Cohalan and Devoy, 23 June 1920.

[44] Dudley Edwards, *Eamon de Valera,* 88.

[45] T. Ryle Dwyer, *De Valera's darkest hour: in search of national independence 1919–32* (Dublin, 1982), 33.

[46] David B. Franklin, 'De Valera's visit to Birmingham, Alabama, April 1920', *History Ireland* 12 (4) (Winter 2004), 30–5.

[47] Michael Hopkinson, *The Irish War of Independence* (Dublin, 2002), 169.

[48] Fitzpatrick, *Harry Boland,* 125.

[49] Hart, *Mick,* 217.

[50] Hopkinson, *Irish War of Independence,* 170.

[51] Dudley Edwards, 'The American identity of De Valera', 11–29.

[52] NAI, DE 2/526, Jan van der Heijde to de Valera, 26 July 1921.

[53] Hart, *Mick,* 264–5.

[54] Tom Garvin, *1922: The birth of Irish democracy* (Dublin, 1996), 57, 96.

[55] Laffan, *Resurrection of Ireland,* 295.

[56] Laffan, *Resurrection of Ireland,* 349.

Chapter III

[1] NAI, DE 2/244, De Valera to Collins, *c.* June 1921.
[2] NAI, DE 2/244, De Valera to Collins, 15 July 1921.
[3] Murray, 'Obsessive historian', 50–1.
[4] Murray, 'Obsessive historian', 50–1.
[5] Hart, *Mick*, 264–306.
[6] Maryann Gialanella Valiulis, *Portrait of a revolutionary: General Richard Mulcahy and the founding of the Irish Free State* (Dublin, 1992), 101.
[7] UCDA, P122/119, 24 February 1963.
[8] UCDA, P122/119, Typescript copy of a letter from de Valera to Pakenham, 24 February 1963, 3.
[9] UCDA, P122/119, Typescript copy of a letter from de Valera to Pakenham, 24 February 1963, 4–5.
[10] UCDA, P122/119, Typescript copy of a letter from de Valera to Pakenham, 24 February 1963, 5.
[11] UCDA, P122/119, Typescript copy of a letter from de Valera to Pakenham, 24 February 1963, 6.
[12] UCDA, P122/119, Typescript copy of a letter from de Valera to Pakenham, 24 February 1963, 7.
[13] UCDA, P122/119, De Valera to Pakenham, 27 February 1963.
[14] UCDA, P122/119, De Valera to Pakenham, 27 February 1963.
[15] Laffan, *Resurrection of Ireland*, 17–20.
[16] Quoted in Hart, *Mick*, 286.
[17] NAI, DE 2/304 (1), Letter from combined delegation to de Valera, 26 October 1921.
[18] Keith Middlemas (ed.), *Thomas Jones Whitehall diary, volume one: 1916–25* (London, 1969), 174.
[19] NAI, BMH, WS of Robert Barton.
[20] UCDA, P150/1495, Instructions to plenipotentiaries from Cabinet, 7 October 1921.
[21] Laffan, *Resurrection of Ireland*, 349–50.
[22] UCDA, P155 (Papers of Kathleen O'Connell)/138, Desk diary of Kathleen O'Connell, 7 December 1921.
[23] See Ronan Fanning *et al.* (eds), *Documents on Irish foreign policy: volume I 1919–1922* (Dublin, 1998), 361.
[24] Fanning *et al.*, *Documents on Irish foreign policy:I*, 361.
[25] Lee, *Ireland 1912–1985*, 48–51.
[26] Dudley Edwards, *Eamon de Valera,* 110–18.
[27] Dudley Edwards, *Eamon de Valera,* 110–18.
[28] UCDA, P155/138, Desk diary of Kathleen O'Connell, 23 December 1921.
[29] Murray, 'Obsessive historian', 52.
[30] Keogh, 'Eamon de Valera and the Civil War', 54–5.
[31] Thank you to Deirdre McMahon for this information. See also Deirdre McMahon, *Republicans and imperialists: Anglo–Irish relations in the 1930s* (London, 1984), 1.
[32] Eunan O'Halpin, 'Dorothy McArdle: *The Irish Republic* (1937)', *Irish Historical Studies* xxxi (123) (May 1999), 389–94.
[33] UCDA, P150/657, De Valera to Mary MacSwiney, 11 September 1922.
[34] In an editorial in *The Bell* 10 (3) (June 1945), 190.
[35] Quoted in Keogh, 'Eamon de Valera and the Civil War', 45–74.

36 Garvin, *1922*, 14, 49–50, 160.
37 Diarmaid Ferriter, *The transformation of Ireland 1900–2000* (London, 2004), 256.
38 Ferriter, *Transformation*, 254.
39 Garvin, *1922*, 49–50.
40 Laffan, *Resurrection of Ireland*, 424.
41 Gibbons, 'Engendering the state', 261–70.
42 *Irish Times*, 5 May 2001.
43 *Irish Times*, 18 December 2006.
44 *Sunday Tribune*, 3 November 1996.
45 De Valera to Joseph McGarrity, 10 September 1922, quoted in Seán Cronin (ed.), *The McGarrity papers* (Tralee, 1972), 124.
46 Macardle, *The Irish Republic* (London, 1968 edn), 708.
47 UCDA, P150/1826, 19 May 1923.
48 UCDA, P150/1818, Item 10, 31 May 1923.

Chapter IV

1 Laffan, *Resurrection of Ireland*, 437.
2 Laffan, *Resurrection of Ireland*, 438.
3 Coogan, *De Valera*, 361.
4 Coogan, *De Valera*, 364–6.
5 John Regan, *The Irish counter revolution, 1921–1936* (Dublin, 1999), 268–9.
6 Regan, *Irish counter revolution*, 268–9.
7 Travers, *Eamon de Valera*, 24.
8 UCDA, P150/2011, 17 April 1926.
9 UCDA, P150/2028, 14–20 June 1927.
10 Travers, *Eamon de Valera*, 25.
11 UCDA, P150/2110, Browne to de Valera, 6 October 1927.
12 Peter Mair, 'De Valera and democracy', 32.
13 Donal Ó Drisceoil, 'The "Irregular and Bolshie situation": republicanism and communism 1921–36', in Fearghal McGarry (ed.), *Republicanism in modern Ireland* (Dublin, 2003), 45 and Henry Patterson, *Ireland since 1939: the persistence of conflict* (Dublin, 2006), 18.
14 Richard English, *Irish freedom: the history of nationalism in Ireland* (London, 2006), 328.
15 Patterson, *Ireland since 1939*, 18.
16 Figures cited by John M. Regan, 'The politics of Utopia', in Mike Cronin and John M. Regan (eds), *Ireland: the politics of independence 1922–49* (London, 2000), 34.
17 Eunan O'Halpin, 'Parliamentary party discipline and tactics; the Fianna Fáil archives, 1926–32', *Irish Historical Studies* xxx (120) (November 1997), 581–91.
18 Brian Farrell, 'De Valera: unique dictator or charismatic chairman?', in John P. O'Carroll and John A. Murphy (eds), *De Valera and his times* (Cork, 1983), 35.
19 Brian Walker, *Parliamentary election results in Ireland, 1918–92* (Dublin and Belfast, 1992), 237.
20 Cited in Maurice Manning, *Irish political parties: an introduction* (Dublin, 1972), 57–9.
21 Manning, *Irish political parties*, 57–9.
22 Cited in Richard Dunphy, *The making of Fianna Fáil power in Ireland, 1923–48* (Oxford, 1995), 313.

[23] Dunphy, *Making of Fianna Fáil power*, 313ff.

[24] Peter Mair, *The changing Irish party system* (London, 1987), 37–40.

[25] UCDA, P150/2097, 10–23 January 1933.

[26] Breandán Ó hÉithir, *The begrudger's guide to Irish politics* (Dublin, 1986), 67–8.

[27] Ged Martin, 'De Valera imagined and observed', in Dermot Keogh and Gabriel Doherty (eds), *De Valera's Irelands* (Cork, 2003), 84–104.

[28] Seán O'Casey, *Autobiographies, volume 2, Inishfallen, fare thee well* (London, 1949), 4.

[29] Martin, 'De Valera imagined and observed', 97.

[30] UCDA, P150/3097, 20 February 1957.

[31] Diarmaid Ferriter, *What if? Alternative views of twentieth century Ireland* (Dublin, 2006), 200.

[32] Ferriter, *What if?*, 204.

Chapter V

[1] Garret FitzGerald, 'Tensions between civil servants and ministers', *Irish Times*, 14 September 2002.

[2] Travers, *Eamon de Valera*, 27.

[3] Joe Lee, 'De Valera approached foreign politics with caution', *Sunday Tribune*, 12 November 2000.

[4] Lee, 'De Valera approached foreign politics with caution'.

[5] John W. Dulanty to Joseph Walshe, 18 January 1932, quoted in Ronan Fanning *et al.* (eds), *Documents on Irish foreign policy: volume III 1926–1932* (Dublin, 2002), 897–9.

[6] *Sunday Independent*, 7 November 2004.

[7] Michael Kennedy, 'Joseph Walshe, Eamon de Valera and the execution of Irish foreign policy, 1932–8', *Irish Studies in International Affairs* 14 (2003), 165–85.

[8] Fitzpatrick, *Harry Boland*, 125.

[9] Deirdre McMahon, 'Maurice Moynihan (1902–1999), Irish civil servant: an appreciation', *Studies* 89(353) (Spring 2000), 71–7.

[10] NAI, DT, S2246, Walshe to de Valera, 12 March 1932.

[11] UCDA, P150/2183, Walshe to de Valera, 13 June 1933.

[12] Crowe *et al.* (eds), *Documents on Irish foreign policy: IV*, 16.

[13] Crowe *et al.* (eds), *Documents on Irish foreign policy: IV*, 229.

[14] Crowe *et al.* (eds), *Documents on Irish foreign policy: V*, 256.

[15] Fitzpatrick, *Two Irelands*, 149–52.

[16] McMahon, *Republicans and imperialists*, 239–83.

[17] UCDA, P150/2517, MacDonald to de Valera, 17 May 1938.

[18] NAI, Department of Foreign Affairs (DFA), 5/220, De Valera to Thomas, 6 August 1935.

[19] See Crowe *et al.* (eds), *Documents on Irish foreign policy: V*, xvi.

[20] NAI, DFA, 26/31, 20 September 1932.

[21] Michael Kennedy, *Ireland and the League of Nations, 1919–46* (Dublin, 1996), 177.

[22] Deirdre McMahon, 'Ireland, the Empire and the Commonwealth', in Kevin Kenny (ed.), *Ireland and the British Empire* (Oxford, 2004), 208–12.

Chapter VI

[1] Bowman, *De Valera and Ulster*, 35–89.

[2] NAI, DE 2/266, De Valera to Collins, 13 January 1921.

[3] Quoted in Garret FitzGerald, *Ireland and the world: further reflections* (Dublin, 2005), 84.

[4] See Lyons, 'De Valera revisited', 60.

[5] Bowman, *De Valera and Ulster*, 308.

[6] Bowman, *De Valera and Ulster*, 308.

[7] McMahon, *Republicans and imperialists: Anglo–Irish relations in the 1930s* (London, 1984), 101–50.

[8] De Valera, *Memoir*, 205.

[9] UCDA, P67 (Papers of Seán MacEntee)/155, Draft letter from Seán MacEntee to Eamon de Valera, 17 February 1938.

[10] Bowman, *De Valera and Ulster*, 308.

[11] UCDA, P150/2517, De Valera to MacDonald, 30 May 1938.

[12] UCDA, P150/2548, De Valera to Chamberlain, 12 April 1939.

[13] See Ferriter, *What if?*, 117.

[14] Ferriter, *What if?*, 122.

[15] Crowe *et al.* (eds), *Documents on Irish foreign policy: V*, 438.

[16] *Sunday Independent*, 3 December 2006, 34.

[17] FitzGerald, *Further reflections*, 88.

[18] UCDA, P150/2548, Item 11, 26 June 1940.

[19] Patterson, *Ireland since 1939*, 58–9.

[20] De Valera, *Memoir*, 224–5.

[21] McMahon, *Republicans and imperialists*, 181.

[22] McMahon, *Republicans and imperialists*, 241.

[23] NAI, DT, S14440, De Valera to Costello, 7 April 1949.

[24] UCDA, P150/2940, Rugby to de Valera, 18 February 1948.

[25] UCDA, P150/2940, De Valera to Rugby, 17 April 1957.

[26] UCDA, P150/2940, Rugby to de Valera, 18 May 1957, and de Valera's reply, 8 June 1957.

[27] McMahon, 'Ireland, the Empire and the Commonwealth', 182–220.

[28] Eunan O'Halpin, 'Long fellow, long story: MI5 and de Valera', *Irish Studies in International Affairs* 14 (2003), 185–203.

[29] McMahon, 'Ireland, the Empire and the Commonwealth', 213.

[30] UCDA, P150/2955, Radio talk by de Valera from New Delhi, 15 June 1948.

[31] UCDA, P150/2955, Nehru to de Valera, 18 June 1948.

[32] NAI, DT, 96/6/247, N.G. Nolan to R.K. Tandon, 21 March 1967.

[33] NAI, PRES, 2003/18/66, Ó Flathartaigh to Brooks Peters, 7 July 1972.

Chapter VII

[1] Mair, 'De Valera and democracy', 35.

[2] J.G.A. Pocock, 'The limits and divisions of British history: in search of the unknown subject', *American Historical Review* 87 (2) (April 1982), 311–64.

[3] Regan, *Irish counter revolution*, 309.

[4] Fearghal McGarry, *Eoin O'Duffy: self-made hero* (Oxford, 2005), 203.

[5] McGarry, *O'Duffy*, 232.

[6] McGarry, *O'Duffy*, 269.

[7] Regan, *Irish counter revolution*, 361.

[8] Eunan O'Halpin, 'The army in independent Ireland', in Thomas Bartlett and Keith Jeffery (eds), *A military history of Ireland* (Cambridge, 1996), 407–31.

[9] O'Halpin, 'Army in independent Ireland', 328–9.

[10] Patterson, *Ireland since 1939*, 20.

[11] See Brian Hanley, *The IRA 1926–1936* (Dublin, 2002) and also Brian Hanley, 'The rhetoric of republican legitimacy', in Fearghal McGarry (ed.), *Republicanism in modern Ireland* (Dublin, 2003), 172.

[12] Fearghal McGarry, '"Too damned tolerant" republicans and imperialism in the Irish Free State', in Fearghal McGarry (ed.), *Republicanism in modern Ireland* (Dublin, 2003), 80.

[13] Ronan Fanning, 'The rule of order: Eamon de Valera and the IRA', in John P. O'Carroll and John A. Murphy (eds), *De Valera and his times* (Cork, 1983), 60–73.

[14] Seán MacBride, *That day's struggle: a memoir 1904–1951* (Dublin, 2005), 123.

[15] Richard English, 'Socialist republicanism in independent Ireland', in Mike Cronin and John M. Regan (eds), *Ireland: the politics of independence, 1922–49* (London, 2000), 84–97.

[16] UCDA, P150/2590, Transcript of radio broadcast, 8 May 1940.

[17] O'Halpin, 'The army in independent Ireland'.

[18] Lee, *Ireland 1912–1985*, 223.

Chapter VIII

[1] McMahon, 'Maurice Moynihan', 71–7.

[2] J.M. Kelly, *The Irish Constitution* (2nd edn, Dublin, 1984), xxvi.

[3] Kelly, *Irish Constitution*, xxx.

[4] J.M. Kelly, G.W. Hogan and G.F. Whyte, *The Irish Constitution* (3rd edn, Dublin, 1994), xci.

[5] J.M. Kelly, G.W. Hogan and G.F. Whyte, *The Irish Constitution* (4th edn, Dublin, 2003), ix.

[6] Kelly, Hogan and Whyte, *Irish Constitution* (4th edn), ix.

[7] Colm Tóibín, 'Inside the Supreme Court', *Magill* (February 1985).

[8] Joe Lee, 'A Constitution as much for war as for peace', *Sunday Tribune*, 15 October 2000.

[9] Brian Farrell, 'De Valera's Constitution and ours', in Brian Farrell (ed.), *De Valera's Constitution and ours* (Dublin, 1988), 198–208.

[10] John Cooney, *John Charles McQuaid, ruler of Catholic Ireland* (Dublin, 1999), 94.

[11] Cooney, *John Charles McQuaid*, 94–107.

[12] UCDA, P150/2395, Item 17, McQuaid to de Valera, 15 April 1937.

[13] UCDA, P150/2395, Item 21, McQuaid to de Valera, *c.* April/May 1937.

[14] UCDA, P150/2419, Handwritten report from Joseph Walshe for Eamon de Valera, 22 April 1937.

[15] UCDA, P150/2419, Handwritten report from Joseph Walshe for Eamon de Valera, 22 April 1937.

[16] Joe Lee, 'How de Valera finished his 1937 Constitution', *Sunday Tribune*, 22 October 2000.

[17] Garvin, *Preventing the future*, 220.

[18] Mair, 'De Valera and democracy', 44.

[19] *Irish Press*, 5 October 1949.

20 Diarmaid Ferriter, *Lovers of liberty? Local government in twentieth century Ireland* (Dublin, 2001), 16.

21 NAI, DT, S4964, *c.* April 1933.

22 Ferriter, *Lovers of liberty*, 16–17.

23 Joe Lee, 'Centralisation and community', in Joe Lee (ed.), *Ireland: towards a sense of place* (Cork, 1985), 84–64.

24 NAI, DT, S10677B, Browne to de Valera, 12 February 1940.

25 NAI, DT, S10677B, Browne to de Valera, 7 June 1940.

26 Dáil Debates, vol. 105, 3, cols 569–70, 16 April 1947.

27 John Whyte, *Church and state in modern Ireland, 1923–70* (Dublin, 1971), 73.

28 *Irish Independent*, 30 October 1939.

29 NAI, PRES, 2003/18/66, 'Day in the life of the president', *c.* 1972.

30 Archive personal papers of Sir Andrew Gilchrist (Churchill Archives Centre, Gilchrist Papers, GILC 14B), 27 February 1967.

Chapter IX

1 Fitzpatrick, *Two Irelands*, 230.

2 McGarry, *O'Duffy*, 229.

3 UCDA, P150/2878, *c.* 1933.

4 UCDA, P150/2886, July 1934.

5 John P. O'Carroll and John A. Murphy (eds), *De Valera and his times* (Cork, 1983), 5.

6 Coogan, *De Valera*, 36.

7 Coogan, *De Valera*, 658.

8 Dublin Diocesan Archives (DDA), Papers of Archbishop John Charles McQuaid, Government Box 5, A138/b/XVIII/5/33, Health Bill 1952, McQuaid to Reverend Gerald P. O'Hara, 7 November 1952.

9 Cooney, *John Charles McQuaid*, 169–70.

10 UCDA, P150/2652, Correspondence between McQuaid and de Valera concerning the Commission on Unemployment, 17 December 1943.

11 Cooney, *John Charles McQuaid*, 171.

12 Cooney, *John Charles McQuaid*, 193 and 336.

13 John Bowman, 'At the disposal of the archbishop', *Irish Times*, 6 November 1999 and 13 November 1999.

14 NAI, DT, S13444, 'Health Services: Reorganisation and Development (including legislation) 1944–1953', *c.* April 1953.

15 Ronan Fanning, 'Catholic bishop's role in the Health Act of 1953', *Irish Times*, 13 and 14 February 1985.

16 Fanning, 'Bishop's role in the Health Act'.

17 Fanning, 'Bishop's role in the Health Act'.

18 Eamon McKee, 'Church–state relationships and the development of Irish health policy', *Irish Historical Studies* xxv (98) (1989), 193.

19 McKee, 'Church–state and Irish health policy', 193.

20 Evelyn Bolster, *The Knights of Saint Columbanus* (Dublin, 1979), 70.

[21] Frank Pakenham, *Avowed intent: an autobiography of Lord Longford* (London, 1994), 59.
[22] C.S. Andrews, *Man of no property* (Dublin, 2001 edn), 241.

Chapter X

[1] Quoted in Angela Bourke *et al.* (eds), *Field Day Anthology V* (Cork, 2002), 145–8.
[2] Máire Cruise O'Brien, *Same age as the state* (Dublin, 2003), 141–3.
[3] Garvin, *1922*, 97.
[4] UCDA, P150/657, De Valera to Mary McSwiney, 11 September 1922.
[5] UCDA, P150/667, Markievicz to de Valera, December 1919.
[6] Bourke *et al.* (eds), *Field Day Anthology V,* 150.
[7] Catriona Clear, 'Women in de Valera's Ireland', in Dermot Keogh and Gabriel Doherty (eds), *De Valera's Irelands* (Cork, 2003), 104.
[8] Yvonne Scannell, 'The Constitution and the role of women', In Brian Farrell (ed.), *De Valera's Constitution and ours* (Dublin, 1988), 123–37.
[9] NAI, DT, S9880, Betty Archdale to de Valera, 14 June 1937.
[10] NAI, DT, S9880, Louie Bennett to de Valera, 24 May 1937.
[11] NAI, DT, S9880, Lucy Kingston to de Valera, 13 May 1937.
[12] NAI, Papers of the Joint Committee of Women's Societies and Social Workers, 98/14/15 (1), Minute Book 1935–39.
[13] Margaret O'Callaghan, 'Women and politics in independent Ireland, 1921–68', in Angela Bourke *et al.* (eds), *Field Day Anthology V* (Cork, 2003), 130–1.
[14] O'Callaghan, 'Women and politics in independent Ireland', 130–1.
[15] O'Callaghan, 'Women and politics in independent Ireland', 111.
[16] Ivy Pinchbeck, *Women and the Industrial Revolution* (London, 1932).
[17] Catriona Clear, '"The women cannot be blamed": the Commission on Vocational Organisation, feminism and home makers in independent Ireland in the 1930s and 1940s', in Mary O'Dowd and Sabine Wichert (eds), *Chattel, servant or citizen: women's status in church, state and society*, Historical Studies 19 (Belfast, 1995), 180–6.
[18] Dáil Debates, vol. 67, col. 64, 11 May 1937.
[19] Clear, 'Women in de Valera's Ireland'.
[20] Mary O'Dowd, 'Interpreting the past: women's history and women historians, 1840–1945', in Angela Bourke *et al.* (eds), *Field Day Anthology V*, 1103–4.
[21] De Valera, *Memoir,* 325.
[22] A portrait revealed in de Valera, *Memoir*, and Coogan, *De Valera*, 690–1.
[23] In the books *Fantastic Summer* (London, 1946) and *Uneasy Freehold* (London, 1944), See Gerardine Meaney, 'Identity and opposition: women's writing, 1890–1960', in Angela Bourke *et al.* (eds), *Field Day Anthology V,* 968.

Chapter XI

[1] Robert Fisk, 'Turning our backs on the fire of life', *Irish Times*, 19 October 1999.
[2] Quoted in *Village*, 13 May 2005.

[3] Brian Girvin, *The Emergency: neutral Ireland 1939–45* (London, 2006), 320–31.

[4] Girvin, *The Emergency*, 320–31.

[5] Girvin, *The Emergency*, 181–220.

[6] Girvin, *The Emergency*, 200–19.

[7] Girvin, *The Emergency*, 9–13.

[8] Girvin, *The Emergency*, 233–5.

[9] Terence Brown, 'Responses to the Emergency', *Irish Times*, 17 March 2007. Clair Wills, *That neutral island: a cultural history of Ireland in the Second World War* (London, 2007).

[10] Wills, *That neutral island*, 391–417.

[11] See Girvin, *Emergency*, 256–75

[12] In a letter to the *Irish Times*, 7 February 2007.

[13] Ferriter, *Transformation*, 389.

[14] FitzGerald, *Further reflections*, 77.

[15] UCDA, P150/2597, Cosgrave to de Valera, 9 and 16 July 1940.

[16] UCDA, P150/2597, De Valera to Cosgrave, 13 July 1940.

[17] Ferriter, *What if?*, 97.

[18] O'Halpin, *MI5 and Ireland*, xiii.

[19] Ferriter, *What if?*, 101–2.

[20] R.M. Douglas, 'The Pro-Axis underground in Ireland, 1939–42', *The Historical Journal* 49 (4) (2006), 1155–83.

[21] Douglas, 'Pro-Axis underground in Ireland', 1155–83.

[22] Ferriter, *What if?*, 99–101.

[23] Ferriter, *What if?*, 99–101.

[24] Diarmaid Ferriter, 'Apologies for the past not the answer', *Irish Times*, 7 February 2005.

[25] Dermot Keogh, *Jews in twentieth century Ireland: refugees, anti-Semitism and the Holocaust* (Cork, 1998), 192.

[26] Michael Kennedy, 'Irish diplomats in Germany', *Irish Studies in International Affairs* 10 (1999), 68.

[27] *Irish Catholic*, 7 January 1937.

[28] Mervyn O'Driscoll, *Ireland, Germany and the Nazis: politics and diplomacy, 1919–39* (Dublin, 2004), 237–8.

[29] Cormac Ó Gráda, *Jewish Ireland in the age of Joyce* (Princeton, 2006), 191.

[30] Ó Gráda, *Jewish Ireland*, 126.

[31] Nick Harris, *Dublin's Little Jerusalem* (Dublin, 2002) and Katrina Goldstone, 'Elegy for a disappearing community', *Irish Times*, 4 June 2002.

[32] *Irish Times*, 30 January 2007.

[33] Girvin, *The Emergency*, 1–29.

[34] Dermot Keogh, 'Dev and the Code Dearg', *Irish Times*, 20 May 2006.

[35] Niall Keogh, *Con Cremin: Ireland's wartime diplomat* (Dublin, 2006), 84–94.

[36] Keogh, *Con Cremin*, 112–29.

[37] Dermot Keogh, '"Making Aliya": Irish Jews, the Irish state and Israel', in Dermot Keogh, Carmel Quinlan and Finbarr O'Shea (eds), *Ireland in the 1950s: the lost decade* (Cork, 2004), 252–72.

[38] Dermot Keogh, 'Dev and the Code Dearg'.

[39] McMahon, '*Maurice Moynihan*', 72.

[40] UCDA, P150/2676, Items 3 and 4, De Valera to Brennan, 21 May 1945.

[41] NAI, DT, 97/6/563, 8 August 1966.

[42] Cathal O'Shannon in an interview with Shane Hegarty, *Irish Times*, 6 January 2007 and *Ireland's Nazis*, broadcast on RTÉ One, 9 and 16 January 2007.

[43] David O'Donoghue, 'State within a state: the Nazis in neutral Ireland', *History Ireland* 14 (6) (November/December 2006), 35–9.

[44] Deaglán de Breadún, 'Berry view of Anti-Jewish feeling was rejected by colleagues', *Irish Times*, 3 January 2003.

[45] De Breadún, 'Berry view of Anti-Jewish feeling'.

[46] Fisk, 'Turning our backs'.

[47] *Irish Times*, 14 September 2006.

Chapter XII

[1] Garvin, *Preventing the future*, 112–13.

[2] Garvin, *Preventing the future*, 113.

[3] An archival recording held in RTÉ and quoted in Ferriter, *What if?*, 128.

[4] David Fitzpatrick, *Two Irelands,* 197.

[5] Ferriter, *Transformation*, 398.

[6] Brian Girvin, *Between two worlds: politics and economy in independent Ireland* (Dublin, 1989), 93.

[7] Quoted in Dudley Edwards, 'The American identity of de Valera', 11–29.

[8] Mary E. Daly, *The buffer state: the historical roots of the Department of the Environment* (Dublin, 1997), 215–21.

[9] Ann Marie Walsh, '"Root them in the land" Cottage schemes for agricultural labourers', in Joost Augusteijn (ed.), *Ireland in the 1930s: new perspectives* (Dublin, 1999), 47–67.

[10] Daly, *Buffer state*, 221.

[11] Cormac Ó Gráda, *Ireland: A new economic history 1780–1939* (Oxford, 1994), 439–41.

[12] Ó Gráda, *New economic history,* 439–41.

[13] Joe Lee, 'Squaring the economic and social circles', in Philip Hannon and Jackie Gallagher (eds), *Taking the long view: 70 years of Fianna Fáil* (Dublin, 1996), 54–64.

[14] Girvin, *Between two worlds*, 61.

[15] NAI, DT, S9636, 'Small farmers in west Cork', *c.* May 1937.

[16] NAI, DT, S13413A and B, 'Encouragement of early marriage', 22 December 1943.

[17] NAI, DT, S13413A and B, 'Encouragement of early marriage', 22 December 1943; *Farmer's Gazette*, 11 December 1943.

[18] *Irish Times*, 7 July 1947.

[19] *Irish Times*, 7 July 1947 and *Irish Independent*, 10 May 1960.

[20] Garvin, *Preventing the future*, 140–5.

[21] Garvin, *Preventing the future*, 154.

[22] Garret FitzGerald, 'Eamon de Valera: the price of his achievement', in Garret FitzGerald (ed.), *Ireland in the world: further reflections* (Dublin, 2005), 68–91.

[23] Mary Daly, *Industrial development and Irish national identity* (Dublin, 1992), 171.

[24] Ferriter, *Transformation,* 372.

[25] O'Faoláin, 'Eamon de Valera', 1–18.

[26] UCDA, P150/2756, Items 4 and 5, 1947–8.

[27] Dunphy, *Making of Fianna Fáil power*, 260.

[28] NAI, DT, S1344A, 'Health services, reorganisation and development', 28 September 1943 and *Irish Times*, 25 February 1944.

[29] Joseph Robbins (ed.), *Reflections on health: commemorating fifty years of the Department of Health 1947–1997* (Dublin, 1997), vii.

[30] Raymond James Raymond, 'De Valera, Lemass and Irish economic development, 1933–48', in John P. O'Carroll and John A. Murphy (eds), *De Valera and his times* (Cork, 1983), 119.

[31] Brian Farrell, 'The unlikely marriage: de Valera, Lemass and the shaping of modern Ireland', *Études Irlandaises* 10 (December 1985), 215–23.

[32] UCDA, P150/2648, Item 1, 27 January 1943.

[33] Garvin, *Preventing the future*, 67.

[34] Anthony Cronin, 'This time, this place', *The Bell* xix (8) (July 1954), 5–7.

[35] NAI, DT, S11582C, 29 August 1951.

[36] NAI, DT, S11582C, 23 July 1951.

[37] NAI, DT, S11582C, 30 August 1951.

[38] *Irish Press*, 31 August 1951.

[39] *Irish Independent*, 11 September 1951.

[40] NAI, DT, S11582D, 'Irish Community Trust', 30 January 1954.

[41] *Irish Times*, 6 September 1951.

[42] NAI, DT, S11582D, Louie Bennett to de Valera, 13 October 1951.

[43] Catherine Dunne, *An unconsidered people: the Irish in London* (Dublin, 2003), 225–7.

[44] *Irish Times*, 22 January 2005.

[45] *Irish Times*, 24 July 2000.

[46] Interview of Tim Pat Coogan by Brendan Bradshaw, *History Ireland*, 12 (2) (Summer 2004), 40–5.

Chapter XIII

[1] *Irish Press*, 19 October 1957.

[2] De Valera, *Memoir*, 118–19.

[3] Lee, *Ireland 1912–1985*, 135.

[4] Lee, *Ireland 1912–1985*, 671.

[5] Andrews, *Man of no property*, 238.

[6] Terence Brown, *Ireland: a social and cultural history 1922–2002* (London, 2004), 183.

[7] Alison Healy, 'Priest complained Irish was not spoken by Gardaí', *Irish Times*, 4 January 2005.

[8] Brian Fallon, *An age of innocence: Irish culture 1930–60* (Dublin, 1998), 11.

[9] Brown, *A social and cultural history*, 146–7.

[10] John Banville, 'Memory and forgetting: the Ireland of de Valera and O'Faoláin', in Dermot Keogh, Carmel Quinlan and Finbarr O'Shea (eds), *Ireland in the1950s: the lost decade* (Cork, 2004), 21–30.

[11] Peter Martin, *Censorship in the two Irelands 1922–1939* (Dublin, 2006), 86.

[12] Brown, *A social and cultural history*, 138.

[13] Dáil Debates, vol. 163, col. 731, 4 July 1957.

[14] Martin, *Censorship*, 125–7.

[15] Martin, *Censorship*, 210–11

[16] Wills, *That neutral island*, 299.

[17] Wills, *That neutral island*, 187.

[18] *Irish Times,* 3 March 2007.

[19] Fallon, *An age of innocence*, 14.

[20] MacCartney, *NUI and de Valera*, 41.

[21] MacCartney, *NUI and de Valera*, 47.

[22] Bowman, *De Valera and Ulster*, viii.

[23] Brian P. Kennedy, '"Better sureshot than scattergun", Eamon de Valera, Seán O'Faoláin and arts policy', in Dermot Keogh and Gabriel Doherty (eds), *De Valera's Irelands* (Cork, 2003), 115–32.

[24] Michael Viney, 'No great link to the old sod', *Irish Times*, 7 October 2000.

[25] Gearóid Ó Crualaoich, 'Dev's other Ireland', in Dermot Keogh and Gabriel Doherty (eds), *De Valera's Irelands* (Cork, 2003), 155.

[26] Cormac Ó Gráda, 'Making history in Ireland in the 1940s and 1950s: the saga of the Great Famine', *Irish Review* 12 (1992), 87–107.

[27] UCDA, P150/526, 22 May 1960.

[28] Henry Davis, *Moral and pastoral theology* (New York, 1935).

[29] Sean MacConnell, 'De Valera, priest ponder the morality of taxation', *Irish Times,* 2 March 2000.

[30] *Irish Independent*, 29 April 1957.

[31] *Irish Press*, 29 April 1957.

[32] *Manchester Guardian*, 2 May 1957.

[33] *Irish Independent,* 30 April 1957.

[34] UCDA, P150/3110, Letter from Patrick O'Brien, secretary of the *Gaelic Weekly* Limited to de Valera enclosing cuttings, 11 May 1957.

[35] UCDA, P150/3110, De Valera to Padraig Ó Caoimh, *c.* 12 May 1957.

[36] Archive personal papers of Sir Andrew Gilchrist (Churchill Archives Centre, Gilchrist Papers, GILC 14B), 27 February 1967.

Chapter XIV

[1] De Valera, *Memoir*, 90–2.

[2] *Irish Times*, 11 December 2000.

[3] *Irish Times*, 25 November 2000.

[4] *Irish Times*, 25 November 2000.

[5] Fitzpatrick, *Harry Boland*, 125–32.

[6] Fitzpatrick, *Harry Boland*, 197.

[7] Fitzpatrick, *Harry Boland*, 13.

[8] UCDA, P155/139, 4 August 1922.

[9] De Valera, *Memoir*, 327.

[10] UCDA, P155/103 (1), De Valera to Kathleen O'Connell, 2 October 1952.

[11] UCDA, P150/249, 7 April 1956.

[12] UCDA, P150/3559, Seán MacEntee to Marie O'Kelly, 3 September 1975.

[13] Michael Fitzgerald and Antoinette Walker, *Unstoppable brilliance: Irish geniuses and Asperger's syndrome* (Dublin, 2006), 87.

[14] Fitzgerald and Walker, *Unstoppable brilliance*, 87.
[15] Fitzgerald and Walker, *Unstoppable brilliance*, 88–98.
[16] *Irish Times*, 14 August 2004.
[17] De Valera, *Memoir*, 180–2.
[18] Fitzgerald and Walker, *Unstoppable brilliance*, 109.
[19] Fitzgerald and Walker, *Unstoppable brilliance*, 116.
[20] Fitzgerald and Walker, *Unstoppable brilliance*, 87.
[21] As reported in *Irish Times*, 4 August 2004.
[22] R.F. Foster, *W.B. Yeats: a life II: the arch poet 1915–1939* (Oxford, 2003), 470–1.
[23] O'Faoláin, 'Eamon de Valera', 7–16.
[24] O'Halpin, 'MI5 and de Valera', 185–203.
[25] Martin, 'De Valera imagined and observed', 84–104.
[26] Pakenham, *Avowed intent*, 62.

Chapter XV

[1] Tim Pat Coogan, 'De Valera's begrudging attitude to the Big Fella', *Irish Times*, 31 January 2005.
[2] J.R. Hill (ed.), *A new history of Ireland VII 1921–84* (Oxford, 2003), 682.
[3] Mark O'Brien, *De Valera, Fianna Fáil and the Irish Press* (Dublin, 2003), 85.
[4] Noël Browne, *Against the tide* (Dublin, 1986), 234.
[5] O'Brien, *De Valera*, 102–12.
[6] John Horgan, *Noël Browne: passionate outsider* (Dublin, 2000), 205.
[7] O'Brien, *De Valera*, 107–9.
[8] O'Brien, *De Valera*, 107–9.
[9] O'Brien, *De Valera*, 107–9.
[10] *Irish Times*, 16 September 2006.
[11] *Irish Times*, 19 September 2006.
[12] Ferriter, *What if?*, 117–30.
[13] Hill, *New history of Ireland*, 294ff.
[14] UCDA, P150/3497, Item 5, Lemass to de Valera, 15 July 1959.
[15] Farrell, 'The unlikely marriage'.
[16] Farrell, 'The unlikely marriage'.
[17] *Irish Times*, 22 January 1969.
[18] *Irish Times*, 22 January 1969.
[19] De Valera, *Memoir*, 253.
[20] Viney, 'No great link'.
[21] F.S.L. Lyons, 'De Valera revisited'.

Chapter XVI

[1] *Irish Times*, 18 September 2003.
[2] Maurice Moynihan (ed.), *Statements and speeches by Eamon de Valera* (Dublin, 1980), 466.

[3] Harry Bohan and Gerard Kennedy (eds), *Are we forgetting something? Our society in the new millennium* (Dublin, 1999), 5.

[4] J.J. Lee, 'A sense of place in the Celtic Tiger?' in Harry Bohan and Gerard Kennedy (eds), *Are we forgetting something? Our society in the new millennium* (Dublin, 1999), 71–83.

[5] See *Irish Times*, 20 December 2006.

[6] NAI, DT, 2004/21/65, Dr Bryan Alton to Jack Lynch, 2 January 1973.

[7] NAI, DT, 2004/21/65, Dr Bryan Alton to Jack Lynch, 2 January 1973.

[8] UCDA, P122/100 (3), Máire Ní Murchú, Irish Red Cross, to de Valera, 24 February 1971.

[9] John Horgan, *Seán Lemass: the enigmatic patriot* (Dublin, 1997), 339–47.

[10] Cruise O'Brien, *Same age as the state*, 151.

[11] *Sunday Tribune*, 7 January 2007.

[12] Andrews, *Man of no property*, vii.

[13] *Sunday Independent*, 3 December 2006.

Index

Page numbers in italics refer to documents and photographs.